To Carol,

You are a true blessing!

Arlene Mann Kelly

Girl With The Windblown Bob

by

Arlene Mann Kelly

1663 Liberty Drive, Suite 200
Bloomington, Indiana 47403
(800) 839-8640
www.authorhouse.com

First published by AuthorHouse 11/17/04

ISBN: 1-4184-6607-7 (e)
ISBN: 1-4184-6605-0 (sc)
ISBN: 1-4184-6606-9 (dj)

Printed in the United States of America
Bloomington, Indiana

This book is printed on acid-free paper.

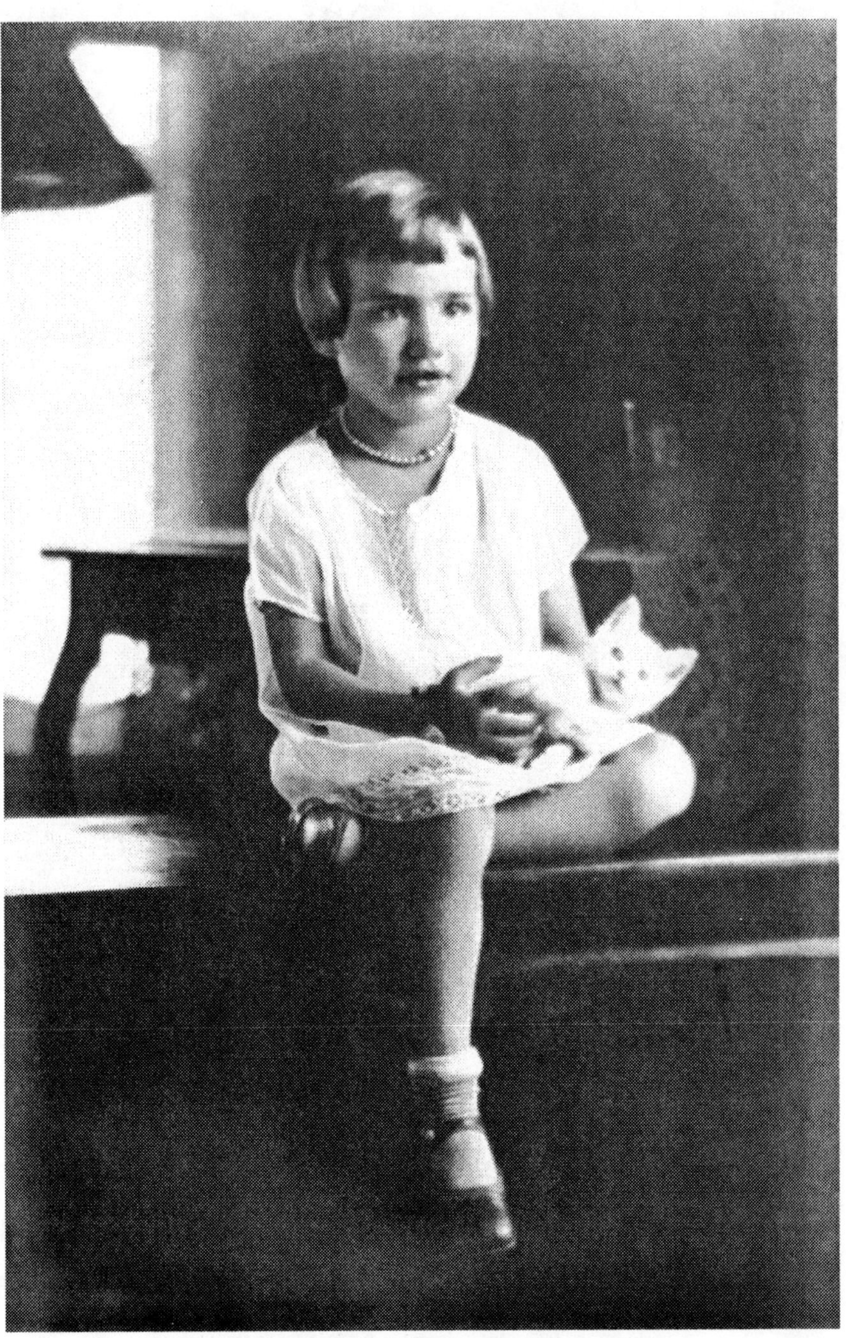

The Original "Girl with The Windblown Bob"
Arlene Mann Kelly

My Thanks

To Bob, with my love,
Who so cheerfully became the
"House Husband," keeping the home fires
blazing while I burned up the computer.

and

To Sydney, the good daughter
who forced me to become
computer literate, and for
keeping the "critter" up and running,
heeding my every cry for help!

and

To God, who faithfully
supplied every elusive word
I was searching for!

FOREWARD

What a tremendous relief to awaken on January 1st, of the year 2000, the first day of the new millennium, to find the shower spouting water, the lights, furnace and coffee maker all working. Airplanes had not fallen out of the sky. Cars, trucks, and trains had not become mute piles of junk, and ships at sea were not stranded in the middle of the ocean.

To our further relief, the business, financial, and technological worlds were up and running as usual. That first cup of coffee couldn't have tasted better that morning, especially since it was hot, and we could sip it while lounging around in our pajamas in comfortably warm homes, supremely grateful that we'd survived, unscathed, into the next millennium. So what could have thrown the fear of God into us simply because we were entering a new year?

I believe one reasonable answer, perhaps even the root cause of the problem, could be the global fixation with technology. The world, it seems, now worships at the altar of technology. This lightning-speed tool has forced us onto a fast track highway of super knowledge. We're swamped and sinking in a quagmire of data. Daily we're given more facts than most of us want. Masses of people are even giving their lives to information. That aside, however, today (good or bad) we can find anyone or any bit of information we choose.

As with most things, it started out gradually, but before long, we'd become the victims of an information-explosion fallout. The glut of information we'd been fed, in the year 1999, coupled with a media run amok, in my opinion, shared the responsibility of worrying us with uneasy threats, dire warnings and nervous predictions of a calamitous event about to be unleashed upon the world.

Whiffing a story of such magnitude, the media could not resist regaling us daily with dark and sinister warnings of this computer glitch and its disastrous consequences. We were warned to buy, save, hoard, barricade, and even arm ourselves against our neighbors. For all we knew, our screwy but sane world was coming to an insane halt. We shouldn't have been surprised, however, because we'd been receiving these warnings of the terror to come for too long.

For the past year, we were forced to contemplate the grim news of our imminent ruin. From that, one could have assumed that our earth was on a collision course with a rogue planet, or we'd become the target of a hostile foreign nation that had perfected an atom bomb, or the sky was going to fall. So what was this terrible tragedy hovering over us, threatening to annihilate us? Strangely enough, that danger, threatening to bring life to a close, was a peril much closer to home.

We knew from the beginning, the source of this internal dilemma. This huge catastrophe was the result of one tiny error! The capability of advancing the date, by just one day into the next century, had not been built into our computers! It was this simple malfunction that had been holding the citizenry captive with apprehension. Worse yet, the fallout from this failure had been prophesied by no less than the top electronic wizards of our time—their predictions becoming virtually synonymous with Armageddon.

Now, spreading such alarming computer stories as this—to the non-computerized set who have already thrown up their hands, dismissing this new device as "too complicated," as well as to the seasoned computer "experts"—is as sure to spook them as a herd of wild horses catching the scent of a cougar.

In addition, recognizing the dominant grip the computer world holds on the population in general, you can be sure that much of the senior segment of our world, already baffled by a world of technology they don't understand, is going to get a little worked up about anything computer experts get excited about. Everyone, however, whether they were willing to admit it or not, seemed to pay attention; recognizing the fact that, "What you don't know really might kill you." It's enough to say that the media did little to reassure us.

Amazingly, to the relief of everyone, and to the validation of those who had seemingly refused to take the warnings so seriously, life as we knew it appeared to have survived this fatal flaw; so we could probably assume that the destruction of the civilized world was still up for grabs. The dismal failure of this grand, but flawed, design, proved, once again, that human fallibility still has the capability of outwitting technology.

In the world where I grew up, such events as this weren't a threat; but I suspect that if they had been, they would have been handled with the same good old-fashioned common sense that our forefathers employed in dealing with the complex problems of their age. *Common Sense* was the name of their guidebook; and it was ours.

Of course this was in that pre-dawn age, BC (before computers) when everyone was forced to do arithmetic with a pencil, paper, and brainpower—still a valid computer, even if we had to count on our fingers. So for those of us from a calmer era, marking the end of another year—even if we'd had the great good fortune of living through such an extraordinary event as the end of a millennium—meant only that we got to stay up until midnight so we could shout, "Happy New Year" out the front door to neighbors already asleep in bed. Tomorrow would dawn just as gloriously uneventfully as it had from the beginning of time.

Although many consider this period a time of hardship (among other things, not having been blessed with the myriad of laborsaving devices we have today) this calmer, kinder, and slower world, where people actually had time to stop and gather a few rosebuds, was our reality and our security.

This is the world in which I lived. It is a place that everyone really should know about. Quite possibly, by pausing to look back at this special time, one might find a reality grip for the things that go speeding through one's life. It might also have the additional benefit of slowing one's heart rate down to a normal pace as they ponder these things of yesteryear.

So let's throw open the window of time and space and take a backward glance at the world as it was, at least my recollection of it, during the early part of the Twentieth Century.

Together we'll explore this strange and wonderful *other world.* It's a world that may be entirely new to many; or it may be a comfortably familiar place waiting to invite those of my generation back for a revisit.

It is the story of a distinct kind of world, seen through the eyes of a young girl who lived through the years of the Great Depression, then on through World War II. Although observed by a child, the story is told by the woman she became; a person who found that world quite a wonderful place, even in the midst of the worst of that time.

Come ride with me in a Model-T Ford (who could beat that for fun) with side curtains instead of windows, and join in some hilarious adventures revolving around this old car. We'll visit a working household cave and savor the feeling and the very essence of its musty, dark presence while viewing the contents of this underground cavern.

Experience the amazing joy of a first telephone, a first radio, a first electric washing machine, electric light bulb, first movie and first car ride.

On this space-odyssey, you'll experience the happiness of penniless kids, and learn why they didn't always understand that they were penniless. View our holidays and our home life, and join in the antics we devised for having fun. Find out how each of these events became so special.

The word "*Depression*" conjures up many negative images: soup kitchens, unemployment lines, bankruptcies, and groveling misery. It may come as a surprise to learn that many people living through this super rough period made it through intact; not only by just surviving, but surviving reasonably well under the circumstances. These stalwarts were somehow able to see beyond the oppressiveness of their present, and keep future expectations alive, being unwilling to remain forever shackled to their debilitating past, or defeated by the dismal nature of those years.

Through it all, these hardy folks managed to draw strength from a source buried deep within their souls, hearts and minds. It was by dipping deeply into this rich spiritual supply that their needs were met, compensating them in large part for their unfairly-dealt hand, even restoring a goodly measure of humor where there was little.

It's my hope that every visitor coming along on this time adventure will learn something about its people; and because of them, will gain a greater insight into the many opportunities awaiting future generations of this world.

These bright and exciting prospects are their heritage; a legacy of hard-won benefits bequeathed to them by those of my generation and the many generations who came before. This, then, is the story of a few of our gentle, loving, hard working, ancestors, and their struggle to carve out a new life in a continually changing world. Because of their struggle, they have provided a legacy for future generations; underwritten by the dogged determination of some others who picked up the obligation where their forefathers left off.

CHAPTER 1

It was a different time, another place, a mere blip on the radar screen of history. It was that much-maligned and unlovely period known as the Great Depression, although it was neither of those to many of us born into that era, for it was all we knew. That times were hard, no one could deny. But people rise or fall according to their own personal circumstances, and their strength and ability to deal with them. In that regard, it is my recollection that our family generally seemed able to manage the proverbial two steps forward to every step back. Of course this assessment was made from the viewpoint of a child who was neither shielded from, nor scarred by, any intimidating repercussions of a depressed economy. It simply was!

My discovery of the world as it was in my own personal time slot in history, began during this period known as the Great Depression Years of the 1930's, and my recounting of it continues on through World War II. However, in the interest of painting a more accurate picture of the significant change these years made in everyone's lives, I must first tell you a bit about some of the remarkable people responsible for helping bring about this change. I'm referring to a few of my ancestors, who were major contributors to their slice of the world, and to my own personal gene pool as well. The contribution made by these folks influenced the future of a notable portion of American history, as well as shaping my own destiny.

Fortunately some of my more creative forefathers had the prudence to record many of the historical family facts of our story and preserve them in several books. One of my sources is a book called the Keese Family History, from 1690 to 1911.

This book traces my father's family through his mother, Hannah Anna Keese Mann, back to 1690, while also making reference to the Bowne Family (whose family intermarried with the Keese Family) whose history dates back to 1595, beginning in England. So it was that the Bownes of Flushing, Long Island, became a further addition to our history through the marriage of John Keese, of Keeseville (named for the family) Long Island, to Mary Bowne, of Flushing in 1722. Of course, if anyone in the family possessed enough curiosity to dig up the complete pile of family skeletons, it's likely that our origins could be traced even further back--and why not--all the way to Adam and Eve.

A recent brochure brought back from Flushing, lists the Bowne Mansion as *"The oldest house in Queens County, the original section being built in 1661 by John Bowne, a member of the Society of Friends (Quakers). Bowne's successful opposition to Governor Stuyversant's religious intolerance restored freedom of religion to the colony of New Netherland. It is believed that the house served as a station on the Underground Railroad in the years before the Civil War.*

As it looked then…..

As it looks today!

Dining room and kitchen of the Bowne Home
Dining room (below) and (above) kitchen of the Bowne Home
.....as seen now with the original furnishings

"The Bownes were among the first who embraced the principle of Friends in this country, for which they suffered much under the Dutch government. John was persecuted, fined and imprisoned and finally banished, sent to Holland, for allowing Friends to hold meetings in his house. Having been sent a prisoner to Holland, he was released after a time with an order to the provincial government, not to molest peaceable citizens.

He built a house at Flushing in 1661, in *which they gave room to Friends to hold their monthly, quarterly and yearly meetings for many years. These peaceable meetings being held in his house incensed the populace against him, but his quiet perseverance and peaceful submission won the victory after much suffering. Hannah, his wife, became a minister and traveled much in America and twice crossed the ocean to Europe, where she labored extensively in England, Ireland and other parts of the Continent. And when all was accomplished that seemed to be required of her, she returned to London in peace and quietly resigned her breath.*

The book was *"Dedicated To The Descendants of John and Elizabeth Titus Keese."* My grandmother, one of eight children, was born June 25, 1868, to Jason E. and Lovina O. Keese, my great grandparents. Back it goes, all the way to John and Elizabeth Keese (and even further) with a listing of their descendants. The preface of the book states: "*John and Elizabeth Titus Keese, were noble people, not warriors, not religious zealots nor enthusiasts, but Friends, a peaceable people, bred and brought up in the society where it was taught that 'It is better to suffer wrong than to do wrong.' "*

This book is an historic treasure as it contains much personal information, written in the antiquated style of those times, such as: *"He replied that his head felt so badly that he did not think he knew anything. He seemed to be sinking, and was helped on a lounge, where he soon ceased to breathe, having attained the patriarchal age of nearly eighty-seven years,"* and, *"She was a blithe lassie five years his junior, well formed and intelligent, with auburn hair."*

Ah ha! The mystery has now been solved! The "*blithe lassie*" referred to here was my great, great, great grandmother, Sarah. I now know why sunshine has always brought out the formerly hated red highlights in my own hair. Sorry Grandma, I'm sure you were a ravishing creature who swept grandpa Stephen off his feet. Eleven children surely attest to that fact.

There follows an engaging labyrinth of genealogy; a poem written by a male member of the family as he lay on his deathbed, obituaries, and accounts of the trials of getting settled in a new territory. There is much poetry, many pictures of grim-looking relatives (who give the appearance of just having eaten a bucket of rusty nails) and detailed accounts of daily living. (It could be assumed here that the dour-looking expressions on their faces came from their less than rollicking lifestyle—or maybe it was the photographer's idea).

Reading through this old account has convinced me that the glorified romance of opening and settling a new land, as it is commonly portrayed today, is grossly distorted. Life in the wilds, as written in this book, proved to be no Sunday school picnic, for it described many stories of the arduous struggle by these sturdy people to conquer the land. One such story, told by the author about his father, Stephen Keese, tells of the anguish created by the depressed economic times: *"The times were dull and wages low; 50 to 75 cents per day was about all a man could command. He said the children came faster than money.*

But Father loved his children and six were born to them in the eleven years they lived in Ohio. In the year 1836 they decided to go to Indiana, where there was government land they could enter. They borrowed $100 from a friend to purchase the land, and father went on ahead to clear the land and buy them a house to live in. Mother Sarah, remained in Ohio until autumn, then she and four of their five (at the time) *remaining children came out in a covered wagon."* (One child had died in infancy.) *"Elizabeth was left with her grandmother in Ohio."* (She was probably either too young to make the trip, or perhaps ill.)

One revealing quotation describes an exhausting incident along the way: *"The road was bad, through the woods, and it took four good horses to draw the wagon, and then they stalled many times in the mud."* The book indicated that Sarah had also brought along two good cows and a pony.

Poor, dear Sarah! In this age, we are so accustomed to the comfort and luxury of our world that it stretches the imagination to be able to understand the misery and horror of the rough trip that faced this courageous frontier woman as she set out with her small brood. They were headed for only "*God knew where*," to join Stephen in some wild and unknown wilderness. Who can really understand the grit that it took to contend with every fickle condition of weather, the constant need of foraging for food to add to the meager supply of staples necessary to feed her family in the wilds, as well as tending to everyone's daily needs (like bathing and finding safe places for their toilet) while continually remaining on the alert for predators?

It was up to Sarah to protect her family from wild animals lurking nearby who had a particular fondness for stalking humans on the trail. These, and the many unforeseen and unpredictable tribulations involved in such an expedition would have been a daunting and terrifying misery for anyone, but especially so for a woman who, from her pictures, appeared frail and small. Her clothing must have deceptively hidden a body of steel, and an iron will.

The account did not mention a companion, or a male guide, so it is possible she made the trip alone with only her four children to help her. One can be sure they weren't just along for the ride. Kids born in this rugged new country were expected to pitch in and share equally in the chores, which was one reason for having many children. They were taught to work, at times being put to jobs that were hard enough to challenge the endurance of an adult.

From some deeply hidden source, Sarah found the necessary reserve, the strength and the extraordinary courage to command a team of four horses—taking them through dense woods, and over dangerous rivers and rocky streams on this long and grueling journey. The unbelievable rigors of this arduous undertaking took their toll. Sarah was sorely tested in her constant fight to ward off total exhaustion. This endeavor, requiring steely, unwavering nerves, and the stamina of Atlas, was a challenge for the most stalwart of men making the same trip, but was inconceivable for a woman, traveling alone through the backwoods, with four children.

From her photo in the book, one would assume that Sarah was a lady who would find herself more at home presiding over tea parties than struggling with a team of horses, or the enslavement of helping settle an obstinate land. Surely her determination in the face of such peril and adversity, must give new meaning to the words stamina, endurance, courage, love, loyalty, and yes, even nobility.

It's unlikely that there has ever been a more exuberant and wildly-exciting reunion in the history of mankind than the one that took place the day this band of worn out, travel-weary adventurers made it by horse and wagon from their home in Ohio, to Indiana. There they joined husband and father, Stephen, in their new home in a clearing in the woods, which was described as: "*a small cabin with a wide porch on the north side.*"

Sweltering in a tall stand of prairie grass, tangled vines and thorny bushes, on the near side of the cabin where he was struggling to clear a new field from this inhospitable virgin prairie land, Stephen stopped for a breather. He had just taken a large blue bandanna from his pocket and was wiping away the sweat, dripping from his face, when he glanced up and spotted the wagon containing the determined little band of trail-weary but hearty travelers just as the team topped the nearby rise. The vision now forming before his unbelieving eyes was something of which he had been dreaming through endless days and countless lonely nights!

With a wildly whooping shout, dropping the reins of the team he was using to plow this fertile, but weed-choked patch of land, Stephen began yelling and waving to attract the attention of his family as he started frantically running toward the wagon. Leaping over split-rail fences and newly-hewn tree stumps in his feverish haste to throw his arms around his advancing family, he ran like one possessed.

Having gotten glimpses through the trees, of what they were hoping was a cabin up ahead, the children began calling out to him, leaping and flinging themselves headlong off the wagon at their first sight of Stephen. The lot of them, nearly delirious with excitement, raced wildly in their eagerness to get to him, stumbling and falling as they ran. Sarah, too, threw all caution aside, tossing the reins of her team into the air, no longer mindful of, or caring where the horses went, in the raw emotion of this moment and her relieved need to feel herself enveloped in the strong, loving arms of her beloved Stephen.

Months of pent-up nerves, and the strain of excessive toil, now found instant release in Stephen. The stunning joy of seeing his family insulated Stephen from any conscious awareness of the piercing thorns and stinging nettles that were ripping into his clothing and exposed flesh as he plunged headlong into the brush. Simultaneously laughing and weeping with excitement, mindlessly leaping over thickets of wild underbrush, his only thought was of reaching his dear family and smothering them with kisses and scooping each one into his longing arms.

Stephen was sure his heart was near bursting from shock, and the overpowering elation of glimpsing this wonderfully bedraggled crew coming toward him over the rise. Breathless from the exertion and excitement of racing to reach the little group, he collapsed into their midst, throwing his arms open wide in his frenzied effort to clutch them all at one time. Joyful tears swam in every eye of this reunited family. The children, wild with excitement, clung to their father in happiness and relief-filled emotion, knowing that at last they were safely home.

It was some time before the newcomers were to view the interior of their new home, being caught up in the extraordinary emotion of the moment, which kept them hugging and dancing with excitement, and basking in the reality of each other. Then, sinking to their knees, their first official act as a reunited family was to offer up one of the world's most undeniably sincere prayers, giving thanks to the Almighty for bringing them through the wilderness and its terrors, delivering them safely home. A euphoric state of happiness engulfed the reunited kin that day.

Once calm again reigned, and delirium gave way to near exhaustion, this trail-roughened company's thoughts predictably returned to what they had been anticipating (forever it seemed). For too long a time they had dreamed of a roof over their heads to keep them dry and warm, and a man to protect and stand between them and further dangers. Now it was becoming an honest-to-goodness reality. Halleluiah!

A thrillingly new and intoxicating sense of freedom re-energized the children as they ran on ahead to explore the cabin thoroughly. That done, in their fevered excitement of trying to take in every new sight as soon as possible, they once again poured outside their new home to go exploring. Running and tumbling in the fields with all of the energy and exuberance of young colts, these healthy, work-toughened children took full advantage of this free time, knowing that the farm and its chores would all too soon become part of their daily routine. For now, however, nothing would dampen their free spirits as they romped with untiring enthusiasm, for they were home! As the family grew, the cabin was added on to many times and was eventually replaced by a larger frame house.

There were many more poignant and moving excerpts in the book, including a portion of a poem (resembling a will) written a few days before his death, by Stephen R. Keese: (evidently the same Stephen Keese who is mentioned above, but written much later).

"My wife and I are old and gray
And do not know how long we'll stay.
Bury me plainly and decently when I die,
And let not a stone tell where I lie.
Plant some tree (pine or cedar) o'er my head,
My body will nourish it when I'm dead.
I do not like to see costly white stone
Watching over flesh and bones."

Religion was of primary importance to my stalwart and faithful forefathers. Having embraced the Quaker faith, they formed many Friends groups and continued in this faith through the years. There are accounts of many preachers in the book and many other people of worth, some of wealth and some of meager means, which gives a family tree stability and roots. To support those facts, the author added this note about his (my) family: *"It appears from different accounts that many of my ancestors for four or five generations back were accounted of as among the worthys of that day in our society."*

He was obviously as proud of the family as am I. Most importantly, there doesn't seem to be one horse thief among them.

It does, however, appear that they remained true to the Friends faith throughout the remaining pages of the Keese Family History—my grandma Hannah's family.

CHAPTER 2

My grandfather Mann's family, also had a rich history; one that helped to influence and develop another vital segment of Americana. Grandfather R.E.L. was born to Henry Thomas and Elizabeth Birks Mann. Henry, my great grandfather, was born in Covington, Kentucky, June 3, 1827. Henry T. and Elizabeth had four sons, two dying in infancy.

The source of this information was taken from family stories and the *Laurel Iowa Centennial 1881-1981,* which mentions that Grandpa was named after General Robert E. Lee, Commander-in-chief of the Confederate Army in the Civil War. Reading historical novels about the South, especially those set during the period of the Civil War, has always piqued my imagination. Through them I feel closely connected to Grandpa.

In the spring of 1998, my husband and I were traveling through Georgia where we stopped at the small town of Andersonville, a short distance down the road from the site of the infamous Confederate prison camp of the Civil War. In a quaint little shop, propped up against a wall, stood a painting of General Robert E. Lee. Had we been heading on south toward our vacation destination I might not have been able to resist the temptation to buy the picture. But since we were heading home, having already spent my *mad money* on other "gotta have its" while we vacationed in Florida during the winter, reason took over, especially when I saw the price tag of $100. Instead of buying the painting, my husband held it in the light while I took a picture, figuring someday to display the photo next to my grandfather's picture. Somehow I still regret not splurging and buying the painting, as it was beautifully done.

My grandfather, Robert E. Lee Mann, was born on the homestead just north of Laurel, Iowa, September 26, 1868, twenty-four years after his father, Henry Thomas Mann, had come to Iowa by covered wagon and oxen from Springfield, Illinois, having moved there earlier from Kentucky.

Henry had met and married Elizabeth Hicks and together they homesteaded the land north of Laurel. Their history states that: *"He was actively involved in the affairs of the community, and the country, and endeavored to aid every enterprise that was for the public good. He saw the wilderness transformed into one of the most prosperous sections of the United States. Story has it that Jesse and Frank James stopped at his house late one afternoon and stayed all night."*

The family has always claimed this Jesse James story, and I know it to be true, because several of my cousins and I heard all about it while visiting our grandparents on the farm, one uncomfortably hot July day. As predictable as kids are, though, we hadn't noticed the heat at first—being totally unaware of the relentless temperature for the better part of the afternoon, as we ran about absorbed in our own pursuits. We'd only become aware of our discomfort when our clothes began sticking to our skin, and perspiration drenched our faces. It was then that we spotted Grandpa sitting in a lawn chair, canopied beneath the dense shade of the many stately trees surrounding the lawn. The trees, like sentries, rimmed and cooled the spacious lawn, their dense foliage providing nature's own perfect air conditioning.

Running over, we flopped down beside him on the sweet, lush grass, to recover and cool off. Sprawling lethargically around Grandpa's chair, we began moaning and groaning about how hot we were. In an effort to take our minds off our misery, Grandpa began telling us the story of Frank and Jesse James, who had visited the farm and had asked to spend the night. We were instantly captivated by the story he began relating to us.

Jesse James was an outlaw; but since those days when he roamed the country, robbing and killing, he has become one of the world's famous (or perhaps infamous) legendary characters. Some labeled him America's Robin Hood, while others called him a cold-blooded killer. He was born in 1847, and began his life of crime in 1866, after serving in the Civil War. At the age of 19, Jesse, with his brother Frank, began robbing railroad express cars. We were startled to learn that their very first train target was the Chicago and Rock Island express near Adair, Iowa, on July 21, 1873, where they got $2,000 from the safe and stole the passengers' valuables.

Grandpa's high-spirited audience excitedly agreed that it was probably right after that robbery that the James brothers stopped at my great grandfather's farm, since their daring robbery might have logically sent them east looking for a place to hide out. We were totally enthralled by the story Grandpa was relaying, and hung on his every word as he told us about the James brothers next reported "job."

That job came two months later in Kansas City, Kansas, where they stole $10,000 from the fairground. In 1873, the year of the great "train heist," my grandfather would have been five years old, so he could have had some recollection of their visit himself, but it would seem more plausible that the story came to him from his parents.

We spellbound kids were like blank pages, sitting enraptured, eagerly soaking up every drop from the inkwell in which Grandpa was penning his dazzling story. Visions of those two notorious bank robbers—who had spent time right here on this very spot where we were sitting—took vivid form in our eager, fertile imaginations. The farm began to take on an entirely new look for this bunch of awe-struck kids as he pointed out the places where the James boys had walked, stabled their horses, and the very place the "boys" had spent the night in the barn.

Grandpa explained that their visitors' conversation did nothing to alarm my great grandparents, undoubtedly because they had not heard of the exploits of these two at the time. "Just two very nice men," as I remember Grandpa's description of them. After breakfast that next morning, the visitors went peaceably on their way, leaving nothing exciting or legendary in their wake. This sketchy story, however, continues to thrill every new generation of family members; the romantic tale of the James Boys will forever be linked to our family. Who could believe our fantastic good fortune, not only to be hearing a story like this, but to also be part of a family in which it actually happened?

On that same magical summer afternoon, Grandpa, continued to keep his audience thoroughly spellbound through his good-natured and delighted retelling of another larger-than-life story involving the family farm. This account, too, held his eager, mouth-gaping grandchildren, at rapt attention.

This awesome war story has also been handed down through the generations of the Mann family. During the Civil War, a part of Cox's Army, Union soldiers under the leadership of Brigadier General Jacob D. Cox of the Army of Ohio, was traveling through Iowa on their mission to protect the railroads (of which there were many in Iowa) and offering civilians, loyal to the Union, protection from southern sympathizers.

Who couldn't recognize a certain irony in this situation since these Union soldiers had chosen this particular farm on which to camp—a farm whose owner would later name a son (my grandfather) Robert E. Lee Mann. It would indeed seem strange if these soldiers hadn't picked up some clue that they were camping on a farm being occupied by transplanted southerners. Perhaps the soldiers' presence was intended as a warning; maybe they were keeping an eye on a "Confederate sympathizer;" or it may have been merely a luckless happenstance.

The lawn of the Mann farm was large and beautifully kept, with many majestically towering pine trees offering deep shade. It must have appealed to the soldiers as a perfect place to bed down for a spell. With Great Grandpa Henry's cooperation, the soldiers pitched their tents and camped for a time. So it was that our great grandparents, who may have had little choice but to cooperate, given the dire condition in which they found themselves, made sure that the men were fed and made comfortable. Then again, one would expect nothing less from southerners than courteous southern hospitality.

Although the situation may have appeared relatively harmless, the Mann family was, at the same time, keeping particularly close watch over their young 'uns, making sure they were safe and protected from any undesirable elements.

That the event actually happened was never in question, but since Grandpa was not born until after the war ended, the story he brought to light for us that day must have been another incident he had heard from his parents, told and retold over the years. It was a riveting recitation of the occurrence for us, his grandchildren, just as he told it. It was incredibly surprising for us to learn that rough soldiers—with guns, horses, and tents, and maybe even bandaged wounded—had actually visited, and even camped on *our family's* farm.

Our imaginations were working overtime, conjuring up the sight of that small army actually camping on this very lawn—Grandpa's lawn. Eventually the sobering thought of these soldiers preparing to leave the farm—off to fight yet another battle where they might be killed—brought a few grim reflections.

Our games, for the rest of the day, were reenactments of what we imagined things might have looked like, taking place right here in this historic but familiar place. Leaving for home wasn't nearly as difficult that day as it usually was, because we couldn't wait to get home to tell our friends. We had suddenly become the exciting characters of Grandpa's stories—brave soldiers fighting the enemy. We were oh so proud, arriving home, rushing out to repeat the stories to our friends. Our heads were swelled with conceit and pride. How "special" we were to be able to claim our "distinguished, famous family."

So it was that grandpa Robert was born on this homestead, into this pioneer home and family. The account goes on to state that: *"On March 27, 1889, he was married to black eyed, raven-haired Hannah A. Keese, a native of Indiana."*

Hannah Anna and Robert E. Lee Mann

What a terrific description of my grandmother, Hannah Anna Keese Mann—for she was all of that, and much more. Grandma Hannah was a tall, very straight, imposing woman with a commanding presence, and in her later years, rather heavy-set. She was used to being given her own way and she tolerated no nonsense. That she had strong opinions was widely recognized; neither did she want for the courage to express them. With her grandchildren, however, she was loving and kind, and to us, seemed much softer than her imputed perception.

She became a volunteer for the Red Cross during World War I, and weekly was driven by horse and buggy into Marshalltown, approximately ten miles away, to help roll bandages. Knowing my grandmother as I did, it would not have been hard to imagine she might have been the one who organized it. Among my possessions are the heavy, black wool, Red Cross cape and the small, black, straw hat Grandmother wore, covering the bun on the top of her head, when she was doing her volunteer work. The uniform, cape and bonnet will soon be 100 years old.

Grandma was also a member of W.C.T.U. (Women's Christian Temperance Union). Many who knew her might have described her as "militant." How she must have admired Carry Nation, the great ax-wielding agitator for temperance who was the founder of the cause. Unlike Miss Nation, however, Grandma obviously confined her opposition to energetic rhetoric, since no physical confrontations were ever mentioned.

The story is told about Grandma Hannah that one day as she was walking along a street in Marshalltown, she overheard some German people speaking in their native tongue. Anti-German sentiment was epidemic at the time because of our country's involvement in World War I, and the American people's *hatred* for "the Kaiser." What Hitler became to the world during World War II, the Kaiser represented in World War I.

In her characteristically outspoken, uninhibited quick-tempered mode, black eyes snapping, Grandma marched up to these innocent and unsuspecting immigrants, and in her usually direct manner said, "You had better start learning to speak English since you are now living in America." Their undoubtedly shocked reaction was never reported, but to these startled newcomers her biting remarks probably did little to endear their new country (or her) to them. While Grandma took no prisoners, she was somehow able to retain her much-respected, lady-like demeanor, and everyone who knew her treated her with great deference. One might wonder if it was partly out of fear of invoking her displeasure.

Grandpa R.E.L's happy nature proved a providential counterpart for Grandma's rather "starchy" countenance. He was a man with a quick smile and a jolly laugh who liked teasing his grandchildren. We didn't need to be coaxed into doing chores with Grandpa since it was unusual fun for us—shelling corn, by feeding the dried ears into a hand-operated sheller and cranking to remove the kernels from the cob, feeding the livestock, or fixing a fence, among other things. Tagging along with Grandpa, lending a hand with the jobs he gave us to do, was always interesting, partly because he never thought our steady stream of questions too bothersome, or even too many; and because our part of the chores was never too hard since he did most of the skilled labor and hard work.

"R.E.L.," the account continues, "*was about five feet ten and a half, and stockily built and he raised Spotted Poland China hogs, Clydesdale and Percheron horses. He and Hannah lived in a house, believed to have been built, by Henry Thomas. Later they added on to the dwelling, and it became known as the Mann house. It had large rooms, with a kitchen, dining room, sitting room, parlor, music room, bedroom and open stairway on the main floor, with four large bedrooms and bath on the second floor. "R.E.L,"* a successful and enterprising farmer, "*and Hannah had four children: Mayme E., lovely and artistic; Claude Jason, a quiet man of sterling character and integrity; LeRoy Thomas, (*my dad) *a fun-loving young man and veteran of WWI, and young vivacious Ida, also with musical talent.*

" The four children attended the 'Mann School' located on the corner just north of his house." "LeRoy married Alvina Otillia Pischel, a cheerful young lady with outstanding musical talent and leadership qualities. Together they raised their three children in a religious environment. The children are Maxine, Maurice, and (me) *Arlene,"* the later links in the family chain.

By inheriting this particular background, which includes grandparents who were all farmers, I'm sure I have been given a greater appreciation for the land and for those who labor to tame it. I'm thankful for my ancestors who had the vision to see the unlimited possibilities of this new land and its ability to provide for, and nurture future generations, and who also possessed the obstinate courage and determination to make it happen. For me they raised the bar of achievement considerably, a necessity for attaining higher goals.

CHATPER 3

My origins, having thus been accounted for, I now begin the account of my entry into the story. So, in the immortal words of another aspiring author, *Snoopy*, the talking dog character in the popular cartoon *Peanuts*, I begin.

"It was a dark and stormy night*...!*" No…. this, I realize, is not a good beginning for me as there is no supportable clue as to what kind of day or night it was on the day of my birth. I am, however, positive that it was on January 27, which would suggest cold and snow, since the place of my birth was Faulkner, Iowa. All available evidence leads me to believe my birth was at home, but whether in town or on a farm is unclear. There remains the impression, however, of Dad's summoning the doctor and being told that it was too snowy for him to get there. Whether he was late, or made it at all, will remain a mystery for all time. Since phones did not appear to be in general use at the time, it is puzzling how Dad contacted the doctor. Though this question will remain forever unanswered, my entry into the world was completely successful, coming in at a lusty, six and a alf pounds.

Faulkner was one of those legendary wide places in a country road that can be missed, as the old saying goes, "if one sneezes while passing through." Had they published a newspaper in that

Lilliputian hamlet, my arrival would quite possibly have been the sole piece of news for the day, the week, or even the month, with the possible exception of the discovery of any stray cow, pig or pet dog that may have accidentally frozen to death in a snowdrift somewhere by the road.

My birth added one more name to the Mann family line: Mother, Alvina Otillia Pischel Mann, Father Leroy Thomas Mann (widely known as Roy), sister, Maxine Cavanaugh, and brother, Maurice Robert. It's my belief that I was rather well received, as I don't remember any abuse from my siblings, at least not until I grew old enough to defend myself.

When I was very young, my family moved from Faulkner to Whitten. Whitten was, at the time, another very small, but rather active little rural community nestled among farm fields that edged up to what I will grandly call our city limits. The town is located on a line, as the crow flies (undoubtedly a much more comfortable means of travel than most country roads at the time) roughly somewhere near the center point between Eldora and Marshalltown.

Dad, skilled in any area of farm work, decided to try his hand at blacksmithing. He spotted and bought a building suitable for a blacksmith shop, which he outfitted and opened for business. A blacksmith shop was a welcome addition to any farming community in those days, since horses were used to work the farms and they were in constant need of shoeing. Dad not only applied shoes to horses' hooves, but he repaired harnesses and fixed broken wagons and other farm equipment. Repairing machinery was a large part of his business from which he supported our family for many years in this small community of Whitten.

During these growing up years, a visit to our Grandfather Mann's large and handsome old country estate home was always the most exciting time imaginable for us kids. Mom and Dad would load us up in our old Model-T Ford (that had side curtains instead of windows) and drive, traveling over dirt and gravel roads from Whitten, through Marshalltown, then on south toward Laurel. It was at that moment when we rounded the big bend in the road, spotting the large red barn that stood some distance behind the house, that told three *antsy* kids we were almost there.

Perhaps you've never had the privilege of riding in a Model-T Ford car with side curtains. Any trip to Grandpa's farm meant traveling over twenty-eight slow miles of gravel road in the sweltering sauna heat of an Iowa summer or the bone-chilling, lung-freezing, frigid, hoarfrost of an Iowa winter.

These winter trips especially, in which we were never warm, despite being completely immobilized under a load of heavy lap robes and blankets, is one of the major reasons why we are now so thankful for the ultimate luxury of heated and air-conditioned modern cars, with seats designed to keep one's bones from becoming rearranged. That last quarter-mile was the hardest to endure for it seemed to stretch on forever. The temptation to jump out of the car and run ahead was held in check only by the stern voice of our dad telling us to, "Settle down."

Turning into the driveway, which rounded the large flower-edged lawn, up to the gate behind the house, was the nearest thing to heaven as life itself could be for me each time we visited. The suspense was nearly unbearable as we watched Grandma and Grandpa throw open the door and rush down the walk to meet us. After the hugs and kisses, and their amazed comments, "My, how much you've grown!" it was up the porch steps and into Grandmother's large, old-fashioned kitchen, with the wonderful smell of roasting meat filling the room. Of course that delicious aroma was coming from the innards of her large, old, wood-fired black range.

Waiting on the sideboard were Grandma's special pies or cakes, and every kind of prepared canned, pickled, and freshly harvested edible that any garden could produce. The large dining room table was set with her finest china and crystal, and it was hard to wait until dinnertime. So as not to appear as gluttonous as we felt, we kids would spend the next few minutes inspecting and rediscovering the look and feel of our Grandparent's house.

The kitchen was typical of country kitchens in those days. Just as it was in our own home, the same wood burning range that Grandma used for cooking and baking, also warmed her cozy kitchen. Typical of most women of that age, she knew how to build fires in that stove. She lifted the round iron lids on top of the stove with an iron handle resembling a curved fork that fit into small indentations on the lids.

Removing the lid, she would add smaller pieces of chopped wood to get it going, and coal and larger pieces of wood to keep it burning longer.

On the far right side of the stove was a large reservoir that was kept filled with water. Because of its proximity to the fire box in the stove, the water was always hot and ready for all-purpose use—from washing dishes, to scrubbing floors, or anything else requiring hot water. The large oven was amazing because it was always hot when the stove was fired, with no visible way to regulate temperatures to suit the requirements of baking a cake or roasting a huge chunk of meat.

Today's ovens require individual heat settings for each of these items, but then it was necessary for the cook to rely on how hot the oven felt when she quickly stuck her hand inside. It wasn't unusual, also, to see my mother throw a small handful of water on the top of the stove, watching to see how high the water danced on the black lids. From this she could tell the right moment when the oven was ready to bake her particular food item. Of course, we knew she wasn't practicing voodoo, or witchcraft, but was simply Mom being Mom, leaning on years of experience with a wood burning cooking range.

In addition to its fluctuating heat peculiarities, this type of stove made other demands for its care and maintenance. It was a weekly routine in our own home, after the stove had cooled or was cold, to rub its surface with stove polish—a thick, black paste, which could accurately be compared to black shoe polish—with about the same smell. After spreading the gooey paste over the entire stovetop we rubbed and polished until the surface shone with a beautiful black patina. While mother was proud of the results of our vigorous polishing it must have taken her longer to wash the clothes we were wearing than it did for us to shine the stove. Our hands remained dyed black for days. About the time they started looking presentable again, it came time again to polish the stove. None of us kids escaped being conscripted for this detestable ritual.

In between polishings Mom would often grab a large piece of crumpled-up waxed paper and rub it over the stovetop—whether the stove was hot or cold. It didn't seem to matter to her, for she seemed impervious to the searing heat; and she was able to renew the gloss with the waxed paper. It met her test, at least temporarily.

Mother could plunge her hands into the hottest, or the coldest water imaginable, and she was never burned from her many waxings of the stove. Even though it would seem she mistreated her hands with all of the rough work she did, they were always soft and smooth. Daily, Mother used a hand lotion that was a mixture of glycerin and either bay rum or rose water that she had prepared at the drugstore. There was something very pleasurable about watching my mother apply the lotion with her long, deliberate, and graceful motions. I loved smelling and feeling her hands, after the treatment; their softness was a comfort.

Another maintenance requirements for these black behemoths, was making sure there was always firewood available. So the job fell to us kids to keep the wood box, sitting next to the stove, filled so Mom could start her fire whenever she needed to.

Always starting the fire in the same way, by grabbing a piece of old newspaper and crumpling it, she placing it in the firebox first. Then came a few very small pieces of kindling, and on top, larger chunks of wood. It didn't take long for the stove to become hot enough to cook a meal.

Although we were required to handle these chores, none of them were harder than we were able to perform; they were only inconvenient when we were involved in doing something more interesting. And although we "groused' a bit, at times, we knew we wouldn't get out of doing them because everyone had jobs to do and we did them without too much argument. That's what families did. Everyone pulling together, working in harmony, in my mind, is the glue that bonds a family.

While waiting for the grown-ups to finish getting the meal on the table, after our arrival at Grandpa's farm (knowing it would always take longer than expected because of the inevitable "catching-up-chatter" going on among the adults) we kids took advantage of that time to revisit the rest of the large house beyond the kitchen and dining room.

Stepping from the linoleum-covered floors of the kitchen and dining room, into the carpeted, high-ceilinged sitting room, parlor, music room and bedroom on the first floor, the house took on a noticeable difference. Matching carpets adorning each room were of an Axminster-type wool weave, centered with a floral pattern that was repeated in the border extending around the perimeter of each room. Since there was little, or no padding under the carpet, the muted resonance of our footsteps on the rugs, lying directly on wooden floors, sounded only slightly hushed. The echo produced, as we walked, gave the large rooms a rather cavernous feeling. We kids were somewhat intimidated by the austere formality of this part of the home, so our visits never got out of hand, or our play there, too rambunctious. Somehow each of these rooms seemed to command restraint and good manners.

The "attention-getting" feature of this part of the house, was its furnishings. Each room was furnished with an extravagant collection of glistening, shiny-black, stiff, horsehair-covered sofas and chairs, so grand in their day. However, I can't remember the last time I saw a piece of this type furniture in any furniture or antique store, so they must either be buried at the bottom of a landfill somewhere, burned, or they've joined a collection of historical artifacts in some out-of-the-way museums.

It's understandable that their popularity didn't last too long because the horsehair sofas and chairs, while striking and quite grand to look at, were rigid and rather hard to sit on. The coverings on these large pieces of inflexible home furnishings gained their name because of the fabric from which they were actually made—horsehair.

Due, simply, to their large imposing nature, these pieces of furniture didn't suggest a place for lounging, as we know it today. Ladies of that day, however, didn't "lounge;" they were expected to be *lady-like* and decorous as they sat. But because their dresses were most always voluminous, with outlandish undergarments adding to their girth, women of that era undoubtedly found the firm, wide, slick surfaces of the furniture quite practical for their needs, allowing them easy access on and off, with ample space to spread out their dresses.

My grandmother's parlor also contained a collection of decorous tables of all shapes and sizes, most of them covered with doilies.

Of course there were the usual pieces of china, books, and other treasured *objets d'art* decorating the room as well as a number of paintings on the walls. Some of the pictures were of our ancestors, and a few which were done by my Aunt Mayme, who studied art at the LeGrand Academy in Grinnell and at the college in Cedar Falls.

Aunt Mayme also had a great talent for china painting. I now have one of her delicate pink creamer and sugar sets, hand-painted with small roses, sitting on a shelf in our over- fifty-year-old walnut corner cupboard that my husband built in manual training class when he was a young lad in school. Grandma's parlor, because of its formal and stylishly grand furnishings, had a rather imperious air and we children preferred to play outside, or in Grandma's sitting room. Perhaps that was her choice as well.

One unique and unusual "picture" gracing a wall of the living room was a favorite of my sister, Maxine's. It was a curious brown wreath mounted inside a deep shadow-box frame. The wreath was intricately intertwined with flowers, and was really quite beautiful. But horror of horrors (from my perspective) it was all made from human hair. While continually fascinated with the idea of this ghoulish piece, I could never desire it, or even understand why she would want it as much as she did. This type of "art," popular at the time, could be found in many homes of that period.

In the summertime, Grandma often placed flowers in the large rooms; but the windows were never open to my recollection, giving that end of the house a rather dark appearance. Perhaps it was grandma's personal war against the inevitable dust that rose off the dirt and gravel road that kept her windows closed. Summer heat didn't seem to be a great problem, however, since the house was tall—a lofty two-story structure whose large rooms and high ceilings kept the house naturally cooled. In addition, the house was shaded by the many tall trees surrounding it. With draperies drawn to keep out the hot morning and afternoon sun, they managed quite well. Between the parlor and music room were polished, wooden, sliding pocket doors, which met in the middle to close off the rooms from one another if the need arose. A perennial pastime of mine, as a youngster, during our too-infrequent visits to my grandparents' house, was pretending to be riding up and down an elevator. Using the music room as my elevator, I found it great fun to repeatedly open and close these sliding doors.

My experience with elevators, to that point, had been limited to those occasional trips to Marshalltown, the only close town large enough to boast of one or two buildings tall enough to require the use of an elevator. What grand fun to "ride up and down" in the music room until I tired of the game. The music room was furnished much like the parlor, but included a piano, in addition to another scaled down collection of the same horsehair-covered sofas, chairs, tables, and bric-a-brac. It was a wonderful room and indeed, a marvelous house.

It was in the huge parlor of that house that my grandmother was "laid out" when she died, for it was the usual practice in those days for the deceased to be brought back home to be "shown" and visited until the time of the funeral. The main function of funeral homes then was merely to prepare the dead for burial. They had not become, as we know them today, highly private places to hold the bodies and "shield the squeamish from the distasteful state of death," a given for which I am very thankful indeed.

Grandma and I had made a pact, when I was very young, that if one died first, the survivor would **make sure** the other one was dead. Grandma devised that agreement to allay my fear of being buried alive. In our small town of Whitten lived a neighbor lady who delighted in telling us kids scary stories as we played with her children on the front porch in the evenings. It was one of her darker stories that instilled this terror in me at a very young age.

It was about a man whom she claimed had actually been buried alive. I was nearly paralyzed with fear as she recounted the gruesome details. And because I harbored this morbid thought for such a long period of my life, it isn't surprising that this irrational fear raises its ugly head at odd moments to plague me, even today. Negative ideas such as this can become so ingrained in a small child's mind that they have the ability to damage the psyche for a lifetime. We need to be careful about the stories or jokes we tell a child!

Grandmother died in the year 1938, when I was thirteen. We, of course, answered the call to come when we got the news of her death, but we didn't leave home until later the next day. By reaching the farm after dark on the day she was brought home for viewing, the gloom of nighttime seemed to magnify the weirdness of the entire affair for me.

While the house and the living room were exactly the same as they had been the last time I had visited, something now felt horribly changed, depressingly different. The room had taken on an unfamiliar, stifling, and gloomy heaviness that made it hard for me to breathe. Standing in the doorway, in the cheerless presence of the many mourners, all of my old fears came rushing back as I haltingly stood there, wanting desperately to turn and run back out to the car.

Resolutely, however, I entered the familiar parlor where she lay. Stepping through the doorway, it was as if some invisible presence was pressuring me from behind, pushing me, cutting off all avenues of retreat. I remember thinking that my heart would surely stop if I went any further, for I seemed to be cloaked in a cloud of gloom.

In an attempt to shore up my sagging courage, I kept reminding myself that it was my sacred duty to keep my vow to Grandma, of making *absolutely* sure she was dead. So it was, that through this constant mental prodding I faced the ghastly fact that I had no choice but to cross that room, even if it killed me. I had to find out for myself whether or not my grandma was *completely* and *irreversibly* dead

Determination alone gave me just enough courage to force my fear-stiffened knees to bend, propelling me across the room. Not at all certain I would remain vertical for the entire trip, I nevertheless managed to continue onward (on some very shaky legs) while all the time, being keenly aware of the unseen force that kept prodding me forward.

Cautiously weaving my way among the large number of people standing about in small groups, visiting in hushed, inaudible tones, I reached the coffin—which had appeared from the doorway to be at least a block away.

Reaching the casket I was met by a ghastly, shocking sight! I had been told that my grandmother would be lying in this large, ornate box in the far corner of the room. Instead, she had been replaced by a life-sized, waxen, unresponsive, replica of a person bearing the same image as the one who used to comb my hair and make pancakes for my breakfast.

Looking at her still, silent, frozen features—although as dignified and imposing in death as in life—now made death a grim reality. The discipline of forcing myself to touch her hand must have come from the "sacred" promise I'd made. The cold, hard, lifeless response to that touch, gave me my answer. I had fulfilled my sacred obligation, and I knew beyond all doubt that my grandma was *truly dead.*

Things were never quite the same after Grandma's death. There was never to be another of our famous little picnics down in the grove; a favorite event we shared because of our mutual love of picnics. Some of those times I suspect these little outings were to distract me from my recurring bouts of homesickness during my overnight visit to the farm.

The grove was one of Grandma's favorite places and had become mine as well. On the spur of the moment she'd ask me if I'd like to go on a picnic. "Oh yes Grandma, let's," always came my excited reply! Quickly she would pack a little lunch of whatever was available; sandwiches or left-over fried chicken, hard-boiled eggs or fruit, and many times a piece of pie or cake. Filling a large fruit jar with cold milk, lemonade or iced tea, she would then pack it all into a basket, cover it with a cloth, and off we'd go.

It didn't take long to find just the right spot, usually near the small brook running along the far edge of the grove. Together we would spread a blanket and the small tablecloth and sit under the dense shade trees to eat.

Bird watching, trying to identify the species, was our usual pastime at lunch, and after we'd eaten we'd often lie back on the blanket to digest and watch fat, billowing clouds form and re-form in the wind, leaving us laughing with surprise as we spotted misshapen bears, mutant elephants, cars, weird faces, and mountainous scenes as they drifted and fused into still other identifiable objects.

With the remains of our picnic cleared away, Grandma usually suggested we take a walk through the grove, over to the animal pens where we would stop to have a look at the cows. This was high adventure for me, a town girl. At times, if we were lucky, we got to see some newborn, wobbly little calves doing their best to stand up and walk.

Leaving the cows, our pathway usually led to the pigpens, which were generally pretty smelly places. However it was worth enduring the odor to watch the pigs rooting around. They were usually covered with dried mud from wallowing in the available puddles. The sound of their grunting and squealing got downright raucous when they were fighting for position by shoving and nudging each other for a place to stick their snouts in the feeding trough. I really didn't like all the noise they made and I became alarmed, afraid some of the smaller pigs were being hurt.

After the pigpen check we next visited the hen house to look for eggs. Grandma taught me how to find the eggs in the nests. This was a new experience and it took a while for me to stop feeling squeamish about reaching under the hens, feeling around for eggs. One finds out pretty quickly that chickens don't like being disturbed when they're sitting on their nests. I guessed it was probably because they were trying to protect their eggs.

In any case, they became distressed and agitated as I hesitantly slipped my hand beneath the hens to retrieve the eggs. At the disturbance the hens would begin clucking and jerking their stiff, sharp-clawed legs about. These nervous actions were startling enough to cause me to yank my hand back in surprise. But the straw in the nests was warm to my hand, the hens' feathers soft, and Grandma got the grand announcement every time I discovered some of their beautiful brown eggs.

Our egg hunts were usually successful, and more often than not we would come home with a basket full of these natural wonders. Of course, finding the eggs oneself made breakfast the next morning an even bigger event. We generally had eggs with our pancakes at Grandma's breakfast table. I still smile, recalling the sight of my grandfather preparing his breakfast, for his routine never varied. He would begin the ritual by pouring homemade sorghum out onto his plate, adding softened butter, then, mixing the two around and around with the tip of his knife until it was just the right creamy consistency. This perfect mixture was then ready to put on his pancakes. Back at the house after our little excursions, when the eggs had been carefully put away, we were often faced with a more painful chore. We were usually forced to spend the next half-hour picking nettles and cockleburs off our stockings and clothes. It was even more painful if I'd taken off my shoes and stepped on one with bare feet.

These pesky critters came from weeds that were hidden in the tall grasses of the grove. Without warning, these sneaky little hitchhikers silently grabbed onto anything they touched so tenaciously, yet so stealthily, that we were usually unaware of them until we were back at the house. Getting these prickly, sticky nuisances off our clothing was not an easy job because each one had to be picked off by hand. This could be a painful procedure, particularly when they stuck to our hands and drew blood.

Grandma's picnics were great fun. I still love picnics, but it is always I who must suggest our summer picnic outings to my (prefer to eat inside) family, having to prod and wheedle them to go along with the idea. But I'm sure Grandma would be proud of me.

During Grandma's funeral, it suddenly occurred to me that never was there to be another night spent snuggled up next to her when I awoke in that big house and was afraid. My favorite comfort, while cuddled next to her in her big, warm bed was the promise of a trip, next day, to Marshalltown where she would treat us both to a banana split at what was then the stylish Fantles store. She never failed to keep that promise, for sure enough, the very next day she and I would get dressed in our Sunday best, and Grandpa would drive us into Marshalltown for our stroll about town and our treat. Sometimes the two of us would visit a few stores for a bit of shopping, and occasionally Grandma would find something for me that she believed *I needed.*

As hard as it was for me to absorb, it was also becoming apparent that there was never to be another visit to our family by Grandma and Grandpa—together. At that point, I felt the need to sit down and cry until there were no more tears.

This new emotion engulfed me like a tidal wave and left me feeling devastated—as if I'd been completely deserted, that I had lost something of great value that could never again be found—an overwhelming emotion for someone of any age. In that moment I became irrational, and furiously angry with God, and wanted to run and shout at Him to give my grandmother back to me. How dare He do this—I didn't want my life to be changed. It was too soon for this to happen, and I wanted God to change things back like they were. Little could I understand just how selfish and self-absorbed were my thoughts. Too young to fully comprehend it at that moment, it would be time, and maturing in faith, that would bring the comforting answers from God that I so desperately wanted.

Grandpa Mann suffered most of his adult life from rheumatoid arthritis. The only way I would ever remember him walking was with a side-to-side gait, much like the rocking motion of a boat tied up to a dock post. This infirmity slowed him down considerably as he walked. Many times I would see him rubbing his knees and hands as he sat down to rest after having come in from the barn or the field. He was remarkably plucky about his ailment, however, and didn't complain overmuch about it. Such was his nature that he compliantly accepted the reality of the situation, stoically enduring the pain as "just one of those things." When his health finally forced him to give up farming, he eventually left the farm, moving out of the house in which he was born.

The old homestead then became home to my Aunt Mayme and Uncle Frank Ward, and their son Robert. Although we visited the farm many times after my granddad moved, and there are many happy memories of playing on the spacious lawn and the farm again, it had ceased to be Grandpa's farm. The furnishings were changed, of course, and the big rooms had taken on a different appearance. The farm was later sold to "outsiders." The house fell into disrepair little by little; one occupant, wanting to modernize its appearance, removed the entire front porch with its pillars. This architectural travesty totally destroyed the grandness and integrity of the structure, leaving me, and perhaps the rest of the family, heartsick.

The last owner of the house had great plans for completely renovating the home and had just finished restoring the inside when it caught fire and was burned beyond repair. The house was torn down and three small tract homes now stand on the old home site that had played host to the family, the famous and the infamous in past centuries. Endings can be devastating!

CHAPTER 4

We didn't get to know my mother's parents—Grandmother and Grandfather Pischel. They both died before my sister, brother and I were born. The total written account of their lives came to me from my cousin Carrol Appel, who answered my inquiry about our grandparents with a copy of a newspaper account dating back to 1918. The headline read *"Three Killed When Train Strikes Auto."* From this account I was able to learn as much about my grandparents as I have seen written about them. Mother, of course, would occasionally recall memories of her parents, but too many specific details were left untold.

The newspaper account goes on to state: *"Three persons were killed, one instantly, when the Chicago Great Western No. 6, the Chicago passenger train, struck an automobile on the highway crossing in Melbourne at 10:25 Monday night. The victims were Mr. and Mrs. Ginter Pischel of Melbourne, and Ernest Lucher, the latter a young carpenter of the Laurel neighborhood who was employed by Pischel."* At this point I must correct the newspaper's misspelling of Grandpa's name—it was actually Gunther, not Ginter, as stated.

"Mrs. Pischel was killed instantly, her back and neck being broken. Her husband died after being brought by the train to this city, as did also Lucher. Lucher died at midnight and Pischel at 1 o'clock. The victims of the accident were on their way, in a new Ford

sedan, to the Pischel farm, nine miles southeast of Melbourne. They approached the highway crossing just east of the station without seeing the train from the south, which does not stop at Melbourne, and was running at high speed thirteen minutes late."

Elsewhere in the account it states that since they were riding in an enclosed car, with the train station and other buildings obscuring their view, they neither heard nor saw the train coming. Evidently the train hit the car squarely, throwing it, and its occupants, 100 feet or more down the track, reducing the car to splinters, fatally injuring the passengers..

Grandpa's right leg was broken just below the knee and his face was bruised. The account goes on to read: *"The Pischels are well known in the Melbourne-Vancleve-Laurel neighborhoods, where they have lived for many years. Mr. and Mrs. Pischel have spent the twenty three years of their married life on the farm southeast of Melbourne until recently they left the farm to go to Melbourne. Their home in town, however, was not quite ready for them, and they were staying at the farm."*

"Before her marriage to Mr. Pischel, Mrs. Pischel was the wife of Adolph Osterhagen. Mrs. Pischel was born in Leipzig, Germany, and was 61 years old. She was married to Mr. Osterhagen in Germany, and came to this country thirty-four years ago, settling at Freeport, Ill. There Mr. Osterhagen died twenty-seven years ago. Six months after her husband's death Mrs. Osterhagen came to this country, (Iowa) *living south of Melbourne and at Laurel, and three and one-half years later became the wife of Mr. Pischel. Mrs. Pischel is survived by seven children, four of whom are by her first marriage. Mr. Pischel was a native of Schwartzburg, Germany and was 52 years of age. He came to this country twenty -seven years ago, remained in New York City a year, and then lived for a few years in Jasper County before he took Mrs. Osterhagen as his wife. Mr. and Mrs. Pischel were members of the German Reform Church near Baxter."*

Mother's Family –the Osterhagens and the Pischels

L to R: Pauline, Anna and August Osterhagen, Bill, Adolph and Helen Osterhagen,
Cordie and Louise Appel, Mom Alvina, and Carl Pischel
Front row: Grandpa Gunter, Harold Osterhagen, son of Anna and August, and Grandma Willhelmina

The account did not mention the fact that two of these children were twins—my mom, Alvina, and Pauline, her sister. While these hardly seem like twin names, in that German household where they were raised, the family pronounced the names "Alveena" and "Paulina."

These facts, as reported in the newspaper (of the car-train accident and the deaths of my grandparents and the "hired man") were sketchy and all too brief for my satisfaction. While the newspaper article did give me a poignant glimpse of their tragic and untimely deaths, the story left me with an aching spot in my heart that would never be healed by the joy of knowing them personally.

Their deaths came as they were on their way home from a happy day of visiting with my mother and father. My grandparents had just learned they were to become grandparents again. Mother was pregnant with my sister Maxine. But they would never meet any of the three of us, their daughter Alvina's children.

A copy of my parents' marriage license lists my maternal grandmother's full name as Minnie Wilhelmina Carolina Herzog Osterhagen Pischel. I recently learned that the name Herzog is a royal German name that can only be used by royalty (at least that's the story that was told to me). Imagine my surprise! After informing several of my relatives of this piece of stunning news, their typical response was that they'd always suspected they were of royal blood. I'm sure this can bear some looking into, as I certainly wouldn't want to miss my chance to be known as, Duchess, Lady, Dame or any other fancy royal title. Princess Arlene sounds good. Grandfather, however, was listed only as Gunther Pischel—go figure!

On those occasions when Mom told us stories of her childhood, they were invariably centered around life on their farm. One such tale was told about how her father harvested ice blocks from the frozen river near the farm—hauling them by horse and bobsled to the icehouse where they were buried in straw, sawdust and wood chips. This insulation was evidently sufficient to keep the ice safely frozen during the summer months. Ice cutting was done with some very primitive saws and drills, making it a backbreaking operation.

It was very necessary for this job to be done, however, as it was important for farm families to have ice available for food storage, and for its most important use (according to me) making ice cream. Most farms of that era had an icehouse. It wasn't hard to recruit men for this job as it was the custom in those days, for groups of farmers to join forces to help each other get the ice out of the river.

Perhaps it was even looked on as next thing to having an "old boy's club" party. Perhaps these communal projects were the farmers' way of learning the latest news around the county, with some of that news even being suitable for passing on to their wives. These times of working together undoubtedly provided the camaraderie and convivial good feeling that came as a result of merely having a group of guys to talk to. Farms, then, were generally rather isolated, and a farmer's mode of transportation, when he wanted to visit a neighbor, took a good deal more effort than merely hopping into the truck.

I'm now wondering at what point we stopped being that same community of caring neighbors who were available and willing to drop everything and come to the aid of anyone who needed their help. When did we become so independent and remote? Oh, I'm sure there are still a few of us aging old dinosaurs around who still like to chat and talk with anyone who nods at us, but it still seems true that most everyone in the present age has become addicted to *busyness*. As one who is never shy about expressing an opinion or two, I'd like to sneak in my own theory about this.

Seems to me that today we live in a jungle of communication and information—computers, televisions, radios, telephones, faxes and the like—that demands our full attention. Perhaps it follows that hectic activity would become a natural by-product of an attitude that says, "Who can take the necessary time to get to know an acquaintance in a very personal way?" It's sad, but too true, that we can scarcely find the time, or the will, to shout hello over the fence, so we compensate with a wave as we rush into our houses from a busy day away from home? Granted, it takes time to cultivate a friendship, and our easy mobility efficiently removes us from the home scene where comfortable neighborly friendships are most apt to flourish.

Our jobs, with couples working away from home, do little to invite casual conversation over coffee with neighbors. While this may seem an exaggeration to some, the trend is one I'm sure we all can recognize. The probability of losing warm and loving friendships, because they were never allowed to develop, seems to me too high a price to pay for any of the questionable benefits of our fast-moving, high-tech world. I'm reminded of a song that was popular a few years back, that sums up my feelings about the pitfalls of too much avoidance of others. The song was: *People Who Need People*. Somehow that idea warms the cockles of my heart much more than, *Sorry, I don't have Time For You!*

Locking our doors these days must surely be another form of isolation and a sign of our times, which almost never happened in an earlier age. Our forefathers trusted their neighbors who came by, and even strangers who might have stopped. Because of this trust their doors were nearly always left unlocked. Neighbors felt comfortable stopping by to borrow things from one another, and did so without waiting for permission if there was no one at home to give it; but they were faithful to make sure borrowed items were returned.

Again, it's hard to know just when the habit of locking doors became the thing to do. While I was a young married woman, Bob and I decided to take our children on a little trip. Since we were going to be gone for a few days, a neighbor mentioned that it might be a good idea if we locked the house while we were gone. We had moved to Des Moines by then, but continued to feel as safe in our unlocked house as before when we lived in the small town of Waterloo. After thinking it over, we decided that it might be wise to listen to the neighbors' warnings. They had been shocked to learn that we didn't lock our doors, even at night, and had lectured us properly on the foolishness of being so trusting.

It was settled then that we would start the habit of locking up, a radical new concept for us. This new resolve was almost shattered before it got started when not one of us—mom, dad or the kids—could find the key to the house. We were all given marching orders, and the search began in earnest. We were instructed to hunt in every possible, and in every impossible, nook and cranny until we located the key. After what began to seem like a futile search, Bob finally located the unused key stuck away among the legal papers we'd been given when we bought the house. The locks, so unaccustomed to being turned, were stiff at first, but through perseverance the doors were finally secured and off we went, marking another reality milestone in our lives—though a rather unpleasant one. Up to this point we had felt so secure in our home, not even knowing that we needed to be afraid. Now we knew!

Mom told great stories about growing up on the farm. A favorite was the summer a ferocious rainstorm swept across their family farm. As summer storms often do, this particular cloudburst, that had directly hit their farm, produced baseball-sized hailstones that ruined their entire crop. Grandmother Pischel must have been "my kind of gal" for instead of sitting down in tears, she hurriedly gathered up some of the hailstones, and with them, made ice cream.

How I long to have known this spunky little woman with the lively spirit, the courage, and the imagination to turn a disaster of this proportion into a celebration. Undoubtedly, she possessed that special brand of character that enables one to look past the dark cloud straight into the silver lining. That was my Grandmother, Minnie Wilhelmina Carolina Herzog Osterhagen Pischel.

Now I'm sure I know where my mom learned the art of looking adversity in the eye and daring it to defeat her. From what I have gathered through conversations over the years, these two women were, as the saying goes, "cut from the same bolt;" for although they didn't look especially alike, they were similar in so many ways. I've never known a stronger more dependable or harder-working woman than my mom, and the same was said about Grandma as well.

From the pictures I've seen of Grandma Wilhelmina, however, I would have to say, comparing the two, that Mom had her beat for looks. But since it was decreed somewhere in the original old-time "*bible of photography*" of that day, that smiles had to be banned from photos, perhaps Grandma's looks would have improved had I seen her in person. I hope that would be true because in the few pictures we have of her, Grandma looks a bit tired and like she might have been sucking a lemon just before the camera clicked. Mom, on the other hand, always had a sweet countenance about her—a quality she carried throughout her life.

It was on the family farm that mother learned her love of "a glass of cold beer on a hot day." Because of their German ancestry it would have been an unnatural denial of their God-given heritage had the family not kept a keg of their home-brewed, 20th century-style German "Coca-Cola," on hand. But it was rare—like almost never—that we kids ever saw her drink a glass of beer, or anything else of an alcoholic nature. I suspect this was due in large part to my Grandmother Mann's strict attitude against drinking alcoholic beverages. When Mom and Dad were married, they lived for a time with Dad's folks

Grandma Mann, as mentioned, was a member of the Women's Christian Temperance Union, and Mom would never have thought of crossing or disrespecting her in any way, so she undoubtedly gave up that occasional glass of beer, at least for then.

As in my dad's family, Mother's family also possessed a strong work ethic. Both families, having been born and raised on farms, like people everywhere who labored in the fields, knew the meaning of hard work. This lesson was passed on to all of their children.

Mom and her twin, Pauline, eagerly started taking piano lessons, but it wasn't long before Mom found it had become her responsibility to keep her sister, who loathed practicing, motivated and faithful to that hated exercise. Aunt Pauline, it seems, was very clever at being absent when it came time to do the chores or to practice, and so it fell to Mom to finish most of the jobs. It stood her in good stead, however, as she is remembered for both her piano playing and her "work-brittleness."

The twins (l to r)...Pauline and Alvina, with sister Louise and mother Wilhelmina

(left)
The twins grown up…
"Alvina and Paulina"

In the interest of fairness, however, it must be mentioned that my Aunt Pauline was a vivacious and fun person; we kids were excited when we knew she was coming for a visit. She could always think up exciting things to do, and sometimes played with us just as if she were a kid herself. Being as generous and loving as she was fun, Aunt Pauline gave great gifts. It was she, who one Christmas, gave me my child's roll-top desk. I adored that desk then, and even now it sits as a reminder of her in my home.

From the first moment that I received my desk, teaching became my full-time occupation. Every doll, dog and cat in residence, visiting friends, and make-believe students were required to attend classes. I became the most officious and probably one of the most offensively hands-on teachers the world had ever known. Dolls got spanked when they couldn't answer a question. From the moment

I first sat down at my desk every morning, it never failed to stir in me a feeling of authority that fed my ego gloriously. **I** was the teacher!

Aunt Pauline, this sweet-natured and fun-loving girl we all adored, could, however, occasionally shock us all with a startling display of explosive temper that was surprisingly foreign to her usually placid nature. In her later years she could get so worked up over a game of canasta that her heated remarks could turn the air blue! This, of course, sent the rest of us players into spasms of laughter while she sputtered and fumed because she was losing. Accusing the lot of us of cheating, she generally threatened never to play again, but she always did and we couldn't wait to challenge her whenever she came for a visit. Because of her tirades, I began taking the game seriously so I could win as often as possible, insuring another display of explosive entertainment for the rest of us game players.

One weekend, when she was a young woman, Aunt Pauline and a man, who was to become my Uncle Jim Draper, arrived quite unexpectedly at our home in Whitten, from Marshalltown. Having been injured in the war, he had been a patient at the Veterans' Home there, where she was employed at the time.

My parents didn't know of their plans in advance, but they had come to our house to be married. Because Jim had been married before, they had been unable to find a minister who would perform the ceremony in Marshalltown. Aside from the fact that Pauline wanted her twin sister to be present for the ceremony, the couple had come to Whitten, hopefully in search of a minister. Mom and Dad made hasty calls to the church in search of a pastor. Eventually one was located who agreed to officiate at the ceremony.

What a flurry of activity ensued as Mom hastily pulled together a wedding—quickly making a wedding cake, gathering bouquets of flowers and arranging the house to accommodate the ceremony and a small reception. Aunt Pauline was flush with excitement as the time drew near. I can still see every detail of her wedding dress, which, at the start, shocked and disappointed me because it was colored. From my experience with weddings I knew this couldn't possibly be a wedding gown because it wasn't white. It was, however, a lovely, soft color called sea-foam, a shade of very pale greenish-blue; and after seeing my aunt in it, I accepted the fact that, like the bride, the dress was beautiful, if unconventional.

The dress was made of chiffon, underlined with a slip of the same hue. Two soft ruffles formed the sleeves over each arm. The cut of the dress reminds me of the styles being worn today; form fitting, with a straight skirt flaring gently near the bottom. Her dress reached to her ankles. To complete the ensemble she wore a matching sheer, large-brimmed hat and white pumps.

With the hubbub and commotion of the plans and work behind them, Pauline was now able to relax, knowing that her sister had once more come to her rescue by providing a perfect wedding. She was a radiant bride, carrying a bouquet of pale pink roses, which complemented her unusual but striking wedding dress.

The ceremony was held in the living room of our home, and seemed to me to be the most glamorous and exciting event I'd ever been part of. The wedding, though small, went off smoothly, after which we celebrated with wedding cake and the dainty extras Mother had been able to prepare, all artfully arranged on her decorated table. Mom had a knack for making things attractive and she had outdone herself, even in this short time, for her sister's wedding. As the reception ended and the newlyweds were preparing to leave, we were caught up in an outburst of family laughing, hugging and kissing all around; then away they went. The bride and groom jumped into their car and disappeared.

Just as quickly as they had appeared (springing this rather hectic surprise), as quickly it was over and the happy couple was gone—too soon it seemed, leaving in their wake a feeling of anticlimax, and Mother, undoubtedly, in a state of collapse. Although the house was yet happily aglow and alive with the still lingering special aura of love and romance that surrounds a wedding, there came with it also, a feeling of loss and void. The excitement was over and there was nothing left for us to do but change out of our wedding clothes and clean up after the party.

Aunt Pauline died at age 87, January 26, 1986, seven years before Mother Alvina, who died three days short of her ninety-fifth birthday on August 13th in 1993. The twins were born August 16,

1898. When asked for an explanation of the cause of Mother's death I was able to put it as simply as this: "It was as if she merely came to the end and stopped." Quietly and peacefully this saint had gone home. There were some similarities between the twins and some differences that naturally occur when twins begin living apart. However, on the occasion of each of their deaths, a remarkable and lovely coincidence took place that seemed totally fitting and right for these twins. Our son, Tim, not too long out of Seminary, officiated at the funeral services of both Mother and her twin sister Pauline, thus sharing a beautiful continuity in death as they had through life. Dad died in 1967, of an aortic aneurysm at the age of seventy.

CHAPTER 5

Mom and Dad were married on August 1, 1917, at my mother's farm home. Mother's wedding day gave new meaning to the expression that, "traditionally, something always goes wrong at a wedding." Little did she know that what happened to her would someday become a spellbinding tale to be passed down through the generations. She was able to laugh about it in later years, but at the time she was living through it, hysterical tears would probably have seemed more appropriate. She could have even been wondering all the while about the possibility of having a nervous breakdown on her wedding day. Her harrowing experience was tormenting enough to cause any bride to envision an ominous black cloud hanging over her head, subtly suggesting she cancel the wedding.

The main source of Mother's anxiety arose over her wedding gown. Mother had special-ordered her gown from a department store in Marshalltown months in advance of the wedding day. The sales people assured her that all was well and her dress would arrive in plenty of time. She was horrified to learn that as late as her wedding day the unthinkable had happened; the dress, whose arrival she'd been fretting over, had still not arrived.

Frantically, she returned to the store to choose another dress. She had no choice but to pick something from among the dresses they had in stock. Busily searching for a dress from among the available choices, she became hidden from sight in the dressing room. This was indeed unfortunate because it led to the next traumatic event in her day. Because it was closing time, and she was out of sight for the moment, she became locked in the store when they closed for the night.

How she could have been overlooked seems unimaginable, but perhaps the sales personnel had been locked in also. At that point in her day, all of her best-laid plans must have appeared doomed. There had been one seeming disaster after another. Many less determined brides might have viewed the entire fiasco as an ill-fated omen and dissolved into a heap of tears. However, help was summoned; and in time she was mercifully rescued.

With dress in tow, she jumped into her buggy and drove the lively team of horses home at breakneck speed, a fact that would surely have distressed her father had he known. Then, pulling into the driveway and throwing the reins around the hitching post she raced into the house to get ready, with only moments to spare. Finally dressed, with just enough time to regain her composure, the wedding proceeded without further trauma.

I found it an interesting side note to the wedding that my Aunt Retha Pischel had provided her homemade crème puffs for the reception.

That which had begun as an ill-fated day of nerve-wracking obstacles ended on a happy, perfect note. The wedding was beautiful and the bride lived to tell the tale to her grandchildren. Though their wedding got off to a shaky start, my parents' marriage was strong and enduring, surviving for nearly fifty years.

Mom and Dad's wedding portrait was scheduled for a few days after the wedding, which meant another trip to Marshalltown where the photographer had his studio. Dad wasn't happy about having to dress up again for the sitting and Mom always said that was why he looked so stern in the picture. Some things never change.

LeRoy T and Alvina O. Mann
"The wedding Photo"

Because of his impending service in World War I, Dad brought Mother home to live with his parents after their marriage. Fortunately, Mother and Grandmother developed a loving affection for one another; and it was Grandma who nursed Mom through a near-fatal bout of Smallpox.

My parents had been married for just over a year when Dad had to leave, off to serve his country, leaving Mom at home and pregnant with my sister Maxine. To add to the misery of these days of upheaval, a smallpox epidemic of major proportion was raging throughout the country, claiming many lives. Mother nearly lost her battle with the disease.

Maintaining a relentless vigil over her patient day and night, Grandma devotedly nursed my mother back to health, and an even stronger bond was forged between the two of them because of it. Mother once laughingly told me that she secretly suspected that Grandmother relied on her more, and was more impressed with her willingness to pitch in with the hard work, than she was with her own two daughters.

Mother had been trained from childhood to value hard work, and it was probably a natural reaction for both of her new sisters-in-law to see Mom as a welcome replacement for their own position in the family as "indentured servants." My Aunt Mayme, a gentle creature, and artist, undoubtedly found more time to paint, and Aunt Ida, the tomboy, undoubtedly had more time for whatever pleased her.

Aside from the gleeful prospect of having another "drudge" to help with the work, Mother was well received and much loved by both of my aunts. The jobs they considered tiresome, my mother typically found to be opportunities for pleasing Grandma. Mother's willing attitude and her sweet, gentle nature were qualities that quickly endeared her to the family, who soon found her to be nearly indispensable. It could not have been an easy time for her, regardless of the family's acceptance, with Dad being ordered into military service, taking him away from home.

Strong feelings arose among family members, stemming from the fact that my father had been drafted at all. Farmers in that day were given exemptions because it was seen as their duty to stay home and raise the food that supplied the army; and for that reason it was felt that Dad should have been exempt. My Aunt Mayme's husband, Frank Ward, was on the draft board, and it was rumored that it was he who blocked the exemption, thereby having Dad declared 1-A, and promptly drafted.

Years later I learned from my mother that Grandpa had bought the farm across the road from the family farm, and this farm was to have been given to my mother and father. Perhaps resentment was the motive that caused Uncle Frank to make sure that Dad got sent away to the army. In any case, since Dad was no longer there to work the new farm, it was given to my Uncle Claude.

There didn't seem to be any long-lasting resentment among family members, however, since we regularly visited all of the aunts and uncles throughout the years without any animosity. I only heard about these events from my mother when all of the people involved were dead. I now suspect that it wasn't considered proper in those times to discuss private family matters with your children. In questioning my mother about why these things happened as they did, I was merely given a shrug of her shoulders and that settled the matter. I was never to know.

Dad was just days short of being sent overseas when World War I ended. Since he was a man who loved adventure, I suspect he hadn't struggled too hard against being sent off to war. For Uncle Frank's sake, it's a good thing it was my dad, the fun-loving son, who bore the brunt of any possible spite. The time of Dad's service must have appealed to his restless and spirited nature, and he would have undoubtedly welcomed a stint overseas.

Dad, like most all veterans, was proud of his time in the military; we have a picture of him with his entire unit that had trained at Camp Dodge in Des Moines. When he returned home after the war, Mom and Dad moved to a farm of their own and began married life again. Through the years, however, my father, obviously proud of his time of service, never missed an opportunity to meet old war-service buddies and relive his war experience with them by attending every American Legion Convention held in Des Moines.

CHAPTER 6

Earliest memories of life and times as they were when I was young always picture a warm, loving and secure Christian home. We were poor, to be sure, but it wasn't obvious to me at the time. That was due in large part to the creative talent of a mother who made birthdays, Christmases, and other important events in our lives extra special. She would energetically sew, craft, scrimp and save from the meager budget until she could ensure an exciting and wonder-filled celebration for each of her children.

Today they accuse me of being a pack rat, a trait I proudly attribute to the lessons learned at home. If anyone wants something unusual all they have to do is ask me, and more than likely I can produce it—just like my mom. While I would have to admit to being more of a "junkie" than she, however—I'm sure she was a more organized and neater "junkie."

These celebrations at home followed a traditionally grand routine. For each special occasion my mother would lengthen our large, round, Queen Anne-style dining room table to its full size by adding all of the extra boards, of which I believe there were six or seven. It was immense. She would then cover the table with custom-fitted table pads, followed by her very best and very long white linen tablecloth and finest china. My parents purchased the table and chairs, from Mom's half-brother, August Osterhagen, who owned and operated a furniture store, in Melborne, Iowa. Attached to the store, also operated by my uncle Gus, was a funeral home. While this might seem like an odd combination to us, it was not an unusual coupling of businesses in those days.

No party is complete without guests; there were always guests for any of our special celebrations. The one constant for any birthday, the one we could *always* count on, was the assurance of one of Mom's Iowa State Fair, blue ribbon prize-winning, angel food birthday cakes, piled high with a spectacular fluffy white frosting. On other special occasions the frosting might be tinted a very pale shade of green, pink, or yellow to match the season or the occasion. Sugar and water were two of the main ingredients of this frosting, boiled together. The syrup it made needed constant testing to determine whether or not it had reached the right consistency. Dipping the spoon into the boiling liquid and lifting it into the air gave the answer. If this action produced fine, wispy, flyaway threads, then the syrup was ready to be carefully drizzled into the beaten egg whites, folding to blend.

This frosting confection took special handling and required absolutely perfect timing to concoct. We kids were sometimes recruited to help, but because of the deft handling required, we were more often cautioned to stand clear during the process, depending on our age. When this special frosting was piled high on the cake, the sight of it was sure to elicit plenty of "oohs" and "ahhs." To accompany our special birthday cake, we could always be certain there would also be a large freezer of homemade ice cream. Life was good!

Like kids of all ages, I would argue that no one, in my estimation, has ever made ice cream that tasted as good as Mom's. Her ice cream was *always* vanilla flavored—which to me is still the only authentic homemade ice cream flavor.

With that first bite of this "hurt-your-teeth" kind of cold, (found only in homemade ice cream) to the last, luscious melting golden drop in the bottom of your bowl, you knew that you'd just had real homemade ice cream. It was only the wonderfully moist and spongy angel food cake, eaten with the ice cream, that tempered your mouth and kept it from freezing. With this taste treat, the celebration was on. How could any kid possibly feel poor?

Birthdays celebrated at school were also extra special for us kids. It was customary for the birthday child's mother to bring treats for the occasion. My favorite treat for celebrating my birthday at school was always my mom's popcorn cake. This novel creation, which I always felt she had originated, was made from homemade caramel corn, which she usually tinted some pretty pastel shade. The caramel corn was then pressed into her well-worn angel food cake pan. When it was turned out of the pan, it was a glorious thing to behold.

This unusual and spectacular treat, when turned out and sliced into pieces for everyone, always made a big hit with my classmates. To start off the party, there were candles to blow out, and many discordant notes of *Happy Birthday* sung by squeaky-voiced kids who were undoubtedly enduring the singing so they could get to the treats.

I realize now, more than I did as a youngster, that Mother was an outstanding parent. Such knowledge as this can come in dribs and drabs when one is young; but more likely than not, its true impact arrives somewhere around the dawning of adulthood, or even much later for the very dense. While I was always aware of mother's ability to create many things "out-of-the-ordinary," in retrospect, I now see her as a gifted genius at making much from little. God bless her.

Our little house was charming in its own aging way. Although of the same vintage as most of the other houses in our small town, Mom's special touch always managed to make our house a home. One of the house's special features was a porch that stretched around two sides, ending with a small-roofed porch over the front door. This entryway was covered with a mass of pink climbing roses, which bloomed from early summer until late fall and was a favorite place to have our very rare pictures taken. It was there that a prized picture was taken of my brother, Maurice, and I in front of the porch with our grandparents. I was sitting on Grandmother's lap. Incidentally our favorite dog, Spot, was also in the picture.

Me and My siblings
Arlene, Maxine and Maurice

Me on Grandma Hanna's lap, Maurice and Grandpa Robert
In front of the pink rose bush (and dog Spot)

My grandparents, of course, were Hannah Anna and Robert E. Lee Mann. I love repeating Grandfather's name as it always conjures up for me the place of his origin. Looking with fond remembrance at this aging memory reminds me of that front door by which we posed. This door opened off the living room. This room was kept closed in winter to conserve heat, and thrown wide open during the summer months to entice any wandering breeze into the often-sweltering interior of the house. Is it my imagination or were the Iowa summers really hotter in the days of my youth?

Our small home consisted of a kitchen with an eat-in area, a dining room, the living room, and an upstairs with three bedrooms that were never heated—or in the winter, only somewhat heated by radiant heat—meaning any stray heat radiating up through the registers from downstairs. Such heat was negligible, thoroughly chilled, and scarcely noticeable by the time it reached the second floor.

The comfort of our home in the summertime depended largely on cross ventilation. By keeping every window in the house open, it was hoped to capture any stray breeze. Mom engaged her own weapons to combat the heat, which was to close the east windows and lower the shades in the morning, then reversing the process in the afternoon, lowering shades and closing windows on the west side of the house. One is driven to desperate measures when one's brains are on the verge of being fried; these maneuvers helped as much as anything. When the weather became too unbearably hot, Mom had us place our hands in a pan of cold water, and would sometimes soak towels in cold water, wring them out and apply them to our sweaty brows and the back of our necks.

The argument, that our Iowa summers of those days were excessively hot and oppressive, needs no defense for those who lived through them. I recall all too well the many summer nights we kids spent stretched out on blankets on the floor, just inside the open living room door hoping to escape the certain suffocation of our bedrooms. Electric fans, if they had been invented at that point, were not available for home use—at least not in our home.

The intensive heat seldom slacked off at night and even drove us outside to sleep on the lawn during some of the more scorching heat waves. My sister, Maxine, and I were doing just that one very warm, star-glittering evening, when I woke up to find her missing. To awaken in the middle of the night to find myself outside, and alone, was a shock for me! I was almost too unnerved to stir, afraid of what might get me if I moved, and yet, furious enough to want to run into the house and start yelling at her because she'd deserted me.

I lay there for a few seconds trying to decide whether or not my courage would let me make a run for it. By then a cold, wet dew had settled on my skin, and the blanket I was lying on felt damp and uncomfortable, which only added to my already unreasonable machinations. I knew I wouldn't survive outside alone; so, with my heart beating wildly, I decided to risk making a dash for the house. In one quick motion I leaped up off the blanket, stepping into the cool, wet grass. With every slippery, chilly step, the darkness became more ominous, and panic began to claw at me with almost tangible fingers.

I should have realized, then, that I was Olympic material, given the speed at which I raced to the house. Once safely ensconced behind the screen door, my relief was overwhelming. That relief, however, was soon replaced by savage thoughts of revenge as I remembered my sister sleeping soundly in her bed. Somehow reason told me that any confrontation had best be put on hold for the time being, since everyone in the house was fast asleep.

Grudgingly, I retreated to my bed, all the while nursing a growing resentment toward a sister who would treat me in such a perilous and uncaring way. Every instinct urged me to waken her, to scream and yell at her, demanding an explanation for leaving me alone in the dark. Had I been so foolish as to give in to that impulse, it's more than possible I would have wound up the loser for causing a ruckus in the middle of the night. So with an uncharacteristic decision made to put off the idea until morning, I trudged off to bed—but boy, was she going to get it then!

With the dawning of another sunny morning, however, most of the heat of my anger had cooled, and forgiveness for the sister who had so recklessly left me outside to face certain peril, all alone, came a bit easier. With the forgiveness, however, came my stern warning that she was never to do such a wicked thing again. Her teasing apology nearly undid my resolve to forgive, but she was able to convince me that her remorse for her great sin was genuine, so I was able to let go of my resentment and allow her back again into my good graces.

If the summers were indeed hotter, then it follows that Iowa winters were predictably colder in those days. Because the parlor was kept closed during the winter, Dad had to install a round "pot-bellied" stove in the dining room. This stove was fired up early in the morning before we kids were up and was never allowed to die out until the family was in bed at night.

I can imagine that our winter sleeping arrangements would be viewed by some, today, as child abuse. But in those long-gone days, these inconveniences were accepted as completely normal, an accepted part of the routine of our lives. We would have had no thought, back then, of using discomfort as a grievance for assessing blame (siblings excepted). We seemed to have learned the masterful art of suffering stoically through much of what we didn't like. We simply learned to tolerate, without complaint, the bad things, because it never occurred to us that there should be any other recourse. Those of us living in that tranquil, countrified setting had not yet become acquainted with public protests, or personal injury suits—at least not at this level.

Of course, who wouldn't prefer waking up in a warm, cozy room to one displaying a small dusting of snow on one corner of the bed coverlet? This startling event actually happened one morning after driving winds had forced snow through a not-too-well-sealed crack near the roof. But the incident was a cause for laughter and surprise, not resentment. It's a good bet that story was even taken to school—if not for "show," then at least for "tell."

For our long Iowa winter nights my mother made up our beds with flannel sheets that covered featherbed mattresses; and with long-johns and socks, and even stocking hats on the coldest nights, we stayed toasty and comfortable. Throwing off the covers in the morning was another matter—forcefully ejecting ourselves from our warm little nests took a colossal act of courage. Bitter cold slapped us awake the moment the covers were flung off and our feet hit the floor, guaranteeing spasms of violent shivering and chattering teeth.

The race down the stairs, where we dressed in the incredible warmth of the old stove, got the sap coursing through our veins before we reached the bottom step. It was important to keep revolving, as we dressed before the stove, in order to warm our backsides as well as keeping our frontsides from scorching. Many a garment was burned from standing too long in front of one of these fiery-red heaters.

It was this pot-bellied stove that again nearly proved my undoing. On one particularly sub-zero winter day, when the stove had been heated to red-hot, my brother Maurice and I, having been forced to stay home from school as the result of the nasty snowstorm raging outside, found ourselves trapped indoors. Deciding to relieve our boredom by playing "Blind Man's Bluff," we soon found a scarf and the game began.

When it came my turn to be blindfolded, he of course ran off, leaving me to flounder around trying to catch him. In the excitement of reaching and groping for him, as impossible as it might seem since the stove was super hot, I accidentally wrapped my arm around the stove, causing a blister from wrist to elbow. Of course there was near pandemonium in the house, and Maurice was dispatched to run and tell Dad to come immediately.

Since we lived across the street from the doctor, it seems strange that he wasn't called, but instead Dad brought with him someone unrelated to the medical profession, but who was evidently knowledgeable about healing. My vague impression is that this man was connected with faith healing. At any rate, it was truly a miraculous healing, not just because my arm got better, but also because there is not a trace of a scar left on my arm. God's healing, I'm sure.

It was fortunate that Doctor Blaha had his practice in his home, because more than once that short distance was advantageous. I was especially thankful for the short commute when a boil developed on a very personal spot on my anatomy—so painful, indeed, that it hurt too much to walk. Since I'd become too heavy to carry, Dad stood me on our sled while my mother walked alongside, supporting me as he pulled me along. From this picture one can deduce that there was snow on the ground and it was cold. Aside from the humiliating, pre-teen embarrassment over the entire situation, my recovery once again came swiftly!

Iowa winters, when I was growing up, were epics about which fables are written. One of the longest cold spells in recent memory came blustering in the February of 1936, when temperatures didn't get above zero for thirty days, even dropping to as low as 30 degrees below zero on some days. The dangerous cold kept folks mostly inside their houses. It wasn't long before every home became like a prison to those trapped inside, with every person under house arrest. Scarcely anyone ventured outside unless it was a case of extreme necessity, and then, not for long. Cabin fever became the claustrophobic, contagious disease of the season.

Even though the winter was life threatening and treacherously cold, Dad needed to tend to our few animals in the outbuildings. Of course it was also necessary for him to make a few trips for supplies, though not entirely sure that the store would even be open. He closed his shop, going there only to check to make sure everything was still intact and that there was no danger of fire or cold damage. As always when he returned, so bundled up you could scarcely see his eyes through the slits in his snow-packed and icy-stiff scarf and wraps, his bright red cheeks looked as though they had been burned. Mom always met him at the door, frantically eager to help him shed his frozen clothing and get him near the stove to thaw out.

That our winters were ferocious was proven beyond the shadow of a doubt one particularly devastating winter morning. We'd been bombarded throughout the night by a snowstorm that had howled, blasted and raged until it wore itself out. Eager to view the situation, Dad had thrown on his heavy snow gear in preparation for checking outside to determine if there had been any serious damage.

Reaching the door, he turned the doorknob, then tugged, jerked and pulled without success, for it seemed to be sticking. After yanking and tussling with the door for a time, the icy seal was finally broken, but even then he seemed to be having difficulty getting the creaky door to open. With one last gigantic effort the door opened, sending him reeling; and there, to everyone's shocked amazement, we found ourselves staring at a blank wall of snow covering the entire entrance, imprinted with the outline of our front door.

Captivated by this unusual sight, we began laughing in startled disbelief. Wow, was this some sight, or what? For a moment we were so completely shocked that we couldn't comprehend what had happened. We'd never before seen such an incredible spectacle. To say we were dumbfounded by this vision, seems like a poor description of the bizarre scene that greeted us on that eerily quiet morning. Who would ever expect to find one's doorway completely blocked with snow? We were stunned!

Viewing the scene from the outside, it might have appeared that a giant avalanche had obliterated the front of our house, covering most the rest of it as well. From the ground to the rooftop, it was as if a giant snow bomb had taken direct aim at our home, and found its target.

When the reality of the situation finally set in, we kids became tense, but listened quietly as Dad and Mom discussed our options for getting ourselves out of the house. Their suggested solutions for escaping this predicament seemed drastic and far too strenuous, but the situation probably appeared far more threatening and scary to us kids than it did to our parents, or than it actually was. We were still young enough to be certain that we were going to die of starvation, or the cold, or from being buried alive in our house, never to be found again.

I was probably the most intimidated of all, being the youngest, for even the windows were frozen shut, frosted over and covered with snow, completely shutting out the view and darkening the inside of the house. My pessimistic assessment of our grim fate was short-lived, however, because it wasn't long before we heard the shouts of our neighbor, Bill Clough, calling to us from outside the house. His house had evidently not been as dumped on as was ours. In a loud voice he kept shouting questions in the direction of the house to determine if we were all right.

Our joyful response let him know that we were all very much alive and well. He quickly summoned a few more neighbors to help shovel us out, and the rescue operation began. Once the doorway was cleared and we knew we were going to be saved, we kids began jumping up and down, clapping hands, laughing and actually hugging each other—greater proof that a miracle had happened.

The certain death we kids (or maybe only I) had feared, suddenly and magically turned into high adventure. What an adventure to run through the snow tunnel our rescuers had carved outside our door, which could have been likened to the entrance of an igloo. Having been thus freed from imprisonment and certain death by freezing or starving, we were startled to see the bright sunlight that hadn't been apparent from inside the darkened house. We were giddy with relief, and enormously happy to see our rescuers. We were going to escape, and life for us would go on as before, although it would take some time for the front of our house to become completely visible again.

Another unforgettable snowstorm that hit Iowa—one that made our part of the country sit up and take notice—occurred in 1938. It came on the day my friend, Doris, and I had been invited by our next-door neighbors (Omar and Ida Mitchell) to go to Des Moines with them to see the Girls State Basketball Tournament. We had gotten our parents' permission, and the four of us set out in high spirits. We were headed for the big city, thrilled at the prospect of getting to go to some place as large as Des Moines.

We were twelve years old, and felt very much like Alice in Wonderland as we drove into the city that had buildings as tall as skyscrapers. Disappointment followed our arrival there because we didn't get to see much of Des Moines since Mr. Mitchell drove directly to the Drake Fieldhouse, where the games were held at that time. We'd been expecting to drive through the downtown area, which we had desperately wanted to see. Neither Doris nor I had ever been to Des Moines before.

With the prospect of the upcoming ballgame waiting for us, we tried bravely to choke down our disappointment. We followed the Mitchells into the Fieldhouse. Our spirits began to revive as we became caught up in the crush of spectators, carried along by the crowd. We now found it thrilling to be part of the throng entering the Fieldhouse. All of the friendly jostling and noisy clamor, the sound of the basketballs bouncing on the floor as the players practiced, soon worked their magic, and the disillusionment we'd been harboring was soon set aside.

After being seated for a while, we began longing for some of the treats we saw others eating, but we were two small-town girls who were too shy to venture out into such a large crowd to find some of these treats for ourselves (neither did the Mitchells suggest it) so we went without. But even this was only a minor regret to the thrill and the magic of simply being there.

It was getting late by the time we started to leave. Our trip home, as it turned out, was even more thrilling than the games, for it was snowing as we left Des Moines. This should have come as no surprise to us, as snowstorms during the Girls State Tournament are legendary. The snow didn't let up for the entire trip home. The car we were driving was a 1935 Chevrolet. Since cars of that period were not the superheated, radial-tired, luxury, speed-demon limousines of today, we knew it was going to be a cold trip home, and very late when we arrived.

Mr. Mitchell must have begun to doubt his sanity for making such a trip in the first place as we drove down the long stretch of road from Des Moines to Marshalltown in a blinding snowstorm. There was nothing to do but press on. Reaching Marshalltown, we turned onto highway 14, heading north, directly into the full force of the storm, until we reached the turnoff road leading to Whitten.

As if we weren't cold enough by then, what we saw there was even more chilling and alarming. Turning off the main highway, rounding the corner onto the Whitten road, we were stunned by a most disastrous sight—the road had literally disappeared! In fact, it was so covered with snow that even the ditches had been drifted over by the blizzard—and we still had some five or six miles to go. The only things we could see in this pitch-dark blackness were the tops of few fence posts sticking up through the snow here and there, outlining the fields.

With the lights of the car turned on bright (as bright as lights were then), every person in the car snapped to attention in an effort to assist the driver by straining to watch the guidelines, intent on making sure the car, chugging and laboring along, stayed on a straight line in the middle of the road between the few visible fence posts on either side.

In addition to our concern that the car might drive off the road into a camouflaged ditch at any moment, each one of us also had to deal with the voiceless question forming in our minds concerning our fate if the car were to get stuck. Earlier on, Mr. Mitchell had been keeping up a chatty, teasing, line of banter, trying to reassure us that all was well. Now, he no longer seemed as concerned about our need for encouragement and reassurance, for he kept his total attention focused on the road. We knew from his intense concentration, and his white-knuckled, tight grip on the steering wheel, that the situation was getting seriously serious.

I'm sure our imaginations were running in exaggerated tandem about the "what ifs" during this terrifying crisis. I began thinking of Mom and Dad, wondering if I would live to see them again. Oh, how I longed to be home! It was hard to imagine freezing to death. But we were growing colder, and the likelihood of that happening seemed entirely possible, particularly if the old car were to give up the ghost and die. "Come on, car!"

One could almost hear the tension inside the car that night. If tension makes a sound, it's certain that every one of us was straining to hear its noise along with the struggling motor. With muscles tensed, using every ounce of strength we could muster in an attempt to encourage that precious old workhorse not to conk out on us, we kept our attention riveted to that steady chugging sound. Eventually everyone stopped talking, being hard at work mentally pushing, as though our willing the car to keep going was of any help at all. But it was the only thing we knew to do and it was impossible for us not to.

Perhaps it was even that very state of nervous anxiety that helped us endure the cold, as Doris and I, who had been sitting on the edge of our seats, now sat huddled together for warmth in the back seat. We were amazingly calm, under the circumstances; for we didn't make any disturbance or cry, although I certainly entertained the thought. Since we were guests of the Mitchells, however, fussing would have been seen as impolite, suggesting a loss of confidence in the driver—undoubtedly one reason for our silence.

In retrospect, one wonders about the extraordinary power of good manners, for here we were facing possible death, yet sitting mute and accepting. Good manners be hanged—at some point we would surely have to admit that fear was the main reason we were quiet. This nightmare ride home was the most exhausting part of that eventful evening, or of any other evening I had ever had.

It must have been a good old car, because it just kept slogging through the snow despite the fact that a clogged windshield was blinding the driver, and snow continued to build up beneath the fenders. Although lumbering along at a snail's pace, miraculously, the car kept moving steadily forward.

Relief flooded every occupant of our magnificent conveyance the moment we spotted the lights of Whitten shining in the distance. Seeing my house up ahead—as it came into view through a tiny crack in that snow-bogged windshield—was as comforting as stepping into a warm bath. Although limp with fatigue, nervous laughter punctuated my relieved and grateful thanks to our hosts as I stepped out of the car, into a snowdrift that nearly engulfed me. Floundering wildly, I struggled through waist-deep drifts as I made my way to the house.

Once inside the safety of home, a sense of sanctuary enveloped me that was more merciful than anything I had ever known—like warm, welcoming arms—something akin to being enclosed in a down-filled comforter. I was weak-kneed with relief; the tension of the trip had nearly exhausted me. Mom and Dad had been in bed, but were not asleep when I got there. They were fearful for our safety and had been watching the clock as well as the storm raging outside. Mom made me some hot chocolate to drink, got me into some warm pajamas and helped me to bed. Knowing I was safely home with my parents was as reassuring and as happy as Christmas morning.

Since my friend was expected home, the Mitchells must have felt it their duty to continue battling the snow and the bad roads to see that she, too, was delivered safely. Mr. And Mrs. Mitchell were worn out from the strain and stress of our seemingly endless trip as well—tired and thoroughly chilled by the time they had successfully delivered their charges home. Amazingly, everyone made it safely and without further incident that night. But the wild experience we weathered together that night formed a lasting friendship which none of us would ever forget. Because the story could have had a different, or even tragic ending, this would have to be another case of "All's well that ends well."

If memory serves me correctly, the miserable winters we endured in those years were, without a doubt, much worse than our winters now. In fairness, however, extending every benefit for a differing opinion, I should probably concede that the advancement in cars—technology, heating and cooling, better communication, and even better snow removal equipment, may make the weather appear to be better now. Modern technology aside, however, it seems we still like to complain about our miserably cold winters. No matter what the temperature, cold still hurts!

CHAPTER 7

Trying to recall the bad things that inevitably occur in every family, has become much harder for me to recollect than the happy times in my life. It's so much easier to bask in the remembrances of the fun times, the comfortable security of home and hearth, and the consistency of love of family. Surely this is what God intended, when he admonishes us in the Book of Ecclesiastes—to appreciate and love the people he has blessed us with, and not look for our happiness in the relentless pursuit of wealth or pleasure.

We must have adopted that lesson during these lean years, because money was always in short supply in our home. How much of a worry that may have been to my parents was not overly emphasized to us kids—only the caution to be careful with it. Neither were we alone in our struggle, during those hard financial times, for almost everyone in this little town of Whitten found it a challenge to consistently make ends meet. That made us not much different from the rest of our neighbors. Strangely enough, this *mutual lack* blessed us in ways we could not have foreseen—for poverty had become a true social equalizer.

The country had taken a major blow with the collapse of the stock market at the end of the 1920's, resulting in something we children knew only by that hateful name, "Depression." There was scarcely a family left untouched by the devastating results. Many families were victims of oppressive poverty, without jobs, having lost their homes and livelihoods, with despair becoming a way of life. This was the legacy of my generation. With thanksgiving I now realize how secure I was throughout the devastation and hopelessness of the times, by being protected by two parents who drew strength from God and each other, when hope was becoming a dwindling commodity.

Not only did Mom do her best to see that our lives were as normal as possible, but Dad also shared in keeping the deception alive—at least they did for me. It was never inherent in their characters to sit down, wring their hands, and give up. They were both brought up on farms where hard work was the ethic, expected and given. Mom and Dad lost their beautiful new home in Marshalltown during the Depression, before I was born. We would later hear stories about a time when it became necessary for Dad to "pound the pavement" looking for work.

Incidentally, it was from that house that my brother, Maurice, who, when he was first able to walk, ran out of the house after a bath, one day. Mother had turned away to get a towel, and in a flash, Maurice had disappeared from sight. Mother found him gaily racing down the street *stark naked.* The story was used against him many times when we felt he needed to be "brought down a peg."

Maurice was amazingly agile, for a baby. Another day as Mother had become distracted by something, Maurice once again eluded her, vanishing from sight. Realizing that her active little whirlwind had once again disappeared, she began searching the house. What she found was that her baby had climbed up on a table and somehow managed to get himself up onto the clock shelf that was hanging on the wall. There he sat, giggling and laughing with glee, proud of what he had done. This fearless little monkey knew no danger. The fate of the clock.....?

If I could choose one wish—and if mom was alive to hear me say that, she would undoubtedly favor me with one of her favorite clichés, "*If wishes were horses, then beggars would ride*" (meaning we shouldn't waste valuable time only wishing)—my wish would be to have the ability to paint a word picture that would allow you to look back at the scene, and the time, of what would have to be every kid's ideal place to grow up. Since Mom is no longer with us, I'll stick with my original premise in making the wish.

This little town of Whitten certainly wouldn't qualify for that honor because of its grand location, spectacular scenery, wealth, or its proximity to educational, recreational, or entertainment venues. It was instead a rather ordinary little spot that many might describe as a "little berg out in the sticks," typical of many country villages around that time. Quite possibly, for me, that was the very reason, plus the lack of all of those questionable assets, that made it the perfect place to be a child. Seen through my young eyes, it was beautiful.

Life was simple, uninhibited and unrestricted. Joy and freedom are words that loom large in my mind. Money was in short supply for everyone then; but its lack seemed more often to have a strengthening quality that connected neighbors, encouraged friendships and prompted caring. Kids of that era knew that fun doesn't depend on money.

If we became aware of our lack of money, at times, its absence was only a small disappointment to wishing for something we wanted, but had little hope of getting anyway. This lack of possessions didn't make us feel different from anyone else, or even deprived, because most of the rest of our friends were "in the same boat,."(Coupled with the fact that we weren't being constantly enticed with TV and sales ads announcing the "zillion" things we couldn't live without).

Through accepting these small disappointments we learned an invaluable lesson—that happiness and contentment don't depend on one's financial resources. Quite the contrary, because that very lack of ready cash forced us to find alternative means for having fun, and we found it by using our wits. In fact, deprivation and making-do were the accepted lifestyle of the times. Interesting to speculate about whether our present world could profit by a little more of that kind of lifestyle.

Although our frugal standard of living was seen, at times, as mean-spirited and oppressive, these very circumstances were to become super teachers of inventiveness, and motivational character builders of epic proportion for the great majority of less well-to-do kids of that era. Toys were anything we could lay our hands on—with the imagination to see them as toys.

Playtime meant freedom; unsupervised, unorganized, (except for our "pick-up" softball games in the pasture—which were mostly disorganized) spontaneous fun. Being outdoors was where we chose to spend our free time, and most of our exuberance came from the sheer joy of being free to roam and run in the sun and wind without many time- constraints or adult supervision.

As tight as the economy was in the twenties and thirties, my folks somehow managed to make sure our Christmases were very much akin to today's extravaganzas. By comparison, however, there was a distinct difference in the grandness of the gifts. Very often our Christmas presents were handcrafted by Mom or Dad—a new dress or coat, shirt or trousers, or some other needed piece of clothing Mom had made. She did, however, manage to assemble piles of gifts for each one.

One year Dad painstakingly made a porch swing for a family present. He also made an A-frame stand for it to hang on, and our beautiful, dark green, swing sat on our lawn every summer, getting lots of use. It proved to be very well made. The swing is now mine, and is still in good shape. Our "courting swing," is the way my husband, Bob, describes this still-sturdy antique, because it had hung on the front porch of our house when we were dating, and we made good use of it.

My longing to see the old "courting swing" hanging there largely prompted the addition of a porch we recently had built on the front of our ranch-style home. Years of memories came flooding back as Bob climbed down from the ladder after having attached the last chain to the hooks mounted on the ceiling, and we sat, once more, on our beautiful green swing.

Christmas presents were not all handmade by our parents; but it did require that they plan far ahead to be able to purchase something special for all of us. My special gift one year was a Shirley Temple doll. Golly, did I ever want that doll. I had thought about little else from the moment I heard about her; and so, I suspect, did every other little girl who had ever seen a Shirley Temple movie.

Shirley was a child star, reaching the height of her popularity between 1935-1938. My parents sometimes took me to see one of her films, or let me go with my sister; and I'm sure the theater could have collapsed around me without my knowing as we sat, absolutely enthralled, watching Shirley prancing and dancing and acting on the screen. I yearned for that doll so much that just thinking about her made my stomach ache.

It would be a sure bet to say that every little girl in the theater imagined herself up on that screen, wearing all of Shirley's unbelievably cute costumes; for the clothing she wore in her films bore little resemblance to the clothes we wore, which only aroused our appetites to see more of them.

"You know you really don't want that ugly old doll," Dad would tease me for weeks before that special Christmas. Protesting noisily, I would start whining and fussing, and challenging his description of the doll, trying to convince him that I really did want her—no, that I needed her—and that she truly was beautiful. I was still young enough to believe that he was serious, and naïve enough not to know that it was permissible to "stretch the truth" when it comes to Christmas secrets. That is still today, however, my only concession to lying!

After weeks of being warned that I really couldn't expect a Shirley Temple doll for Christmas, and trying valiantly to steel myself against the big disappointment of not getting her, there she was, that special Christmas morning—under the tree—my very own Shirley Temple doll. Could anything in the whole wide world ever again be more wonderful than this? Shirley came inside her own wardrobe trunk, wearing a pale green organdy dress. I found her waiting for me in one side of the trunk, with the rest of her clothing hanging neatly on the other side.

"I'm really mad at you, Daddy," I scolded him, with a mixture of mock anger and relief, "'cause you said I wouldn't get my doll." With happiness flooding over me, I was ecstatic as I gazed at my new treasure. Hugging my new doll, I threw myself into my parents' arms, loving them with such emotion that it brought me to tears. Shirley was beautiful, and she was mine!

My love for dolls insured my getting a new doll each Christmas until I had grown almost embarrassingly past the doll stage. In keeping with my nesting nature (meaning that I loathe to part with treasured keepsakes, or most anything else in which I see value) many of these dolls, even the cracked and pock-marked ones, are now in residence in boxes in my basement. Because of their condition, and my age, these dolls will be forever doomed to rest in peace for the remainder of their shabby existence in dark, airless, cardboard coffins, never to be played with again. But I know they are there and that's a comfort to me in my advancing years.

I can still recall the sweet, adorable look of each new, precious baby as they arrived, and how lovingly each was welcomed into my arms with such unreserved affection. Today my dolls are still good for a warm memory or two when I carefully take them out of their boxes for a look, on those rare occasions when that "Great Ole' Cleaning-the-Basement-Spirit" moves me. Which reminds me that my dolls haven't been looked at for some time!

Our home was situated in the northwest corner of Whitten on the last block of our street. Beyond our house to the north was one last house—large, old and square. On the other side of that house there was a wide grassy strip that was not quite, but almost, an alley. Our family always referred to this strip as "Green Street." This was neither a street nor was it always green. Had the street in front of this last house not curved to the east at that point, or had the road coming west continued straight on, our precious "Green Street" would have been covered with gravel.

Our parents usually knew where to find us, as it was one of our favorite places to play, this tree-lined strip of soft, lush, almost knee-high grass. It was the perfect place for fertile minds to reinvent the world while remaining just out of earshot of mothers who were good at offering suggestions for something constructive we could do with our leisure time.

What gratitude I now feel for that unlimited, unrestricted freedom in which we were allowed to play as children. Today we are all aware of the constant security precautions parents must take. What confidence our parents must have felt, knowing their chicks were safe even when out of sight. Because of the size of our town, however, our whereabouts were fairly predictable, and grownups had the luxury of assuming their children were safe from strangers. There were, of course, the inevitable skinned knees, cut lips, and broken arms with which parents have always had to contend, but that is a seemingly mandatory part of the childhood experience.

Not particularly restricted by boundaries also meant that we weren't always in sight of home. Sometimes we'd wander on north of Green Street, up to the railroad tracks where we found it a really brave and daring thing to walk on the train tracks and across the trestle. Not every kid was brave enough to walk on the trestle because of the way it made your legs get weak and shake when you looked down through the railroad ties to the dry creek bed—about a "hundred miles" below.

Much of our bravado came from seeing how long we could walk on the rails, or across the trestle, before jumping off at the sound of the whistle of the occasional train that came tearing through. Because we thought walking on the trestle was such a keen idea, we sometimes went too far in testing our mettle. The temptation to remain on the tracks too long suddenly turned the speeding train into a roaring tiger if we hesitated longer than was sensible.

The sound of the approaching train whistle made us catch our breath—instantly panic-stricken by the loud blaring it made—particularly if we were somewhere near the center of the trestle. At that point, with every hair standing on end, the message that it was time to "git," came through loud and clear.

It was downright crucial (to avoid falling) that we take extra care to watch our footing as we fled. Moving as fast as it was humanly possible, under the circumstances, we gingerly hopped and jumped across the wooden ties, hoping and praying that God would keep us from slipping through the spaces to the ground below—or even worse—being smashed by the train. This impending threat sent us scurrying like frightened jackrabbits toward the nearest point of the trestle's end where we could safely jump off. Fear, as usual, once again proved to be a colossal motivator, blessing and sharpening our footing skills. Providentially, we made it off every time—frightened but safe—and supremely smug and pleased with ourselves.

The same gratitude I expressed earlier for our unrestricted play time should probably be extended here to cover our miraculous escapes from taking a nose-dive off the trestle or from demolition by the train.

I'm sure I wasn't alone in feeling that my own home was the best place in town, even though it was certainly not the most elegant. Others must have felt the same about their own homes too. But to me mine was the best. The word cozy comes to mind—that feature figuring largely in my opinion I'm sure. Dad and Maurice kept the lawn mowed and Mom saw to it that we all kept things picked-up and tidy.

Just outside our kitchen door stood a water pump that needed to be primed by dumping water into its top. Priming meant pouring water into the top of the pump and furiously pumping the handle up and down until the water comes gushing out. It stood just off the end of the porch to the west. We were fortunate enough to have had a pump inside our house as well, which was attached to the end of the kitchen sink. This pump saved us from many freezing trips outside to get a bucket of water. We mostly used the inside pump during the winter, but that may have been to keep us from freezing outside, or for conserving water, since I believe it was connected to a cistern.

A brick walk led straight out from the kitchen door to a cave where all of Mom's garden produce was stored: potatoes, carrots, sweet potatoes, turnips, parsnips, rutabagas, apples and all of her canned fruits and vegetables. This was convenient because we did a lot of canning then and the cave was the safest and roomiest place to store the results.

Who could forget the canning days? The first requirement for canning, it seemed, was that the temperature must be at least 102 degrees in the shade—or was that in the kitchen? especially on corn-canning day. On those marathon canning days everyone was required to be up early and helping.

After a quick breakfast, corn-canning day began in earnest with all of us being given our marching orders: "go and bring in the corn from the garden." Since it was early in the morning when we began picking, the corn stalks and leaves were still wet with dew as we made our way through the rows.

How uncomfortable and irritating this job was, working our way down the wet rows—dripping leaves striking us in the face and head, soaking our clothing, and bonding garden soil to the soles of our shoes until they became heavily caked with mud. The long-bladed leaves of the cornstalks were sharp enough to inflict paper-cut type injuries on careless pickers, and we got our share of them.

When the bushel baskets were full, we took them to the house and began tearing off the husks—"shucking the ears." Mother's biggest job, it seemed, was to continually remind us to remove as much of the silk as possible. A corn silk floating in a quart of canned corn would have been considered a major flaw in her canning skill—unthinkable.

Mom had kettles of water boiling on the stove by the time the corn was ready to be cut—undoubtedly helpful in raising the temperature of the already steamy kitchen to the required 102 degrees. Actually, the boiling water was to blanch the corn, and to sterilize the jars, caps and lids. Mom's sterilization process would have made a brain surgeon jealous. From my point of view it seemed a little like overkill, but my protests meant little—that was her way—and so it was to be our way!

Next came the best job of all, cutting the corn off the cob. We carefully cut off every kernel, and scraped each cob to be sure we got every bit of "corn milk" that was left clinging to the ear. Not only did this juice thicken the corn a bit, it was the way to make sure we retained all of the flavor possible from the cob. This step in this rigorous procedure covered our hands and arms, and sometimes even our faces, with corn juice; but it also proved to be the most fun for us kids because nearly everyone within range of the big dishpan got splattered. The sight of each splattering rocked us with laughter, and, I suspect, perfected our aim as we scraped.

Come winter, when mom served her gourmet corn, memories of that torturous time of incarceration in her sauna-hot kitchen, somehow seemed less painful. Then too, has there ever been a smell so good as home-canned corn, or the taste? The only other rival for that honor could possibly be homemade bread baking in the oven, or freshly brewing coffee.

We repeated the canning process with each new crop of vegetables or fruit. Once again we were put to hard work in the kitchen. We kids figured the only excuse Mom would consider good enough to get us released from canning would be a raging case of something contagious, or a sudden violent illness. Not many excuses passed Mom's Rorschach test. We learned how to can!

A conversation over lunch with friends recently reminded me of the process used to "put up" pickles, and make sauerkraut. In order to make good pickles at our home, it was absolutely necessary for the cucumbers to be a correct and uniform size. When the sorting was done and all was ready, these "just-right-size" cucumbers were immersed in a large crock of brine, covered and stored until the time they actually became pickles.

Similarly, sauerkraut was made from uniformly thin slices of cabbage. Mom used a large wooden cabbage cutter—a board with two metal blades fastened to a hole in the middle of the board—over which she ran heads of cabbage back and forth, giving her slivers of uniformly-sized shreds of cabbage. This too was packed in a brine of its own juice and salt until it fermented.

Mother carefully packed the large crocks as full as she could get them, and they would then be taken to the cave where they were stored. Each crock was covered with a heavy plate which served as a lid, and in the case of the sauerkraut, the lid had to be topped with a heavy weight. What that was for I have no idea, but I know it was a necessary for Mom. My guess would have been, at the time, that because of all of the fermentation, the cabbage probably swelled up and needed weights to keep it from exploding, or maybe it was to keep the foul smell inside the crock. This is probably as good a theory as you'll get from someone who only now has started to tolerate sauerkraut.

Over the cave, where these canned marvels were stored, once stood an imposing, large, but by then, rather dilapidated, gazebo-type structure. It was a favorite place to play. The sturdy, wooden floor was still intact and there was a hand railing all around. The roof had disintegrated over time. Merely the frame was left standing, reminding one of a sagging, worn out, canopy-type bed without the covering.

The cave entrance was camouflaged with a small overhead platform, and a door covering the steps that led down into the cave, built at a forty-five degree angle, reaching from the ground to the platform. When this door was opened there were eight or ten brick steps leading down to the cave doorway at the bottom.

There is no logical way to describe the smell of a "working" cave. The earthy odor rising up from its depths was a combination of dirt floor and brick walls, all of the stored fruit and vegetables, baskets, burlap bags (known then as "gunny sacks"—can't guess why, maybe a guy named Gunny designed them) an assortment of garden tools, and even a bit of miscellaneous junk stacked around the floor. Shelves, however, were neatly lined with the fruits of mom's (and our) labor—rows of canned green beans, peas, corn, tomatoes, carrots and other vegetables, and every kind of fruit, as well as the pickles and sauerkraut.

If you are ever lucky enough to have this cave experience it will remain with you always—an indelible memory of pungent, musky, smells. The first thing one notices, upon descending to its nether regions, is the tomb-like feeling that surrounds you in the heavy darkness. Its cold, yet insulating dirt walls and floor, chills your bones. I didn't like being there alone, or being asked to bring something in from the cave. When sent, I was always happy to find the thing I'd come for quickly so I could escape back out into the sunshine and freedom. Perhaps this is a clue to the existence of my present-day sense of claustrophobia, undoubtedly learned at an early age. Being sent to the cave was better in the summertime, for it was cool, and a temporary, if peculiar, escape from the heat.

The heavy wooden door covering the steps leading down to the lower cave made a perfect slide for the younger set. We had used it for that purpose so long that its surface, worn smooth and slick, had become shiny. We slid down headfirst, backwards, sitting, standing or any other daring way that would prove our bravery. In a burst of exuberance, one summer day, while attempting to fly down the door in a sitting position—backwards—I was to encounter yet another of my near misses with the "world to come."

Pushing off the small platform, neglecting, in the excitement of the moment, to notice that the door had been left open, I quickly found myself airborne for a short trip down. Landing on my back on the brick floor nearly a quarter of a story below I was momentarily dazed. Once again, another of her children had managed to terrify and traumatize Mom. However, other than having the wind knocked out of my lungs and receiving a few bruises, my life was mercifully spared; more importantly, rather than the embarrassment I'd expected, I was accorded a pretty fair amount of hero status for my daring deed, given to me by my appreciative audience.

Just beyond the cave was a very large, old, tree, which was perfectly formed to accommodate young climbers. Maurice, our budding young inventor-in-the-making, and the instigator of lots of our fun, nailed some boards up the tree for steps. Crawling around in the upper regions of the tree to find a limb sturdy enough to support the weight of the swing he had engineered--a burlap bag stuffed with straw and tied at the top with a long rope—he then attached this marvel to the perfect limb high up in the tree.

When all was ready, we experimental test pilots would wait in the crotch of the tree to catch the straw-filled swing that Maurice would throw up to meet us. With one hand grasping the rope and the other nervously clutching the tree, we would fling our legs around the bag, releasing our grip on the tree, and fly out, soaring like a bird. Feeling as daring as astronauts, or the Wright Brothers, we flew at least five feet above the ground—back and forth, back and forth—swinging just long and high enough to still be able to grab the tree, or the hands of those anxious kids waiting in the tree for their turn.

In yet another of his more creative moments, and because his brain was constantly whirling with neat ideas for still more inspiring ways to have fun, my brother got out the hammer, some nails and boards, one day, and built a pair of stilts for each of us, and our friends. What a noisy racket and goofy spectacle we made, staggering and wobbling, trying to get used to those awkward things that kept wanting to jerk loose from under our arms when we took a step.

The ridiculous sounds of our clunking and clomping on the sidewalk echoed over the neighborhood and must have brought more than one neighbor to their front door to see what on earth was going on. Once we gained a little confidence walking on the stilts it was only natural that the competition would begin.

Running awkwardly on our wooden legs, the race was on. It was war—and it generally disintegrated into a melee of shoving and bumping into one another, while scrambling frantically to remain upright. These skirmishes often ended with most of us falling off our stilts onto the concrete sidewalk, or sprawled in the grass. It wasn't unusual for us bruised and scratched, grass-stained, wounded warriors, to limp home suffering skinned knees and elbows.

The pole-vaulting bar he constructed, one summer, was another of Maurice's great creations. He set up the vaulting bar in the orchard out beside our house. He'd made it from some old lumber and a number of bamboo poles he'd managed to scrounge up from "*only Heaven knows where.*" He was exceptionally adept at finding just the right things we needed for any of our projects.

Everyone wanted to be first to jump, but since he was the boss we had to abide by his rules, so we waited our turn. Running speedily down the grassy course with the long, bamboo pole in hand, straining every muscle, we felt like Olympic athletes as we jammed the flexible pole into the ground (hoping against hope that it wouldn't break) then soaring up into the air and over the bar. After each jump Maurice would raise the bar, but we were not daunted. We accepted the challenge without hesitation—so sure that we could clear it—until we failed, usually landing in a jumble of bar, pole, and cracked shins.

It's sad to realize there are children around who have never had the creative joy of having to depend on such primitive resources for their fun—our main essentials. With regret, I believe the excesses of today often rob our children of their rightful relationship with the proverbial "mother" who found inventiveness absolutely necessary. But then, I was never a kid in the computer age. What do you suppose will they tell their children about their childhood?

CHAPTER 8

As awful moments go, it isn't hard, in thinking back to the absolutely most embarrassing spectacle I ever made of myself, to classify this as the worst memory of my life, and it happened when I was only five years old. What makes it even worse, it turned out to be an incident that was most remembered about me by some of the folks there in Whitten. This harrowing moment, this most horrendous and shameful event, ranks right up there with the worst of the worst. This "never-to-be-forgotten by any of our neighbors within a two-mile radius spectacle," came back to haunt me at the most unexpected times of my life. Another painful part of this ordeal came in later life, when I was forced to gracefully endure the tremendous pleasure some took in reminding me of it.

My shameful experience got its start several weeks before school began. I was nearly delirious with anticipation, and Mother had been forced to endure the fallout of this nervous stimulation for weeks. She was undoubtedly growing tired of my annoying exhilaration, so it was understandable that in her frazzled state, she had become desperate enough to calm me by any means, forcing her to resort to drastic measures. She began asking me, "But what am I going to do at home alone without my little girl?"

This innocent-enough question must have begun to work its way into my consciousness, for something unusual began to happen.

The first day of school finally arrived, but found me harboring a complete change of heart. Whether or not I was expected to walk to school with my brother and sister is unclear. But suddenly, and unreasonably, I totally rebelled at the entire idea of school. Having coaxed, cajoled, teased, and probably threatened me to no avail, Mom and Dad decided I would be driven to school in our Model T Ford with the side curtains that rolled up and snapped open. It was fall and the weather was still warm.

From this point on the fun began! In panicky rebellion, I had taken refuge under the bed. Struggling to retrieve me from my hiding place, Mother managed to grab one of my legs and held on. Then, pulling, dragging, and half-carrying me out of the house, she wrestled me into the car. Before Dad could get the car in gear, however, I had jumped over the car door, through the open window, and had run back into the house. This happened several more times, each time with Mom in hot, and increasingly irritated pursuit. My speed and agility would undoubtedly have set a record for the twenty-yard dash each time I ran for the house that day. This frenzied race was spawned by my near-hysteria, and the frantic search for another, more inaccessible hiding place away from my relentless pursuer.

This went on long enough until both Mom and Dad became red-faced with exasperation. Finally, Mom again managed to capture me; and while still screaming at the top of my lungs, arms flailing and legs kicking, she managed to restrain me in a hold from which there was no escape. Still angry, and stubbornly unwilling to surrender in this war of wills, I nevertheless found myself totally immobilized and summarily wrestled into the car. By then, it was obvious to me that Mom's strength had become "like the strength of ten thousand," and her overpowering, vice-like grip (no doubt spawned from outraged frustration) was so firm there was absolutely no hope of escape. I was her prisoner!

Jamming the car into gear, Dad drove out of the driveway with gravel flying, for what was to become my infamous first day of school! After all of the tussling, I can only imagine the miserable state of disarray I must have presented to the entire school that day. The Principal, Professor James Mabie, by now aware of the raucous situation erupting outside the door, allowed Mother to come in with me—but then ordered her to leave. It wouldn't have seemed normal to me if Mom and Dad hadn't managed to get in a few peeks just to make sure their "little darling" wasn't causing total pandemonium and chaos throughout the halls, besmirching the family's good name and alienating every teacher before she had even started school.

Everyone was in awe of Professor Mabie. He was a very large, ruddy-skinned, and imposing man who tolerated little nonsense; so it wasn't long until this kid began to realize that the "jig was up." Prudence, at that point, seemed to suggest that capitulation might be the better part of valor, and it would be wise to retreat gracefully (if that was still possible) and survive the day. Even in my bedraggled, disheveled state, not only did I survive the trauma and commotion I had created that morning, but at some point I began to decide that I quite liked school and didn't want to leave.

That I felt this comfortable—given my predictably scruffy state of dress, and my disgraceful entrance that morning—was rather shocking, because I was a little "fuss-budget" about my clothes; and I should have felt totally embarrassed by my actions. Because of the staff and student's total acceptance (or so it seemed to me) I was able to relax and become completely absorbed in this wonderful new experience I had been looking forward to for so long.

At noontime, after coming home for lunch, Mother's maverick child was begging to return. That was not to be as school (for first-graders) was only a half-day event for the first week. After my less-than-auspicious first day of school, things smoothed out rather quickly; and mercifully, I suffered no latent recriminations from either teachers or students in the future. There was not the remotest possibility, from that moment on, that wild horses could have kept me home from school.

Learning seemed to come easily for me. I loved a challenge then, and still do. When confronted with a problem that needs solving, my antenna automatically shoots up, and my mission becomes clear. It seems to be my nature to jump in with both feet, even if it necessitates taking the problem out of someone else's hands, resolving it for them.... a common complaint from family members.

Because he lived across the street, Doctor James Blaha, was privy to, and highly entertained, by the explosive goings-on across the street that morning. He managed to keep this disgraceful chapter in my life very much alive. He seldom missed an opportunity to bring this frenzied performance of mine up at the most inopportune moments of my life.

It was he who (whenever he saw me) thought it great fun to force me to memorize a German phrase to repeat to my mother who, of course, spoke German as well as English. Being raised in a German household, Mom hadn't learned to speak English until she went to school. Any time he happened to meet me on the street, or if I was even within calling distance, Doc would hail me over, give me a German phrase to memorize, and grill me until I got the pronunciation right. When my version of the phrase met his satisfaction he would send me home to repeat it to my mother.

Since he was so determined, with this little exchange, I always suspected that the gleeful look on Doc's face meant that the phrase was somehow intended to shock Mom with a bit of naughtiness. Mother was up to the challenge, however, and always took it with good grace and a chuckle. She was, after all, a hard-working German woman who had been given a liberal education in practical communication. She could give it back as well as take it.

I loved to see her face light up with laughter, eyes twinkling, as I labored to deliver one of Doc's little missives through my own awkward translation of German. Sometimes she would coach me in a rebuttal phrase, and send me back to Doc's house to deliver the reply. My pronunciation of the message might have been flawed, but his hilarious reaction to it let me know that he understood. Such warm memories as these, of simple fun being shared by the people of typical small town rural communities, now seem to have existed several lifetimes ago.

Halloween and May Day were two events that my friends and I looked forward to probably more than the adults. My favorite of these two holidays was May Day. I really got into the spirit of this one. Days before the event we painstakingly cut, pasted, wove and colored the perfect May baskets by hand, trying to outdo each other in creating the most beautiful design.

Mom helped us as we filled our frilly, hand-made, construction and crepe paper wonders with popcorn, candy—and the best and main ingredient—the spring blossoms we had just picked off our cherry and apple trees growing in the little orchard behind our house. Because our baskets had to be perfect, we also hunted for violets, lily of the valleys, bluebells, and bridal wreath to top it all off. Because of the overflowing contents, our baskets were obviously rather large. Our neighbors and friends, the recipients of these springtime delights, always seemed surprised and appreciative of all our hard work.

The costumes we wore for Halloween were thrown-together concoctions made of sheets, scarves, grown-up clothing, or anything we could pull together to hide our identities. Struggling to keep our composure, we traipsed, giggling, through town trying hard not to trip on our trailing garments as we headed for our neighbors' houses.

Knocking on doors, rousing the occupants, we made it our brash practice to barge right in when the door was opened. Without a qualm we would tour the house completely, making eerie noises and marching in ragtag parade fashion through every room in the house, putting on quite a show until the "usually amused" owners surrendered and handed out treats. Who could imagine such a practice today? But these self-appointed, mandatory treks through the neighbors' homes on Halloween night were special for us because our intrusions were generally met with enthusiasm and laughter, and a fairly good-natured amount of tolerance.

For me, the trip through Doc Blaha's house was always the most fun and the one I remember best; partly because their home was the first one we "hit" and also, because Doc's house wasn't a place that encouraged casual kid visitors, due to his having his practice there. That made our free access tours even more daring, giving us the feeling that we were the ones in control that time. Of course, the best reason for finding Doc's house fun on Halloween, was because we weren't there on the official business of getting poked, prodded or otherwise treated for some painful ailment.

If May basket Day and Halloween were two of the happiest holidays, the 4th of July was, for me, a nightmare—a terror-filled day. Firecrackers were readily available back then, and the boys in town, my brother included, loved tossing little "finger" firecrackers in the direction of anyone unfortunate enough to be caught in their line of fire.

How I hated the loud "bangs." They hurt my ears, and, incidentally, still do. My 4th of July celebrations were mostly spent cowering amidst the shoes and clothes hanging in my parents' closet, holding my ears, longing desperately for the 5th!

While our parents insisted that we learn to become helpful, they were also wise enough to understand the need for children to experience the sheer luxury of uninhibited playtime. These, of course, are the most easily recalled events, for there were many. "Jacks" was a favorite game we kids played—often, outside on the sidewalk.

My friend, Clarice, and I were playing Jacks on the sidewalk in front of our house on a breezy summer afternoon. It had been raining earlier in the morning, but had stopped just before noon. The sun had come out and Clarice and I had carefully picked a dry spot on the sidewalk to start playing. We were in the midst of our game when a car drove up in front of our house and out jumped my sister's piano teacher.

He was a slightly stocky young man of medium height, in his mid-thirties, with thinning sandy-blond hair, and wearing wire-rimmed glasses. He was someone I scarcely noticed when he came to the house to give the lessons, since he wasn't there to teach me. I usually paid little attention to him.

On that particular afternoon, however, this young man spotted Clarice and me as we were squatting on the sidewalk deeply involved in our game of Jacks. Somehow the sight of the two of us having fun must have triggered some diabolical plot inside his head that became too much to resist. For instead of going directly inside, which he usually did, he veered from the direction of the house, walked up to the place where we were sitting, scooped me up in his arms, and, striding down the walk a bit, set me down, with a jolt and a plop, in the nearest water puddle.

In shock as I sat, stunned, cold and wet, soaking up the rainwater from the puddle, Clarice and I watched him run into the house, laughing as if he was exceedingly pleased with himself. Indignant anger exploded in my brain as I gingerly retrieved myself from my predicament—cold water running down my legs, saturating my clothing,.

With furious tears and dripping bloomers, I stormed into the house to tell Mom about the hateful thing that had been done to me. The sympathy I was expecting came mixed with only slightly-disguised amusement, which made my anger all the more fierce. With a brief word of consolation and a quick change of underwear, Mom insisted that I "get over it and run along and play." I really detest that crazy person, were the thoughts racing through my head that day—a fact of seemingly little concern to him. Neither was I pleased with the amused reaction of Mom and Maxine, who really should have read him the riot act, in my estimation, instead of sharing what I assumed had become a mutual joke for the three of them.

There was no need to be fearful of this teacher on future visits, for he didn't give me another reason to become guarded in his presence. There was never another traumatic incident of this kind. This one-time, uncharacteristic action of my sister's scholarly teacher astonished everyone that day. He instantly reverted back to being his serious and academic self after the first harrowing episode.

My only theory for his irrational behavior of the moment was that he possessed a secret "Dr. Jekyll and Mr. Hyde" complex. To be on the safe side, however, I studiously learned to avoid him, keeping a safe distance where I could observe his movements when he came to give Maxine a piano lesson. And while I never truly warmed up to the man again, I did forgive him.

CHAPTER 9

Times were hard, and becoming increasingly harder for most everyone in those years. World War I had ended in 1919; and in October, of 1929, the stock market crashed, sending the country into a severe depression. The price of stock dropped by 40%, and 9,000 banks went out of business. Nine million savings accounts were wiped out! Eighty-six thousand businesses failed during this time and average wages decreased by an average of 60% for those fortunate enough to still be working. Unemployment rose from 9% to a staggering 25%. Newspaper and radio reports told of stockbrokers and businessmen, jumping from their skyscraper office buildings because of this disastrous calamity that had seen them financially wiped out. The "crash" sent shock waves throughout the country, and, of course, abroad.

While my family experienced this same hard time, we evidently had enough resources to be able to play host to a cousin of mine. Irene Pischel was one of several cousins whose parents, my Aunt Retha and Uncle Carl, needed to "farm out" for a time. They had been financially crippled by the Depression, and since theirs was a big family of six children, feeding and clothing all of them became too great a burden for them to bear alone. Whether or not all of Irene's other sisters and brothers were sent away is unknown to me. Irene and her sister, Kathryn, are the only two I can account for.

Theirs was a religious and God-fearing family, and from my innocent point of view it didn't seem at all fair of God to do this mean thing to that close-knit and loving family. I would later come to learn that God was at work protecting and showing His great love, not only for them but to our family as well. My parents were quick to agree to the arrangement and were happy to be able to lend them a helping hand in this way. How many homes of that era were similarly affected would be impossible to guess—but it was a more common practice—sending children elsewhere to live for a time—than one cared to imagine. The Depression had obviously brought many people a good deal more than monetary heartache.

My cousin Kathryn went to live with my Aunt Louise and her family, while cousin Irene came to live with us. Even though we didn't know her all that well at the time, we kids were excited that she would be coming to our home to be with us. Irene was a quiet and rather shy girl who suffered from a stiff neck, which made it hard for her to turn her head. To compensate, she generally turned the upper portion of her body when looking in a different direction. A doctor friend of mine made a guess that she had probably suffered from a condition known as Torticollis. The large cord running down one side of her neck was very prominent, extending to somewhere around the clavicle.

This condition looked painful to me, but she seemed oblivious to it, having had it for such a long time. What does seem unnatural about the situation, however, was my own reticence in not continually pestering her to tell how she came to have the condition. But it's possible she might have been born with it, dropped as a child, or, as my friend said, "It could have been the result of any number of reasons."

Irene was a great help around the house; she willingly pitched in with the rest of us to do the housework, washing dishes, laundry and ironing. Mom didn't demand any more of her than she did from the rest of us, but treated her with the same consideration and love she gave the family. It wasn't long before she began to feel right at home, and became a valued addition to the family.

Irene went with us to all of the basketball games, plays, and every school event that we attended. She cheered along with the family when I made a basket for the team, whether we won or not. She went to church with us every Sunday, and got as excited about a family picnic or trip to Pine Lake to go swimming as the rest of us. We were a family. We shopped together in Marshalltown (the few occasions we were there) laid awake in bed at night giggling and gossiping about boys, and other things that girls were giggling and gossiping about in those days, sharing secrets and confidences I would never even share with my sister.

Since homesickness was my constant nemesis, I often asked Irene if she was homesick, having to be away from home so long. I wasn't to learn if she never really was homesick, or if she was just trying to make the best of the situation because her answer was usually, "I miss my folks and brothers and sisters, but I'm not homesick." Part of the reason for that may have been the total acceptance she felt as a part of our family, for there was nothing we did that didn't include her. And since she had always lived on a farm, perhaps living in town, no matter how small, proved to be a welcome diversion as well.

Irene stayed with us for over a year. Her leaving was a sad occasion, parting in the midst of a heartrending and weepy farewell. Saying "goodbye" meant that we were losing an "almost" member of the family. How fortunate for me that my dad was able to provide for us, for unlike Irene, had I been the one sent away to live with relatives, there's a real possibility that I would not have endured the experience, having departed this life from acute homesickness!

During this deeply depressed economic time there were many who were forced to accept government help in order to care for their families; but I knew of only one. Learning about this amazing thing called "welfare," I began thinking that this assistance would be a wonderful thing for our family also, for I had learned that those on "welfare" were treated to such unimaginable things as crates of oranges—even in the winter—as well as many other "*luxury*" food items. So, feeling extremely important to have stumbled upon this important information, I breathlessly relayed the marvelous news to my parents as I burst through the door after school one day.

At the mere mention of this word "welfare," Dad's face clouded up and became set in a stern hard look. Suddenly feeling as guilty as if I'd used a swear word, I soon learned that this was not a subject to be mentioned in front of my dad again; for immediately after my happy announcement Dad gave me a lecture on his idea of the perceived "evils" of accepting government help. He informed me that we would starve before we would accept anything from the government. Had that become an imminent possibility, I'm wondering what the outcome might have been. It was, therefore, fortunate for us that Dad had the resources (meager as they were) and the ability to hunt and fish, to at least keep us fed. My, how attitudes have changed since that time!

After having my bubble burst, so decisively, over my "wonderful" newsflash, and in light of his hostile attitude toward this practice, the subject for me was closed. In those days a man's worth seemed fiercely tied to his own ability to provide for his family. There were many men of that era who shared my dad's attitude about accepting government help.

Two girls in our little town became my closest friends during the very early years. There was Clarice, who had three brothers and a sister, a frail little mother, Eldona known by everyone as "Dony" (rhymed with pony) and a rather rotund father named Bill Clough. Mr. Clough, was the welcome neighbor who organized the rescue party that came to dig us out when our house was snowed in. Clarice's mother took in sewing, as my own Mother did. The Cloughs lived in a small house very near us but somehow managed to cope in their tight quarters, despite the size of their large family. Clarice and I became fast friends, spending as much time as possible together.

Because of the size of Clarice's family, and the many distractions of her mother's cooking and sewing, the living and dining room of the house was usually pretty much strewn with clutter. How they could collect so much paper was one of life's mysteries to me. I found it to be great fun in my younger years to suggest to Clarice that we tidy up her house. Imagine the effrontery—or my eagerness. Unlike Clarice, her mother never seemed to object, obviously grateful for any relief in that realm.

Grabbing the broom, because their floors were hardwood, I would start sweeping with the gusto of a whirlwind. Given the amount of paper we collected, it was necessary to sweep the clutter into several smaller piles since there was usually too much to gather into one. What a satisfying contrast could be noticed as the floor again became visible. It's difficult to explain why this simple task gave me so much joy; but I always experienced a rush of pride when it was done, knowing that we had produced such a miraculous transformation.

Next came the bed making. Again, it's unclear how often the family experienced the bliss of climbing nightly into a bed with straightened covers; but it didn't matter, for if they were unmade when I was there, we—Clarice, prodded more than a little bit by me—and I, once more swung into action, attempting to put the house back into some semblance of order. Remembering those days, it would not be unthinkable that all of the Clough kids had viewed me as some sort of Prussian general, for I was very liberal with directions and orders, and not at all bashful about enlisting their help. (Perhaps I take after my Grandmother Hannah more than I realized.)

With the beds made, the floors swept, the clutter organized or removed, and the furniture dusted, I nearly always felt it was necessary to look around to see what little touch could be added to brighten up the rather Spartan and tight quarters. In summer I would look around outside for a clump of flowers or some other unusual object to make the rooms look a little brighter. Right now it's easy to imagine the head-nodding going on amongst my own children and hear their collective agreement, "Yup, that's Mom for sure!" I still seem to find it essential to find just that right touch to brighten any dull spot in my house.

It didn't seem at all necessary to receive words of thanks or praise for these cleaning sprees, for in those days Clarice and I were together so much that I had almost come to feel like a member of the family. Clarice's tired little mother, Dony, more often than not, seemed distractedly oblivious to the straightened house, although she often smiled her gratitude and I always felt that she was pleased. For me it was enough to run home after these furious bouts of housekeeping, energized and happy, and feeling that here, at least, was one little corner of the world that had been restored to order.

The effort involved was undoubtedly appreciated mostly by me, for the house didn't remain in this state of tidy for long; the many children seemed to believe the place for a piece of scrap paper was on the floor. More charitably, it's entirely possible they were simply oblivious to something as superficially mundane and uninteresting as housekeeping. This small flaw in their organizational skills was never a problem for me, as I loved being with them—they were a fine family and fun to be with, and my feelings for them were not diminished because of it.

Having had the opportunity to meet many of these children in later life and learn of their chosen professions, I am now convinced that tidiness and achievement must surely have been mutually exclusive. For theirs was a family of very intelligent children, whose father fostered their desire to learn and insisted on study. They have proven to be a family of achievers. The papers left so carelessly strewn about were undoubtedly the resulting overflow of much creative homework. Charles, the oldest child, was killed during World War II.

Somehow cleaning our own home seemed more of a chore than it was at the neighbors. First, because I wasn't convinced that it was really very messy; and second, because we were given no option but to "hop to it." Since the idea wasn't totally mine, it probably robbed the entire proposal of any creative appeal. To me, the only result I could see from these furious weekly attacks of compulsory dust and dirt rearranging was that the house sparkled and shone just a bit more than it had before.

Our assigned duties were always laid out specifically, and afterward were inspected for the quality of the work done. I was highly insulted when Mom insisted on inspecting the piano keys for dust, even after I had scaled the keyboard with my dust cloth making sure I'd polished every key, black and white, according to her orders.

About the only part of housecleaning that we kids considered coming close to anything resembling fun, was the floor waxings. In every one of our homes the kitchen floors were covered with the traditional linoleum that everyone else had, and it was an unwritten rule in our house that those floors could never be scrubbed without being waxed as well. After scrubbing and drying the floor, Mom knew instinctively where to find us kids, no matter how well we thought we had managed to disappear. Handing each of us a pair of dads old, worn-out, wool socks, we pulled them on our feet, and "skated," back and forth across the floor until it shone like the gleam in Mom's eye.

We did a major housecleaning twice a year in our home—every spring and fall. That was when we really "tore out the nest." Mother began by wiping down the walls and ceilings with a broom wrapped in a clean cloth. Aside from cleaning, she was giving any resident spiders notice that it was time to vacate their hiding places, and down came every stray cobweb. Curtains were cleaned, windows washed, closets, shelves, and every nook, and all the crannies, were "dug out"!

Come spring, every carpet was hauled outside and hung on the clothesline for it's annual beating. With unbridled fury and youthful exuberance we kids took turns thrashing the rugs with carpet beaters. My how the winter's accumulation of dust would fly.

Initially, the job even started out being fun; we took great pleasure in beating the carpets with all of wild frenzy and energetic, enthusiastic zeal of someone possessed. As our arms began to tire, though, the fun part of cleaning the carpets lost a lot of its luster and we were begging to quit.

The carpets always seemed cleaner to us than they did to Mom; so it was back to the clothesline for more whacking, which by then had really stopped being fun. It was now backbreaking and grueling work. We weren't finished, though, until we couldn't see one more flying speck of dust as we beat.

But Mom taught us well, and I find myself, even today, doing many of my housewifely chores according to many of the rules, and even some of the shortcuts, Mom laid down for us as children. I am not a martyr, however, and could kiss the feet of the inventor of the vacuum cleaner—especially when my husband is wielding it.

These remembrances bring to mind one more of Mother's favorite clichés in this working-together-as-a-family situation, which went: "Many hands make light work," she would remind us often. Unfortunately, there seems to be a movement underfoot these days, belittling the use of clichés. But let's get serious and take a look at what a cliché really is: A cliché, in my eyes, is a subtle, interesting and loving way of making a point—*without the lecture*! On the order of the parables in the Bible—right? A parable being: Making a point through telling a story.

It was under Mom's tutelage that I learned to hang wallpaper, which also seemed more of a chore back then. Before we could start hanging the paper we had to trim off the sides of the long, narrow, too-tightly-rolled rolls of wallpaper with a pair of scissors. Next we sized the walls (painted the walls with paste) and then pasted the long unwieldy, curling strips of paper with a big, heavy brush that had been dipped into the bucket of paste. With the strips of paper sufficiently covered (making extra sure to cover the sides and corners so there were no dry spots) we were ready to hang—the paper, that is.

Now, with the new wider, pre-pasted wallpapers, which come already trimmed and ready to hang, a lot of the misery has been removed from the job. One thing we find now that hasn't changed for the better is the greater amount of paper that it takes to paper a room—and the expense.

When I was papering with Mom we could cover an entire room with one or two rolls, and maybe an extra roll if we did the ceiling, which must be causing smiles among those who have tried to do the job now.

There wasn't any job that Mom wouldn't tackle if she felt it needed attention. The thought of reupholstering or slip covering a piece of furniture—a job that I have done, but not so enthusiastically—didn't faze her. "It's too difficult," weren't words found in her dictionary or even her brain.

Because of it, we kids often found ourselves removing the finish from nearly anything in the house that didn't move. We scraped and sanded every stationary varnished or painted item we possessed if she decided it needed sprucing up—a most hateful job.

My thoughts about that time have now softened toward these work projects, especially remembering the challenge Mom and I took on together—refinishing an old, antique, pie safe. This piece of furniture had belonged to her parents, and she had been the fortunate one to inherit it. She had persuaded Dad to move the cupboard out to the side porch so we could work on it there, going to work with varnish remover, sandpaper, and the most important ingredient of all, "elbow grease."

Despite the hard work, there was something so special and wonderful about the time we spent together that summer, working on the pie safe. The job provided us with lots of time to indulge in "girl talk" as we sanded and scraped away. The conversation usually got around to what needed to be done at the church, a subject that found its way into most of our conversations.

The predictable outcome of these little church chats was what "*we*" needed to do about it—for our family was big on that "doing something about it" part. We talked and laughed as we worked; often giggling about the latest interesting thing we'd heard concerning a neighbor or some event going on in town.

But whatever we talked about, that time became our private moment for just enjoying being Mother and Daughter together. And my, how beautiful that rejuvenated old pie safe looked by the time we were finished with it, but no more beautiful that the bond of love that had been strengthened between the two of us.

Mom continued using that pie cupboard, which her parents had owned, as long as she was still in her home. She kept it in her basement for many years using it for storing excess sheet music, quilting pieces, and craft materials, which seemed to be a favorite project of many of the organizations to which she belonged.

When her health began to fail and she could no longer live at home, Bob and I had the unbelievably difficult job of disposing of her furniture. It was a hard and sad task—closing up her home—but necessary.

Not really wanting to part with anything that was Mothers, it was wrenching to sell her things. Every one in the family had their own homes full of furniture and could not take the bulk of this dismantled household. But there was one piece of furniture I refused to sell, and the pie safe became mine. I discovered that Mother had even taped a note on the back of the cupboard stating that it was to come to me.

Had I known that I would one day become the inheritor of this particular piece of furniture, realizing how highly prized they are as a uniquely charming addition to most any home decor, I am sure I would have pestered Mom to keep it in a better place than in her basement. But because it belonged to her, I should have realized that there was no cause for alarm for it was no worse for wear.

Mother took excellent care of everything she owned. The pie safe now sits in a prominent place in my home and I love it. It would be impossible to estimate the number of loving thoughts I have had of Mom as I see it sitting there.

CHAPTER 10

Usually, Clarice and I walked to school together. It was my habit to walk west down the grassy alley, south of our home, to her house, then through their gate that opened from the alley to their garden that was located behind their house. Opening the gate, I walked on the path past the huge garden, up to the house where I would wait for her to come out. It came to be one of our favorite morning rituals, in the early fall, to pick an apple off their wonderful Delicious Apple Tree to eat on the way to school.

For me, there has never been an apple since that tasted as good as the cold, crisp, freshly picked and juicy apples from my friend's tree. The apples were green, streaked with red. They were heavy and solid, without a blemish. Their appearance was dull rather than shiny-skinned, which made them look even more appetizing. That first bite guaranteed a big spurt of juice. Describing them as the best apples in the world is to me, no exaggeration. However, it should probably be noted here that most of the things we recollect as children, appeared, tasted, or felt better than they actually did at the time. But not these apples!

Clarice was often free to play, and invariably we would head off to spend time over on Green Street, pretending we were going on a picnic; and sometimes we actually brought along some snacks.

Friends often came as well. As usual, I was the self-appointed captain in charge, and instigator of these little excursions—any wonder?

It's evident that even at so young an age, my church held a very important place in my life. It must have been true, because, more often than not, along the way to our picnic site, it was my autonomous decision to stop our bewildered little safari under every shade tree along the way—not because we were too hot, not because we needed to stop and rest—no, it was my solitary judgment that everyone in the group must stop and bow their heads...*to pray.* We must have prayed at least four or five times before we reached our destination. What we prayed about is known only to God; but our playtime, was blessed with obviously clean souls.

The neighbors moved out of the large, old house next door, to the north of our home, and it stood empty for some time. Maurice—once again the mastermind of a lot of our more covert schemes—and his friends, took to sneaking into the old house with their roller skates. Hearing the noisy whirring of their metal skate wheels singing along the hardwood floors of this empty house, made this secret little arrangement too irresistible for me to ignore. Although the boys seldom invited me to come along, it didn't occur to me not to join them anyway, so I usually barged right in.

What fun to whiz through the spacious empty rooms on roller skates. Of course, our skates were not like the wonderful shoe skates with the large wooden wheels kids wear today; ours had to be clamped onto our shoes. This was not an ideal situation—and sometimes it was a totally bad idea—because the shoe soles we wore were often too soft to hold the clamp. That was because our shoes were not always leather, and the soles were made of something called composition, resembling heavy cardboard. This made it necessary to tighten the clamps even harder with a key that came with the skates.

Turning the clamps tighter often caused the soles of our shoes to buckle, forming hard ridges under our feet, pinching our toes. When this proved to be too painful we often resorted to laboriously tying the skates on with a rope. However, for the bliss of taking part in this stolen amusement, we readily tolerated a pretty fair amount of pain and inconvenience. Once we were up and running, the pain was hardly noticed, or simply ignored.

By the time I finally got my skates on, the boys had usually disappeared somewhere in the shadowy recesses of the house, typically racing upstairs, leaving me alone to follow after them. How I hated hearing them clomping and clattering up the steep stairs in their skates, leaving me to navigate those narrow steps by myself. It was a real struggle trying to climb the stairs wearing skates. What a chilling feeling, reaching the stair landing, to find the boys had disappeared out of sight. This seemed to be one of their favorite diabolical pranks—to secrete themselves somewhere in a dark spot out of sight.

That empty old house seemed all the more haunted when all was quiet and I felt alone in it, particularly upstairs. With growing alarm in my voice, desperately wanting some assurance that they were still there, my urgent calling was guaranteed to bring these leaping, maniacal fiends jumping out at me from some dusty, dark closet, accompanied by lunatic gestures and wild howling. Of course my screams satisfied their need to scare the *bejabbers* out of me; unfortunately my reaction only encouraged more of their dirty tricks. While furious with them for being so vile, I was secretly and *immensely* relieved to know that they hadn't deserted me in this creepy old house with all of the unseen ghosts I could feel lurking around every corner.

Louise Hauser was another great pal. Louise's family was the antithesis of Clarice's. Her father owned the implement store and they lived in a larger home in our small town. Somehow playing with Louise took on a quieter tone than the physical fun I indulged in with Clarice and most of my other friends. We often read to each other and played with dolls.

We'd spent one quiet afternoon playing with all of the toys in her room, when we dreamed up an even more exciting diversion. How this came about is anyone's guess, but we decided that I should cut her hair. Let me preface this story by reminding one and all that we were still very young at the time. We must have somehow sensed that this was not to be our finest hour since we decided to play our barber game under her bed. Some premonition may have suggested to us that this daring act needed to be done under cover. The timing couldn't have been worse as our beauty school experiment took place only a few days short of our appearances in the church Christmas program.

Mom had accompanied me to Louise's house that day, where she and Louise's mother, Verna, had spent the afternoon enjoying a visit over coffee. Some time later, Mom called me to "come" as it was time to go home. Her call sent a sudden chill through me, immediately signaling the peril I was in. The panic that gripped me was as like a tourniquet being placed around my chest, shutting off my ability to breathe. Louise and I looked at each other in desperation, then crawled even further under the bed, hoping for a place to escape!

The apoplectic look on Louise's mother's face when she got her first glimpse of my handiwork bore out my apparent need for alarm. Her expression struck my heart with such a jolt that, had I been old enough to fully comprehend God's mercy, that moment would have found me on my knees praying for Him to strike me dead so I wouldn't have to face the wrath about to come.

Coupled with the horror-stricken appearance on my mother's face, simple dread now turned to near heart-stopping terror. At that moment I was certain Mrs. Hauser was considering carting me off to jail, and I was giving up all hope of ever being allowed to play with Louise again. Because of the distressed look on Mrs. Hauser's face, I was also certain that she was in danger of falling over dead, or becoming dreadfully sick, and I would forever bear the shame and guilt of causing this awful damage to Mrs. Hauser's health because of my evil deed.

My state of anxiety must have rendered me nearly catatonic as well, because, before I was fully aware of it, or without understanding how it happened, I was mercifully being allowed to leave the premises with my mom. I had no relieved feeling of escape, however, as I departed feeling totally ashamed and responsible for the disaster I had left in my wake. Although I was free to leave with my mother, the prospect of having to share the sidewalk with *her*, for the walk home, was daunting. After an initial, furious lecture, our fast-stepping homeward trek was completed in stony silence. I was left with no illusions but that my illustrious hairstyling career had come to an abrupt end.

It's not hard to imagine how Louise's hair might have looked in light of the fact that we had crawled under her bed to do the deed, and there was barely enough wiggle room to move, let alone wield a pair of scissors. Even with a full range of motion, under the most ideal salon conditions, haircuts often turn out less than stunning.

My suspicion is that this event became a rousing joke, told out of its perpetrators' earshot, in later years; but at that moment, if it was our mothers' mission to inflict the maximum amount of guilt and shame on two wayward girls, they achieved their desired result.

As parents are sometimes fond of doing, they "hung us out to dry" for a time by allowing us to suffer a little longer. When our time of penance was over, when we'd been forgiven and our slates wiped clean, when the trauma of this life-altering crisis had been weathered, both Louise and I felt immensely relieved that our sentence had finally been commuted.

Given the seriousness of our crime, it took a bit of time for the two of us to begin feeling really comfortable with each other again. I felt relieved and elated when one day Mrs. Hauser and Louise, who were driving to Marshalltown, invited me to come along. Louise was to have her hair cut (professionally) while her mother's hair was being styled. Perhaps there was a wistful expression on my face, bordering on the pathetic, because Mrs. Hauser treated me to a professional haircut in a beauty salon—my very first.

"I'd like a windblown bob, please," was always my response to the local barber, Roy Eggleston, when asked how I wanted to have my hair cut. It was he who had always been my "stylist," and it was he whom I credited with creating the name "windblown bob"—probably after dealing too long with my indecision about how I wanted my hair cut. After rejecting several of his ideas, he then suggested this cut with the wonderful name. I was captivated from the start by the name "windblown bob," as the name appealed to my carefree spirit. From then on my hair would always be cut in a windblown bob.

A windblown bob was hair trimmed just below the ears, with bangs across the forehead. Having my hair cut was always a special time for me. Leaving the barbershop with my carefree new "do," always left me feeling beautiful and ready to face the world. In reality my skinny little frame probably looked even scrawnier when my hair was shortened. Later I was to become aware of the many pictures dating back to that era, along with old pictures of former classmates, which suggested that I was not the first, or the lone recipient of the windblown bob.

Each playtime with Louise seemed to build to a bittersweet climax, making me uneasy, and uncomfortably apprehensive. Invariably it was her habit to suggest that we find our dads and ask for a nickel to buy candy or ice cream. How I dreaded hearing this suggestion, because I knew that extra five-cent pieces were hard to come by for my dad. We had to pass my Dad's blacksmith shop first; and after reluctantly asking, I often heard that Dad sometimes didn't have an extra nickel, or at least not one he felt he could spare. Besides resulting in an embarrassing situation for myself, I also knew that if I did receive the nickel I was asking my dad to make a sacrifice for something frivolous for myself. If I came away empty-handed we would go on to the implement store where Louise would whisper something to her dad, and she was most always handed a dime for the both of us.

While it was pleasant to contemplate the treats we would buy, this practice did little for my self-esteem and I usually found myself trying to beg off treat-time. As a result, my play times with Louise became less frequent than with my other friends whose dads probably didn't have an extra nickel either. But she remained a good friend. Louise developed an enlarged heart and died somewhere around the age of sixteen. At that age it becomes an almost unbelievable loss to lose a friend through death. It is not the natural order of things. I was not alone in the deep grief I felt at her death; our entire town was saddened.

Even in a town as small as Whitten, there were lots of kids with whom to play. Playing with the Wilcox girls, Francis, Helen, Margaret and Avis, was always great fun One of the reasons was because of the empty corncrib that stood at the edge of the lawn behind their house. Recognizing the great possibilities here for a marvelous playhouse, we confiscated this drafty and dirty, cluttered old structure for that purpose, and then set about working like beavers to transform it into our dream house. The corncrib was constructed of loose-fitting slats, with enough space between the boards so that we were able to observe anyone approaching. The tall, old crib had a roof; even on rainy days we had a fairly dry, and rather snug place to play.

Before we could move in, though, we had a lot of work to do clearing out the clutter. So, with brooms in hand we began the laborious task of sweeping (seems I did a lot of sweeping in my youth). The dirt flew as our brooms went into action, fouling the air like a dust storm, as we tackled the thick piles of dirt, cobwebs, and mounds of mouse and bird droppings. In addition there were leftover corncobs and stalks, and even some discarded tools and pieces of useless machinery being stored there. By the time we were as dirty as the corncrib had been, over the course of the next two or three days, our "house" was ready for occupancy.

Next we began planning the furnishing of our little home. We set about scrounging up chairs, tables and accessories, many of which we fashioned out of orange crates, egg crates, doll dishes and whatever else anyone could beg, borrow, or raid from home. As novice homemakers, we were a proud little group as we stood back, surveying our grand and glorious estate over which we'd slaved for days. By the time it was clean and pretty enough to pass our inspection, we moved in. This "house" became the gathering place for much of our playtime over the next couple of years, and we spent hours leading our imaginary lives in our own private sanctuary away from adult scrutiny.

An unused chicken coop, set apart from my own house out in the orchard, was also pressed into service as a playhouse. So again we set about decorating another "house" with the same exuberant determination. Chicken coops, by their very nature, are nastier and even more unsanitary than corncribs, which turned this salvage job into a bigger headache than we had bargained for. But armed once again with buckets of water and mops as well as brooms, we set about in our innocent fervor attempting to decontaminate the old coop as best we could. Somehow the chicken coop never seemed to capture the same fresh "outdoorsy" feeling of the corncrib, regardless of how hard we cleaned. In any case, when we got the place as clean as we could, or felt was necessary, we moved in.

The next days, weeks and months were once again spent being housewives and mommies in our cherished, self-decorated domiciles. Zoning laws had not yet become acquainted with Whitten, so they didn't interfere with our activities. We took our fun any place we found it. And chicken coops and corncribs became prime real estate for little girls' fantasies.

Zoning laws may have been non-existent in our town, but there were other laws in place at the time. For instance, there were laws limiting the movement of anyone contracting a communicable disease. Quarantining the unfortunate family was done through the most obviously embarrassing means of enforcing one of these laws.

Catching a contagious disease, such as measles, mumps, smallpox, chicken pox, or the like, brought the sheriff, who had been promptly dispatched to the home to nail a big sign on the house saying that everyone there was quarantined, naming the disease in very large letters along with the large word "warning," or 'quarantined." This meant that everyone in the family was required to stay inside the house (or at least could not come in contact with anyone else) until the disease had run its course.

These instantly recognizable, detestable signs became unsettling and worrisome notices to everyone in town, shattering the routine quiet of our small community while announcing and spreading the news like wildfire. It's understandable that there was a great deal of concern when illnesses struck, as well as a real need for making sure that news of it made the round quickly. At that time, most of these diseases were not as common, or as easily prevented or cured as they are now, and mothers were fearful for their children and family. Being sick, however, was bad enough, but having a "quarantined" sign attached so conspicuously to your house, warning others to beware of coming into contact with any member of your family, was devastating. It had the additional chilling effect of turning the already beleaguered family into village outcasts for a period. The affected residents were surely made to feel like those who had come under the Biblical injunction for lepers—required to announce, in a loud voice, their unclean status to the world.

If we'd been singled out for this ominous treatment it would have been demeaning beyond belief; but it wasn't usually too long before the forbidding signs began appearing on nearly every house in one form or another, and some even before ours.

What ecstasy when the signs came down, allowing the "cleansed," to become normal folks again. We were overjoyed to be freed from that detestable "plague' brand when the sign came down. Racing out of the house after our forced imprisonment gave us the urge to run out and begin hugging the trees, the grass, the sun, and even the neighbors. The world had once again become user-friendly, giving us its righteous permission to rejoin it.

While Whitten was very small, it did have sidewalks. Roaming, especially after the loathsome quarantine sign was removed from the side of the door canceling our status as a social-pariah, meant that I was again free to indulge in my favorite pastime—roller-skating.

Sidewalks were the prime targets for accomplishing an ambitious goal of mine—which was to skate on every walk in town. From the moment I clamped on my first pair of roller-skates, it seems I metamorphosed into this free spirit that had magically been given wings to fly. These wonderful new contraptions instantly brought a new freedom that let me soar as free as a breath of air. Right then it became my burning ambition to make sure I'd not left one sidewalk *unskated* on, even the sidewalk in front of "mean" Mrs. Quigley's house.

Mrs. Quigley felt very territorial about her sidewalk, and we kids knew we'd be on the receiving end of some major "jawing" and threats, accompanied by additional severe tongue-lashings if she saw us skate down to the corner past her house. But a little screaming wasn't going to keep us from going there, "no siree!"

We were intimidated enough that it made us skate a little faster on that block. There were times, especially if I was alone, or even if there were only two or three of us, when it seemed advisable to reconnoiter and ponder the advisability of making that pass. Of course, since the decision was always made not to avoid this street, we'd then have to summon up enough gumption to skate on, trying, at least, to assume a brave front as we violated *"her"* street, or hang back and risk being called "chicken."

Mom and dad, and most of her other neighbors, knew of Mrs. Quigley's fiery temper, so we were only occasionally scolded—generally when our parents had heard her tirades.

My goal, of skating on every sidewalk in town, was undoubtedly accomplished somewhere in the neighborhood of at least two or three hundred times or more. If anyone had been keeping track, my accomplishment would have undoubtedly set a new world record in the Guinness Book of Records. Just imagine, having set a world record for skating on every sidewalk in Whitten, Iowa more times than anyone else. Now there's a record for you!

CHAPTER 11

Two big and spectacular events happened in our town, but on separate dates, both having devastating results. The old house just north of us (our secret skating rink), and the general store, a mainstay of our economy, and an important asset to the community, both burned to the ground.

Why the empty house burned was puzzling. One theory attributed that fire to the "hobos who rode the rails," and hopped off at our town to spend the night in the abandoned house. We were very familiar with hobos at our house. Rumor had it that these "Knights of the Road" used a secret code that they carved on light poles, mailbox posts, or any other place where they could "mark" a house. This secret code was used to identify houses where hungry transients would be assured of getting a friendly reception and a free meal.

We didn't realize that we were running a free soup kitchen until much later when the mark at our home became evident. But even if mom had known it at the time, her door would have continued to be open to welcome these hungry vagrants who were never turned away. The mark, which was a simple series of grooves cut into the light pole, was never removed.

With the fire engulfing the house next door in flames, Dad spent the entire night on our rooftop. News of the impending disaster spread quickly, and volunteer townsmen rallied around and quickly formed a bucket brigade, handing him pails of water that he sloshed over the roof as the rest of the family watched in fear of his falling.

Because of the water being thrown around, the shingles grew wet, causing him to lose his footing, and what we feared, happened. Slipping and sliding, his arms flailing and thrashing about in the vain hope of grabbing hold of something solid, he shot off the roof like an out-of-control rocket. Empty buckets clattered and ricocheted off the chimney and soaked shingles after him, as he crashed to the ground. He was bruised and shaken up, but not broken. His efforts were not in vain however, because that night, Dad (with the help of a few friends) saved our house.

The service and generous spirit of neighbors, in this kinder and gentler, but difficult time, also gave quiet testimony to the fact that helpfulness and sacrifice were not isolated incidents, but the norm. There would have been no thought, among our neighbors, of not becoming involved. Neither did anyone expect to be paid or praised for what they considered only their Christian duty.

The fire at the general store, which at the time was probably the largest building in town, also happened at night. Because Whitten possessed no warning sirens, we were alerted to the fire by neighbors who rushed to tell us the general store was burning. We kids were in bed, but Mom and Dad were still up when the news came. Being roused from our beds, we quickly dressed and the family ran up to the main street in town to follow the progress of this alarming situation. In a small town with little or no fire protection, it was necessary for everyone to be alerted and accounted for—so no one would be caught asleep in bed if their house should become a fire victim. Even the smallest kids were brought to the scene by their parents.

We could feel the heat of the blaze from several blocks away, and could see the flames, sparks and flashing lights shooting skyward for what appeared to me to be miles into the air. This fire consumed not only the huge building, but also the total inventory of a well-stocked general store. The raging inferno also provided a spectacular and dazzling display of pyrotechnics for all of the shocked, but eager onlookers.

Without realizing the paradox that lay hidden in the disastrous firestorm that night, had these spectators bothered to look up, or even been aware of it, they might have beheld an unexpectedly beautiful sight, even in the midst of the tragedy unfolding before their eyes. What seemed to be lost, to the gathering onlookers, was the startling contrast to be seen far above this maelstrom of blazing flames, arcing and pitching angrily upward. This hot, roaring, fire-breathing beast appeared to be ineffectually raging against a serenely cool and beautiful, night sky.

By directing one's gaze above the flames, one could behold a peacefully tranquil heaven, gleaming with silent, immovable stars. A softly placid shining moon had spread a hushed canopy of quiet over all, hanging there in perfect solitude. From their vantage point the angels in Heaven would surely have regarded this monstrous conflagration as merely a glowing ember in the dark. There were, unfortunately, many who undoubtedly missed the dichotomous nature of these dramatic elements on that fateful night, I'm sure. Somehow this important event became tucked away in my childhood memory bank, to be taken out and looked at later as an important serendipitous event.

At the outset, however, what was important was that everyone in town came running to witness the mass annihilation of this huge building, and the resulting disaster generated by the explosive holocaust. The residents of our town were gathered around in tight, fearful, little clusters—silent witnesses to a major catastrophe, hoping against hope that the carnage would not spread to their homes. Many of the men, including my dad, who, after they had seen the enormity of the fire, spent the night on their own rooftops trying to protect their homes.

As the heat of the fire grew more intense, raging flames launched scraps of flying debris everywhere, forcing spectators to retreat to a safer spot further back. These tiny, red-hot missiles shot off and floated in every direction as little gusts of swirling wind lifted and carried them aloft. Many of them came to rest on rooftops, threatening the homes below. Some of the drifting embers were gently wafted to the ground, while others veered off, settling on startled spectators. Every now and then we would spot someone hopping and jumping around, pounding out the little fires these errant sparks had started on their clothing. A few even landed in our hair.

Firefighters from Union and surrounding communities were called to help. Working feverishly through the night, the men finally brought the fire under control, and it was eventually extinguished sometime the next day. Our fascination with the fire kept us glued to the scene with hardly anyone watching the time. It was probably somewhere around three o'clock in the morning when Mom, noticing how late it was getting, started rounding us up to leave. Even though the fire was still going full blast, she decided it was time for us to go, though we coaxed her to stay—to no avail.

An unhappy trio made the short trip home that night, because we didn't want to be cheated out of any of the excitement. Once there, however, without admitting we were tired, we wanted to crawl into bed. Mom wouldn't let us, though, until we'd washed the grimy soot, smoke and dirt from our faces and hands, and brushed the dead sparks out of our hair. In spite of the turmoil we'd witnessed, and our outraged protests at having to leave the scene, sleep came rather easily to three exhausted kids that night.

The next day, stunned and silent, nearly everyone turned out again for still another disbelieving look at this charred, still smoldering, black pile of rubble that had once been our shopping mainstay. Looking over the burned remains of our once-marvelous general store left observers with a general feeling of malaise. The intensity of what had happened in this place the night before gave new meaning to the description, "the pits of Hell." Days later, the dismal and gaping, charred, black hole that was left on Main Street, gave our little community an unnaturally stark appearance, prophesying a ghost town in progress.

As mentioned before, Dad owned and operated the local blacksmith shop during our early years in Whitten. As a youngster I was often sent there on an errand, or sometimes I would just drop by to see my dad. The first thing one noticed, as they stepped through the door, was the unique odor. Venturing into the dark recesses of the shop one could easily identify the source of the smell as coming from the many objects of iron and steel, leather, and wood lining the walls and stacked on the floor, as well as the burned out remains of the many firings of the foundry.

The interior of the blacksmith shop was always shadowy, probably in part because of the dark nature of the inventory. The few tiny windows in the shop were almost always closed and frosted with dirt. The lights in the shop were always on while my dad was working, even on the brightest day. Dad, in his leather apron, could often be found stoking the furnace with coal, forcing it alive as he prepared to heat a piece of iron or steel. It was a sight that raised goose bumps on my arms whenever I stood nearby watching the fire turn from red to a yellowish-white hot when he applied the bellows.

The bellows was a device designed to produce a stream of air under pressure when the foot-operated pump was set in motion and the hand-operated lever that hung over his head was activated. This dual action forced a rush of air into the forge causing the fire to burn with extreme intensity. It burned with such forceful vigor in fact, that the noise it made resembled the roar of an angry animal. This thundering rumble sent vibrations that literally shook the building, as it snarled.

While the fire was reaching the correct temperature, Dad kept turning and moving the bar of steel or piece of iron in the center of the firepot to make sure it was properly heated. He kept a careful watch, while turning the piece over and over, until it glowed with a fierce, white-hot iridescence. With leather-gloved hands he carefully removed the rod with heavy, oversized blacksmith pliers; then laying it over an anvil, he pounded it with his hammer until he had molded it into the shape he wanted. Once finished, he dunked the still red hot piece of metal into a tank of cold water; causing the water to boil, producing an angry cloud of steam that spit and hissed furiously as it shot in all directions.

Sometimes these custom-made pieces re-bound wooden wheels for farm wagons, made a horseshoe, or even crafted a special tool. The large demand for this type of work wasn't unusual for that period—in that age of the horse. Since times were hard, the frugal thing for a farmer to do was to salvage and mend broken things, not discard or replace them with something new.

It was high adventure to watch Dad clamp a piece of hot metal into his large, long-handled vice (the unwieldy nature of the long handle of the vice caused me more than one pinched hand). After he had secured it, he would shape the metal—at times using a foot pump-operated grinder, which really made the sparks fly as he sharpened or shaped the piece. He could determine how fast or slow he wanted the grinder to go by the pressure of his foot.

This work at the grinder on his workbench produced a shower of sparks that could best be described as resembling sparklers on the 4th of July. After convincing me that I wouldn't be hurt, it still took a bit of courage to pass my hand through these glowing sparks the first time. To my delight and amazement the sparks landing on my hand had only a light, tingly, feathery feeling.

I always felt a bit sorry for the horses, when Dad applied the shoes, for they had to endure having nails pounded into their hooves through the holes in the horseshoes. Dad assured me that it didn't hurt the horse, but rather protected him from the gravel on the road or the rocks and stubble in the field. Proof of that seemed to come from the fact that none of Dad's freshly-shod horses ever gave as much as a snort, during the shoeing, but whinnied and pranced out of the shop with a lively new spring in their step.

I loved visiting the shop with its unusual smell. The only negative part of being there was having to tiptoe around to avoid getting dirty. Even so, Dad didn't seem to mind that I had come (undoubtedly getting in his way). Blacksmithing became a dwindling art with the advent of the automobile; and while Dad did work on a few cars in the beginning, it wasn't long before the need for his services was phased out. We were moving into the world of technology.

My husband, Bob, and I took a nostalgic side trip through Whitten, years ago. I had moved from there some forty years before. We drove around looking for my dad's old blacksmith shop, which was now only a sagging reminder of what had been. Gone were our dear little first home and the homes of our near neighbors. During our tour we drove past the site of the Methodist Church, which was now an empty lot. We were told that the church had burned, but we didn't learn the fate of the other buildings; perhaps they too were fire victims, or maybe they just gave up the ghost and collapsed, dying of old age.

Standing there, looking around at these barren spaces in our town, left me feeling as though a part of my life had been erased; much like laying a dear, loved-one in the ground, forever gone. A genuine sadness overtook me in that moment and wistfully reminded me of the old saying, "You can never go home again." Undoubtedly that's because home, as we remember it, never remains the same, and sometimes it never even remains.

Somehow the sight of the vacant lot where the church once stood filled me with the greatest sense of loss. That small church had been the site of many of my activities, both spiritual and social as I was growing up. I was baptized there, confirmed there, and "walked the aisle" there in response to an altar call publicly announcing that I had become a Christian.

It was an exceptional Sunday when our family wasn't in church, for it was an unwritten, but inflexible rule in our home, that Sunday meant church time. The only exceptions to the rule were the times we went for a Sunday visit to see Grandma and Grandpa, or Aunt Louise and her family or other relatives.

Mom was the pianist for most all of our church services. She played for all of the hymn singing, the choir, and solo numbers, and thus they depended on her to be in constant attendance to "make a joyful noise unto the Lord." Dad was also involved, as a Sunday school superintendent. I grew up believing that the church would have a hard time operating if we were missing.

It was not a glamorous job, but because it needed to be done, Mom cleaned the church every week. She also helped cook for threshing dinners, taught Sunday School classes, and played piano for funerals and weddings. She was involved in every area of that church's life; and because she was, we were. That was all right with me until that fateful day she decided I was old enough, and sturdy enough, to replace her in the role of *the* church cleaner.

That idea did *not* win my immediate approval, particularly since I was given little or no choice but to take the job. Since there was a bit of pay involved, however, they were eventually able to purchase my *almost-willing* cooperation, and the "thirty pieces of silver" helped ease the pain and disdain of it all.

My first day of work found me walking somewhat apprehensively up the tall cement front steps of the church. Opening the heavy main door, I stepped into the darkened building, into the narthex where I then climbed the inner stairs to the sanctuary doors.

Entering the sanctuary through the inner doors, gave me a momentary start. I was stopped by this totally unfamiliar view of the church, which, by then, appeared darker and gloomier than I had ever seen it. This view presented an unusually eerie view of the cavernous room. Hearing my own footsteps echoing as I walked into the room sent pinpricks of nervousness over my entire body, making me wish I had never agreed to do this. Seeing the church from this enormously different perspective was almost too unnerving; and the decision, not to run back home, took some tall reinforcing.

Taking my small amount of courage in hand, now fully assured that I was all alone in this enormous building, I cautiously proceeded to work—in the beginning, moving nervously around the many rooms of the vacant building (glancing, often, over my shoulder to make sure I really was alone) yet all the while, tensely expecting someone to jump out at me from every corner.

Still acquainting myself with this new view of the church, it was effortless to conjure up the ghosts of some of our long-departed saints who had been brought here for last services. To chase away these supernaturally chilling thoughts, I tried hard to remember happier times. These good memories must have effectively chased away the unwelcome spirits, at least long enough for me to do my work—with every light in the place blazing.

The church classrooms were in the basement, along with the kitchen, dining room, furnace room, and supply and junk-filled storage rooms. There didn't seem to be an end to the dusting, sweeping and straightening. One might assume I was used to those tasks with all of my playhouse experience. But this was no playhouse, and the work was even more extensive than our work at home, though not as detailed. Strangely enough, straightening the classroom areas was nearly as satisfying as cleaning at my friends, since it was always necessary to remove last Sunday's litter left by the small-fry "churchies."

Spiffing up the sanctuary was lots more fun than doing the heavier work in the basement areas. Upstairs, the pews could be dusted in a flash. If I felt like taking a shortcut I would sometimes sit on the dust cloth and slide along the non-cushioned pews on my backside. After giving the pulpit, the choir chairs, and railings a good once-over, I would start on the bare, uncarpeted floors, which needed only to be dusted with a mop.

If I finished these jobs quickly, I usually had time to play the piano. After time I got used to being in the big building alone; feeling pretty secure in the knowledge that I wouldn't be overheard, I played the piano and sang the hymns at full volume. It became my objective to hurry through my work so I could play the piano, pretending I was playing for church, or a wedding or whatever, which I did after every cleaning bout. One could be sure, though, that my music sounded more heavenly to me than it did to anyone else had they been listening.

Christmas programs were big events in the life of our church and the times we kids looked forward to the most, including the appearance of Santa Claus. The program, which included singing, recitations, and some version of Jesus' birth, depicting the manger scene with all of the children in angel, shepherd or animal costumes, there were final prayers and songs, and the program ended.

With the program concluded, the audience would suddenly be startled by the appearance of Santa as he came bursting through the back door shouting "Merry Christmas to everyone." Down the aisle he came on the run, larger than life with his sack on his back, which meant candy, and an apple and orange for every child. Christmas candy in those days was always the hard candy variety, often filled with raspberry or other jelly. I detested those! There were also peppermints and others, including the inevitable hard candy ribbons that were pretty to look at but failed the taste test miserably.

What our parents were probably mostly thinking about these pretty, sugary, confections, was how long it would take for them to produce cavities. What the candy lacked in quality was made up for by the excitement of receiving something from Santa. Our expectations in those days were considerably less than those of the children of today, but our fun, and the remembrance of it all could not be exceeded.

Sometimes we are asked to relate our favorite Christmas memory. For me my most favorite Christmas memory came on the Christmas Eve I was eleven. Our family had gone to the evening Christmas program at our church. The program was over, Santa had come and gone, I had changed out of my costume, and the family was bundling into heavy winter coats getting ready for the short walk home.

Opening the church doors we were greeted by a surprising scene taking place before our eyes. We were awestruck by a world that had been transformed into an enchanted fairyland by a new, heavy mantle of sparkling white snow. Since there had been no snow on the ground when we came to church, the sight caused us all to gasp in surprise and laughter at the wonder of it. The entire town lay hidden under a surprisingly thick layer of soft, dazzling, evening snow that continued to fall, as we left the church, obliterating the sky.

In a strange paradox, the brightness of the snowfall, that night, somehow gave the sky an even darker appearance. Venturing out into this *"falling feathers world"* one almost had a sense of being secluded in a tiny, white, private, magical world. Had they been there, I'm certain my grandchildren would have described this phenomenon as "totally cool." So complete was the quietness that one could almost imagine hearing the snowflakes falling.

The huge flakes floated and swirled softly around us, as we walked, dusting my cheeks and sticking to my eyelashes. The fact that there had been no snow on the ground when we entered the church, nor the prediction of any that I remember, made this beautiful surprise so dramatic. The thick white carpet now covering the ground muffled the sound of our footfalls as we walked gingerly over the pristine landscape with care, into a world that had never before seen tracks of man nor beast.

A streetlight down the walk, cast an enchanting golden circle on the sparkling snow, giving the scene an even more ethereal appearance. The quiet had become almost physical. No one spoke, not even a dog barked. I wanted to hold my breath for fear the very act of breathing might shatter the perfect stillness and wonder of it all.

It seemed that each of us, my family and I, walked in a world of our own that amazing evening—each absorbed in his own private thoughts. My explanation would be that we were each relishing and savoring this unique vision in silence, fearful that the marvel of it all might slip away if given voice. It was the incredible beauty of this winter wonderland, falling so softly and silently around us, that made this rarely-experienced event, happening on this particular Christmas Eve, so special that it became my favorite Christmas memory for all time.

So perfect was that wonder-filled night that it would not have surprised me if suddenly a chorus of heavenly angels had appeared in the sky singing *Silent Night!*

CHAPTER 12

The women of our church were a dedicated lot. There could be little disagreement that much of the support of the church came from the activities and effort of these women who worked so hard, and so often, on some project or another.

One of these extremely labor-intensive events took place every summer—the threshing dinners. As was the custom in many farming communities, a group of farmers combined their efforts to help each other with the large chore of threshing. On threshing days every farmer who was able would come prepared to work, or bring his threshing machine. More likely it was one rented machine and a lot of volunteer farmers.

There were many men who came to help, and because they worked from sun-up to sundown, it was customary for the farmers in our area receiving the help to arrange for the church ladies to prepare the noon dinner for all of the men. It would have been a gargantuan task for the farmer's wife to prepare so many enormous meals, so this arrangement benefited everyone. This meant, however, that the ladies of the church were busy almost every day of the harvesting season, cooking meals for these starved threshers. Of course the women's association was paid for their services, and since much of the food was donated, and even baked at home (cakes, pies, etc.) the bulk of their pay went to support the church.

Because Mom was *always* involved, she cheerfully volunteered my services as well. Because of that, my summer days started way too early in the morning at harvest time. Before the sun was even up I could be found in the church kitchen peeling kettles full of potatoes the old-fashioned way (with a knife), scraping dishpans full of vegetables, shelling bowls of new peas, and running innumerable errands "since my legs were younger than theirs." These, and any other chores the women could find for me to do, were my early morning jobs, as well as setting up miles of tables with dishes, napkins, silverware and glasses.

Thinking back to those "sweatshop" days (the days before air conditioning) reminds me of some of the old black and white movies showing women laboring over household chores in primitive kitchens, looking haggard, almost like slaves. And although we worked as hard as they, under what seemed like some of the same basic conditions, we wouldn't have identified with them at all. For in reality, it was almost always fun, working with these good-natured women who, though they were *church ladies*, even liked to joke. Working in a group seemed to spawn a good many silly situations, triggering a lot of laughter and lightening the burden of our work. An added benefit for me was that I got to hear most of the neighborhood news usually reserved for the grownups.

Even the most humbling grunt-work in the kitchen was made easier when the prospect of getting to share these man-sized delectable dinners was in the offing. Great slabs of roast meat, fried chicken, chops or steak, mashed potatoes and gravy, corn on the cob, fresh peas, carrots, or green beans, Jell-o or fresh green salads, pickles and relishes, were the usual fare at a threshing dinner. There were also fresh-baked rolls or bread, and freshly churned butter. The meal was always topped off with the ultimate homemade pie or cake. One could only wonder how the men were able to rise from the table, let alone return to work after such meals. They must have had strong hearts and cast-iron digestive tracts.

Before coming into the dining hall, the men took turns washing their hands and faces outside, and dunking their heads and necks under the pump that stood outside the church, as a way of cooling off as well as cleaning up. After this ritual they seemed to give off a pleasant scent of fresh hot summer air, newly cut straw, hay or wheat, and perspiration that had gone through layers of ozone. It was decidedly a man-smell, and all of the females involved in the meal seemed energized from the moment they made their appearance. The sound of the old pump being used outside was the signal for the kitchen and dining room help to swing into action.

Since it was lots more fun serving than helping the cooks in the early morning, my observation was that there were always more young girls who showed up to help serve the meal than help in the kitchen. Undoubtedly I would have been one of these miscreants if Mom hadn't been so watchful, and efficient at keeping me busy.

One of the dining room assignments for these young servers was to keep the men's glasses full of steamy-cold iced tea. We filled our pitchers from an immense (I'm talking gigantic) stone crock that stood on one of the low, children's Sunday school tables in the corner of the dining room. It must have taken at least two men to move it in there. Large ice blocks were used to chill the tea. These large blocks were the same type as those used to fill the ice compartments of our iceboxes at home. Little trickles of water ran down the side of the huge tea crock as misty vapor rose from the top.

What a job it was trying to keep the men's glasses filled, for their thirst seemed insatiable. They were hot and dry and could empty their glasses almost as soon as they were filled. It was more often the cut-ups who drank as fast as they could to see how quickly we could get there for a refill. Calling us cute, teasing names that flattered us, or sometimes made us blush, they laughingly watched as we ran from glass to glass trying to keep up. Of course there were the inevitable jokers who found it great fun to ask us if we had any beer instead of tea.

The men were all nice guys, some shy, but all friendly, who had come for the serious business of eating. For the girls it was definitely the highlight of the day to be part of this friendly, joking and good-natured group. Harassment would have been the last word we'd have used to describe the friendly fun we girls shared with the men. Innocent flirting and teasing are words that would more easily come to mind.

Some of the other most eagerly looked-forward-to, church-related events, were the church picnics and dinners that the women of our church sponsored. These were almost a repeat of the threshing dinners, with one exception. For the dinners, held mainly in the church basement hall, the women mixed up huge batches of ice cream, with each man taking a turn at the crank of the largest ice cream freezer I had ever seen. Somehow, I'm sure it was only the biggest, strongest men in the congregation who could turn the crank of that monster machine.

It was probably just such times as these, and the fact that Mom made ice cream for almost every special family occasion, which was responsible for my love affair with this wonderful treat. Although it never seems to taste quite as perfect when I make it as it did then, I still keep trying, hoping to get that perfect "do" with my little electric freezer.

Someone recently suggested that it might be the freshly-skimmed cream my mother used that gave her ice cream the extra rich flavor mine seems to lack, (undoubtedly, since my "cream" is often whole milk for the calorie-conscious). That seems like a highly reasonable explanation, but it wouldn't surprise me if Mom also had some special little knack that never got passed on to me, even if she tried. More likely my failure stems from the fact that cooking secrets, and these "special little knacks," didn't occupy many of my waking thoughts at the time. In addition, with that young age came the expectation that Mom would be around forever to keep cranking out her homemade ice cream.

Recalling these calorically-challenged, near "orgy-type" dinners reminds me that although we were still living through the depression at that time, our family ate well. This was probably due to my father's competence as a hunter and fisherman, and the large garden Mom tended, much of the time with the help of her less-than-enthusiastic kids. Mom was pretty keen at sorting out fact from fiction when it came to excuses about why we couldn't help in the garden; so more often than not, we found ourselves dutifully manning the business end of a hoe, chopping and digging away in the garden. Whining never helped. So it was natural that at those times we thought of Mother as a miserable tyrant.

Weeding was the worst, however, and even though our mother kept urging us to get out early in the morning before it got too hot, it seems this disgusting chore usually wound up being done in the blazing sun of our Iowa summers. Mom actually wasn't too much of a tyrant, however, since she could usually be persuaded to let her "slaves" go when the sweat began dripping off the end of our noses. No matter how painful the discomfort of working in the garden seemed to be, it became a point of personal pride when our much-toiled-over fruit and veggies showed up on the table.

The absolutely best thing that came out of our garden was our sweet corn. Who needed anything else on the table when we had just-picked, fresh sweet corn, made even better slathered with gobs of freshly-churned butter. Life was sweet as a child—sitting barefoot at the table, faces covered in melted butter, corn juice running down our arms and dripping off our elbows. Life just doesn't get any better than that in Iowa, or anywhere else.

Because we always seemed to have a cow, I churned many pounds of butter in our square glass churn with the tiny wooden paddles inside. The process started with fresh sweet cream being poured into the churn. Butter seemed to come a bit quicker if the cream had aged for a few days. After the lid, with the gears built into its top, was screwed on, the wooden paddles hanging down inside the glass jar were put into motion by a small, metal, hand crank. Turning that small crank became quite a test of arm power.

The cream swooshed around in the churn—far too long, in the opinion of the one cranking—before much began to happen. Things began looking more optimistic when little pea-sized chunks of butter started forming and floating around in the cream. By that time the cream, which was turning into butter, was beginning to look more like milk. Eventually the little chunks gathered up into one large glob and our job was done.

After the chunk of butter was removed, the liquid remaining had become buttermilk. Mom would turn the big chunk into a large crock, add salt, and with a large wooden paddle, knead the butter back and forth until the salt was worked in, and any buttermilk left in the chunk worked out. On sweet corn, or freshly baked bread, or on anything else for that matter, the flavor of home-churned butter has no equal.

We also had a cream separator in a small, enclosed shed by the porch of our home. After the cow had been milked, it was necessary to separate the cream from the milk. We drank the milk and used the cream for churning butter or for making whipped cream when mom wanted to garnish a special dessert, or top off a dish of strawberries.

The large tank on top of the separator was first filled with milk, fresh from our cow. Then it was necessary to vigorously begin turning the large hand-operated wheel to start the separator and turn the tank. And through the principle of centrifugal force the milk was thrown against the sides of the big tank and down through a series of blades, forcing the milk and cream to separate. I never really understood the intricacies of the process; I just knew it happened.

I suppose that's much the same method used today, though I suspect with much more elaborate and sophisticated machinery. A most essential, and absolutely unavoidable step, was to dismantle and thoroughly wash and clean every minuscule part of the separator after every use. As tired as they might have been, there wasn't a family around who would have skipped that important detail, because to neglect that sanitary step would have soured the next batch of cream and milk.

No matter what Dad brought home for Mom to fix for dinner, she was up to the challenge. While Dad was the one who skinned the rabbits, it was an awesome sight to watch Mom wring the neck of a chicken. We kids would help her catch the chicken, and grabbing it by the head she would swing the chicken round and round, and with a snap it was beheaded. The headless chicken would continue flopping and bouncing around on the ground until it realized it was dead.

After dipping the luckless chicken into boiling water, to make plucking easier, she would then quickly rip the feathers from that hot, dripping, and water soaked, foul-smelling fowl. The odor from dousing the feathers of a headless chicken in hot water was guaranteed to send observers scurrying.

The chickens' skins, according to Mom, always had to be a fresh yellow in appearance—a quality she absolutely insisted on, even when she began purchasing chickens in the store. She instructed us that when purchased chickens were white-skinned it meant they were not as fresh as they should be.

She would also fry as many fish as dad could catch, and it would have been hard to beat either her fried chicken or her fish.

Regardless of how many strange, weird, "icky," or gross purchases (because they were inexpensive) Dad made at the grocery store--pigs feet, brains, tongue, liver and more—by the time they reached the table Mom had magically transformed them into something that was actually fit to eat. But more than that, we liked them. Well, most of them. One staple Mom fixed for almost all of our meals was fried potatoes, to go along with the fried chicken. She was health conscious, though, and made sure we got lots of vegetables. In the summertime we had many fresh green salads made from the lettuce, tomatoes, cucumbers, radishes and greens taken from the produce we grew in our garden.

Dad, generally known around town as L.T., or Roy, was described in one of our family histories as "fun-loving"—a fitting description as I remember him. In the evenings Dad and his friends often formed impromptu groups for their entertainment, as was usual for men living in small towns before the advent of TV, computers, mega sports complexes and the like. Some groups played musical instruments, some played cards, some played baseball, and some just played! I believe dad belonged to all of them.

It became a tradition for a small group of men to go ice-skating every winter. They would drive to Pine Lake, over at Eldora, where they would drive the truck right out onto the ice, and spend the next hour or two racing and playing with all the exuberance of teenagers. When he grew old enough, Maurice was allowed to come along. He undoubtedly learned many of his fearless ways from our dad and his friends.

Dad was also usually ready to make the trip to Pine Lake in the summertime as well when we kids begged to go swimming. He was a good daddy, whose pet name for me, when he was in a teasing mood, was *Toody-Boots,* or at other times, just plain *Toody.* Since this nickname held no relationship to my real name, it was simply a loving reaction to his feeling toward me at the time. Dad would come in from outside, calling to me, "How's my Toody-Boots?" as he scooped me up in his arms, hugging me tightly. This got us both to laughing (me squealing) and then he would give me a high toss into the air.

Rounding the bend off the highway leading to Pine Lake, and driving along the wooded road bordering the lake, we would occasionally catch a glimpse of the lake through the trees. These glimpses were like a shot of adrenaline as my heart started pounding with excitement and anticipation. It was nearly impossible to wait until we could jump into the water. I'm pretty certain my love of water wasn't accidental, because I was born in January, under the sign of Aquarius. And while this fact has no mystical or fortune-telling quality for me, I believe it could possibly hold some significance as an astrological indicator of one's proclivities.

Usually there was a picnic planned along with our outings to the lake, but we kids had little interest in food with the lake beckoning us. More often than not, however, we were forced to wait until after we ate to go swimming. Mom always insisted it was necessary for us to wait an hour after eating "so we wouldn't get cramps and drown."

With time to kill before we could get into the water, we spent much of it exploring the Indian mounds at the picnic site of the Pine Lake Park. At least "Indian mounds" was the legend, and we perpetuated it, whether true or not. These mounds were rather high, gently rounded, grassy knolls that were large enough to have actually been a burial site containing the skeletons of many Indians. There were a number of these mass grave-sites in close proximity over which we irreverently chased each other, oblivious to the fact that we may have been desecrating an ancient tradition by treading on sacred Indian burial grounds. (On a recent visit we noticed new signs that read "Indian Mounds," so they must be authentic).

To reach the lake it was necessary to pass through a tunnel built beneath the road that separated the lake from the picnic area. Passing through the tunnel, one followed a long downhill, tree-rimmed path that ended within sight of the bathhouse, the beach beyond, and finally…the LAKE! We were tearing by the time we reached the bottom of the path as we headed for our first targeted activity, the toboggan slide located at the right side of the beach.

This was, of course, the first order of business at the lake—to climb the steep steps up to the toboggan ride, with all of us elbowing and jostling our way, trying to be first in line. The ride, *the* big attraction at the lake, was a large toboggan mounted on lots of small metal wheels. This thrilling marvel would literally fly down the metal tracks from the top of the tall hill into the water below. The lake was set low in what appeared to be a tree-rimmed crater, rising high in the air on most sides. Just the sight of the toboggan slide sent us charging up the hill, pushing and shoving and jockeying for position in line on the platform.

That line of kids waiting on the platform, and up the steps leading to it, must have appeared to onlookers like a pan of corn being popped as we jumped and hopped up and down on one foot and the other in our eagerness to gain any advantage and hurry the process. What a rush came with the operator's pronouncement, "It's your turn." In a flash we would hop onto the toboggan, clutching the handrail in a white-knuckle "death grip,." hanging on for dear life.

The tension and exhilaration of this intense ride was almost enough to cause one to lose one's lunch. Perched, as we were at the top of the tall platform, sitting on the toboggan, looking down the long drop that was to come, had a tendency to grip the pit of one's stomach, and produce major goose bumps. After making sure the rider was safely aboard, the operator then gave a mighty shove, sending him off the platform with a push that sent the screaming rider flying down the steep incline at a dizzying speed.

The electrifying sound of galvanized ball-bearing wheels whirring on metal tracks, the wind tearing at one's hair and taking one's breath, riders screaming hysterically in panic and terror as they shot down those astonishingly high rails, gave everyone brave enough to risk the trip down, a bloodcurdling, spine-tingling, experience of a lifetime.

Reaching the bottom of the tracks at full speed, the toboggan and rider then shot out over the water for a "speed boat" thrill-ride before slowly settling into the water. As soon as we could pull ourselves, and the toboggan, out of the water, it was back up the hill to do it all over again. We never got enough of this ride; but as more eager kids showed up and the lines grew longer, the waits became endless, so we would retreat for a while to try our luck on some of the other water toys.

This cherished toboggan ride was long ago dismantled, because, in our collective opinions, of a few joyless watchdogs who (obviously having no lives of their own and intent on ruining ours) deemed it to be a danger to riders. This, of course was totally not obvious, or even remotely understandable to us, for there wasn't one rider who wouldn't have gladly risked life and limb to be able to continue tobogganing.

We were to learn, at an early age, one of life's hard lessons imposed upon unbridled fun—if that fun becomes too great, then it is surely someone's duty to find a reason to put an end to it, all in the name of unsolicited protection. Our youthful reactions labeled that decision as cruel as having one's tongue ripped out.

That era of the toboggan ride was also a period of great water toys that were available to us swimmers at Pine Lake. One such toy was a large gray metal barrel that had been fashioned into a large elephant with big ears, a trunk and tail. For us to stay mounted was not only hard, but nearly impossible with other swimmers trying to pull you off. The barrel itself was slippery and hollow, which made it nearly un-mountable because of its turning, tipping and rolling over so easily in the water.

Another much-targeted action ride at the lake was a moving structure—an immense water wheel—probably a little larger than a big satellite dish, which rotated in the water. The wheel was tilted at about a forty-five degree angle and mounted on metal supports and stood in two or three feet of water. The goal was to climb onto the wheel and stay on even if people were turning it in an attempt to force you off. Even scrambling aboard the wheel was nearly impossible, for trying to pull oneself up onto that slippery wheel in wet suits—especially when there were other screaming, tugging, shoving and pulling "wannabe" riders trying to keep you off—was often nearly impossible.

Once on, it was the ultimate challenge to stay on, and we didn't usually manage to do that for long. It was only by hanging on for dear life with our hands while pushing at the other kids with our feet, hoping to force them off, that kept us aboard. As one would expect, this was an extremely tricky maneuver, and a predictably losing proposition, especially with swimmers sloshing water up onto the wheel to make it even more slippery while at the same time turning the wheel hoping to clear it for themselves. The only time we managed to stay on for any length of time was when we were in the lake on a "slow" day, but that was seldom.

The wheel was painted to resemble a giant target. Hardly any rider managed to stay aboard for long, quickly sliding off into the water—sometimes head first, on top of each other, or any other luckless way one could be forced off. It was generally the bigger boys who held on the longest, because by lying flat, they could stretch out their long arms and grab hold of the edge of the wheel.

It wasn't only the kids who enjoyed the lake. Many of our neighbors could be spotted swimming and lounging on the beach at one time or another as well. Mom and Dad occasionally swam with us, which made our swimming time much more fun. You didn't have to yell, "Mom! Dad! Mom! Mom! Mom! Look at me!" quite as loudly when they were nearby in the water. Neither did you have to put up with as many impatient, hard looks from other moms and dads who had turned to "look" at the calling kid.

Since our bathing suits were usually made of wool and were stored in drawers or closets over the winter without a lot of protection from the moths, it stood to reason that swimwear was a prime target for the pesky critters. In our house wool swimsuits were packed away in wintertime, in drawers laced with mothballs. We had little choice but to go to the beach smelling like a moth motel, or risk the embarrassment of exposure through some sneaky hole.

That situation happened the day one of the ladies from our town, also at the lake, and I were there talking. She was sitting on the beach at the water's edge and I was standing in the water just in front of her when suddenly my eyes dropped to a spot on her black bathing suit where I spotted a large hole. No matter how hard I tried to keep from looking at it, my eyes were irresistibly drawn to the spot, making it impossible for me to keep from staring. With each little wave of water that swirled around the hole, I would automatically glance down at the offending sight. She was obviously unaware of it and perhaps I should have told her, but to have pointed out the hole in her suit would have meant admitting to her that I had seen it—which would have been too embarrassing, and probably improper.

The sight of that large dot of white flesh, wet and glistening through an equally large black hole, was unnerving enough to prompt me to inspect my own suit very carefully before every wearing. It now seems hard to believe that a small thing like a misplaced hole could be of such concern, or could cause such embarrassment in light of the "barely-there" suits of today, (or as we observed on the beach at Waikiki—a "not-there-at-all" suit!)

We never dreaded anything as much as the call from Mom or Dad signaling us to come out of the water to go home. Even when my hands and feet had long passed the final stages of advanced prune-syndrome, I was never ready to leave. There was nothing in the world that compared to this idyllic lake and the complete happiness it held for me. This summons meant that our fun in the lake was over until the next time.

If their calls went ignored, the orders from Mom or Dad would only become more commanding and a little louder. So, wet, exhausted, and shivering, after having begged and pleaded for "just a little more time," having already used up the "just five minutes more" we were sometimes given, we reluctantly hauled ourselves out of the water to waiting towels and the long trek back up the path, passing through the tunnel where it was mandatory for us to hoot and howl on our way to our car.

We were never able leave the lake without turning to have one last look. My favorite sports activity, even today, remains swimming; and still the mention of the name Pine Lake floods my memory with nostalgic scenes from my childhood and every precious moment spent there. I'm immediately whisked back to the one place on earth where I once experienced total and unreserved pleasure in a way never to be found again. Pine Lake will forever remain my "Secret Garden" of the heart!

CHAPTER 13

For a time, Dad drove the school bus, which he was also allowed to take home and use. Since this was the only transportation available to us at that time, he would often help us, his own kids, tie our sleds on the back of the bus, and slowly pull us along shrieking with laughter, yelling for him to go faster. Being pulled around town behind the bus made us the envy of all the kids who weren't hitched on. As things are now, Dad would most surely have been arrested for child endangerment; but in those bygone "days of reason," no one's feathers seemed too ruffled by this unusual and thrilling delight.

At other times Dad would drive us out to the mound, a very large, tall hill just south of town, for some tobogganing. It was the closest thing to a mountain we had. As we grew older, and friend's cars became available, there was always a group of exuberant teens anxious to load up our sleds and head out to the mound at the first sign of snow deep enough to slide on.

The nights we were simply dropped off by a parent were the worst, as the temperature always seemed to us to be hovering somewhere below zero. Since the mound was merely a large hill, with no warming-house available, we had no way of getting warm on our own. Of course this was never a problem for us when we started out. We were hot-blooded and boisterous kids who shrugged off warnings of cold, totally ignoring the weather. We never expected to need warming.

What always started out bravely, though, lasted only until the prevailing, shrill north wind, and too many trips down the mound, convinced us we were approaching the tottering brink of freezing. When it seemed we could bear it no longer, and having no car waiting to take us home, reality set in and we knew we were in trouble, facing a serious dilemma. Then we would jump up and down, anxiety written on every face, looking to one another and hoping for an answer about what we should do.

Our salvation often came in the form of a very small, old farmhouse sitting across the road from the mound, and the people who lived there. We hardly knew these folks, but for those times when we could stand the bone-chilling cold no longer, our survival hinged on asking for help, or dying! Then, in desperation we would run across the road, knock on the door and announce our shivering presence, sheepishly begging to be let in for a warm-up.

It's hard to believe we were so reluctant to ask for their help, because we found the people who lived in the house to be most hospitable and kind to the point that they even gave us hot chocolate on occasion. Maybe these folks were more aware of our presence than we knew, and were anticipating our visits, because I also remember being given popcorn by them one night.

Perhaps we'd been sufficiently warned by our parents not to bother them. A neighbor's privacy was always respectfully guarded in the days of my youth. This "learned respect" for others was undoubtedly responsible for our reticence in asking favors from strangers.

At the bottom of the mound was a flat stretch of land, reaching from the bottom of the hill to a small creek, some thirty feet away, which seemed ever to be frozen over—but not always. Invariably there would come a night when some daring show-off would ignore all the warning signs and slide under the wire fence that stood just in front of the creek, and sail out over the ice on his sled.

As one might guess, there were a few icy baths, requiring several emergency trips across the road to the farmhouse, where these soaking-wet, crestfallen daredevils sat, shivering and nervous, awaiting a disapproving parent's arrival. As if it was any wonder, my brother, Maurice, could usually be counted among that ill-fated number. In fact, he was usually one of the improvisers of most of the high jinx that landed this highly energetic bunch in hot water, literally as well as figuratively.

It wasn't too hard. to persuade Dad to take a little time off from work to see to it that his kids had a good time. Around Christmas time he made sure we got to go to the neighboring town of Union, where a Christmas celebration was held each year. The most fun for us, of course, was the arrival of Santa, who handed out bags of treats to the kids. Again, these treats, like the ones we got at church, were the predictable hard candies, apples and oranges, passed out everywhere each year.

Our reaction to the hard candy treats, then, was not too unlike the response you'd get from kids today. Watching children now, gathering candy being tossed from the floats of our holiday parades, one can hardly fail to notice the number of less-than-desirable hard candies still lying near the curb when it's over. These savvy young'uns scramble only for the "good stuff." But since we couldn't expect better, or were ever offered much by way of "good stuff," in Santa's sacks, we gratefully, if resignedly, accepted what we were given. After all, candy was candy.

We quickly went through our sacks, breaking open the unshelled peanuts first since they were the best treat in the sack. By the time we reached home, the candy left in the bottom of our sacks was usually sticky and covered with crushed peanut shells. Since there were so few pieces we really liked anyway, it wasn't hard to recover and wash off the best ones.

Knowing exactly what treats we could expect in advance made the Santa sacks only part of the excitement of the celebration. Going on a trip with Dad made the annual celebration truly fun. Getting to these events was made easier for us when my sister Maxine fell heir to a 1928 Chevrolet car before she was even old enough to drive. One of our neighbors, an old man who was widowed and lived alone, needed someone to clean his house on a regular basis. Any opportunity to make money was always welcomed in our home and

Maxine volunteered for the job since she was eager to start building her college fund.

Joe Baker was quite a well-known character in Whitten. I never really knew what his job might have been during his working years, for he seemed always to have been old and retired when we were neighbors. He was best known in the area for his clogging, a talent which he would eagerly perform for anyone who asked.

Clogging, as currently seen at small town festivals or theme parks, is usually performed in wooden shoes, and is a shuffling and stomping dance. Joe didn't wear wooden shoes, but he shuffled and stomped, sometimes without music, clapping his hands as he kept time to the rhythm. What fun it was to see this jolly old man dancing a jig that was to become a lost art. He kept dancing until age and arthritis forced him to stop, but he was a much-loved, entertaining and gentle man.

Even as a young girl, Maxine was a faithful worker, very industrious and thoroughly dependable. She had been cleaning his home for some time when Joe, who was no longer able to drive his car, completely surprised her, and our family, by giving her the car.

He obviously felt this was a good solution to the problem of disposing of his vehicle. She had been very faithful in keeping his home spotless and in order and he appreciated it very much. Since she was not old enough to drive, it was assumed that it would become our family car. The car was a blessing to our family, for we had been without one for some time. With Joe's full approval, the car became our family car; and it remained our only vehicle for years.

Later, it was Maurice who drove Mother and me out to the country, one very hot summer day, in this car, to visit Mrs. Foote. She had invited Mother out to her farm so the two of them could discuss some church business, and Mom had allowed me to come along. Since the car was new to us I never wanted to miss any opportunity to take a ride.

Mrs. Foote was an amiable, rather large-boned and robust farmwoman, with pleasant features and sandy-gray-colored hair that was assembled rather haphazardly, and twisted into a knot on the top of her head. She didn't seem to notice the wispy strands of hair that fell down around her neck.

Upon our arrival, she flew out of the house to meet us, laughing and hailing our arrival with her characteristically good humor and a warm greeting as we drove into the driveway. For the occasion of Mom's visit, she had discarded her usual apron and appeared in a freshly washed and ironed cotton dress.

We were invited into the house where we sat around the large oak kitchen table, typical of those found in country kitchens at the time. The table was covered with a once bright, but now slightly faded, red cherry printed oilcloth.

Since we weren't offered anything to eat or drink, it wasn't easy for me to sit quietly in Mrs. Foote's kitchen for the length of time the two women sat talking at the table. After studying the fading cherries for a time, I began taking note of each item filling the old fashioned room--the old black range with the ever-present teakettle, the wooden ice box, the kitchen sink, with it's fabric curtain hiding the plumbing below, and the pump standing on the drain board. Kitchen curtains, made from printed flour sacks, hung from the windows. (Most women found many ingenious ways to use this material at a time when enterprising flour companies were trying to entice them to buy more flour by putting it up in floral printed cotton sacks). Every lady had to buy some! I'm sure we even had flour sack printed dresses at the time.

Next to the icebox was a large wooden cupboard with glass doors that showed her neatly stacked plates, cups and glasses. Beside the cabinet, a calendar hung on the wall, and I noticed that she had marked the day's date, probably a reminder of Mom's visit.

Over the table hung a spiraling dark brown, sticky, strip of flypaper that had obviously done its job since there were numerous dead flies attached to it. On a hook by the door was a fly swatter to catch those flies the flypaper missed. And propped in one corner, standing on the brown linoleum floor, was a much-used broom.

I kept giving Maurice surreptitious looks, intended to convey to him that I was on the verge of collapse, and hoping he might find a way to get us out of that predicament. I longed for something more interesting to happen. The fidgets set in in earnest when the women's discussion turned to church business. "Dear Lord, was there to be no end to this meeting?"

After what seemed an intolerable eternity of tedious talk, the discussion finally came to an end. My gratitude almost became too obvious. At last I was to be released from the imprisonment of having to sit still—quietly. After their discussions were over, Mrs. Foote insisted on showing us around the farm, which came as a blessed suggestion and tremendous relief as I flew out of the house. Anything was better than being unwillingly restrained.

After touring the barns and pens, and looking at the animals, Mrs. Foote (had I known her first name I would never have been allowed to call her by it, since Mother insisted we respect all adults by using their proper titles) generously offered us a cold refreshment. I was thirsty and hot and more than ready for a cold drink!

Mrs. Foote was exceptionally proud of her homemade root beer and hurried to fetch it. She invited us to come along with her, however, because it was to be served to us outside, and it was necessary that we come to the yard where there stood a deep cistern, or well. I was fascinated, watching Mrs. Foote reach for a crank, which was fastened to the side of the support beam holding up the protective roof over the well, and surprised as she began cranking the handle.

Watching with interest to see how this little scenario would play out, I was astonished when in a bit, up came a large covered wooden bucket full of homemade root beer. How cold, dark, and inviting it looked. As she poured out the drinks in the tall glasses that she had carried on a tray from the house, appetizing-looking, frosty foam rose to the top of each glass.

My experience with root beer, to this point, had been with the commercially bottled drinks sold at the grocery store we now owned. Even that root beer had never totally captivated my taste buds; the only way I usually took it was in a glass with huge scoops of ice cream camouflaging the taste of the root beer. Since she had so graciously, and with such eager anticipation, insisted that we enjoy a glass of her homemade brew, I figured it would have been rude of me not to give it a small try.

It was, indeed, exquisitely cold, which should have been enough on such a hot day, but there my approval ended. The root beer was strong and the smell repelled me. The carbonation hurt my nose as I gingerly tried to sip this foul concoction. From the others' reactions it seemed they were all enjoying the stuff. Alone in my distaste of the horrible brew, it was a mystery to me how they could have drunk it with such gusto. From that day on root beer has never found its way to a place on my list of drinks that I've tried and liked.

Earlier, her suggestion that we go outside for the tour, had, in itself, come as a welcome reprieve since the inside of Mrs. Foote's house had a most peculiar odor that none of us were ever able to identify. The smell had a caustic property that made my nose sting, and my eyes were on the verge of watering. It was nearly as strong as bleach or ammonia, but was neither one. Nor was it a dirty housekeeping smell, just an uncomfortable one. For all I knew, she might have been concocting a formula for dynamite in her basement.

I could scarcely wait to escape into the fresh air outside. In fact, I was so obviously relieved to exit the house that, because of my antics, Mother took me aside, cautioning me to start acting like a proper guest. I was never sure if Mrs. Foote took notice. Later I questioned Mom about the odor and found that she too had been aware of it, but couldn't identify it. Needless to say, trips to Mrs. Foote's farm became mercifully few—and for me, never again.

The ride out to the farm had been quite beautiful in its own way, however. Aside from the fact that the rural road was dusty and full of ruts, causing the car to bounce around a bit, giving us more than a few jolts, it was still a luxurious trip for me since the entire back seat was mine. I could sprawl out, lie back, fantasize, and soak up the country scenery as it passed by. That day was about as hot as a summer day in Iowa can get; and since the road was narrow, typical of many back roads found in the country, weeds and bushes had grown so close to the road that one could almost reach out and touch them as we passed.

What had made this ride so special, standing out in my mind so vividly, was the moment we came into sight of a large, lush, stand of Elderberry bushes, laden with almost-ripe berries. This particular group of bushes was especially spectacular because of its immense size and its cool inviting appearance as we drove beneath its dense shade. Perhaps this lavish display made even more of an impression on me since my mother wasn't suggesting we stop and pick them.

This was an unbelievable occurrence in itself for my mother never ever saw a "going-to-waste" berry bush she didn't love and want to "de-berry." She could no more pass up an opportunity to pick orphaned, homeless berries than she could spend Sunday morning in bed, which was the ultimate impossibility. I could only surmise that the Elderberries were not, in her estimation, quite ripe enough. Oh joy! Over the years Mom had us picking so many Mulberries that even the smell of them made my stomach queasy.

The tall bushes arching over the road gave me a positively royal feeling as we drove through this shady tunnel, offering a momentary cool respite from the heat, creating for this impressionable child a unique memory.

Note: Lest we be accused of stealing, I would hasten to mention that unclaimed berries of any kind growing along the roadside were commonplace in the countryside, and fair game for those who saw them first. Generally they were lush and plentiful due to God's obvious recognition of the people's need, and His abundant provision for those of that age who had few enough resources.

CHAPTER 14

Leaving this brief glimpse of early rural Iowa, reminds me of another old-fashioned scene so typical of those days, which was washday. Of course, washday *always*, and *without fail*, happened on Monday. Ironing day was *always* Tuesday. That in itself is scarcely news enough to evoke much response from the reader, but there was an amusing twist to wash day in our town that needs to be told.

For many of the ladies in our small hamlet, washday seemed to bring out a latent aggressiveness in some of their usually placid natures. There seemed to be some unforgiving, unwritten rule of competition in the neighborhood to see who could be first to get their laundry on the line on Monday morning.

Any lady "worth her salt" would not dare to be the last one hanging her laundry out on the line for all the neighbors to see, while taking special note of the time. The implication here suggests a lazy nature, which would be unthinkable for any self-respecting housewife. It was sometimes my assignment, as a child, to "Look and see if Mrs. Mitchell or Mrs. Blaha has her clothes out yet." Mondays came *early* at our house!

Laundry was done, back then, in a very primitive washing machine with two rollers on top. The just-washed, wet clothing was rolled through the rollers by hand cranking, thus the name, wringer washer. Some hand washing, done on a washboard, of course, generally preceded that. This innocuous-enough-looking contraption—the washboard—belied the actual amount of hard physical labor required to use it. I would vote for the washboard to be recognized as the international symbol of "mean-work," as well as the method of scrubbing ground-in soil from extra-dirty clothing.

This large, flat board had horizontal metal ridges down its surface. The legs of the board were usually propped inside a sink or washtub of hot water, and the wet clothing was rubbed back and forth over its rough surface, along with a cake of homemade soap until the laundress was satisfied with the result.

Mother was proud of the soap she made, which she insisted cleaned better than any commercial soap on the market. It was made of lye and lard, and whatever else—although I don't think there was much else. Since I was never actively involved in Mom's soap making, about all I remember of the process is the unpleasant smell it gave off.

Since she generally made her soap in the summertime, it was common for her to cook the mixture on a kerosene stove in the little shed outside the house. Maybe she didn't want the house to reek of lye and lard. Her mixtures were cooked and strained until they were just right, with never a speck of foreign matter showing. After cooking, the soap was poured into large pans, and when cooled, cut into small bars. This made her soap a beautifully crafted item that she was proud to share with anyone who wanted some "really good" soap.

It's hard to believe that I started married life using just this same kind of wringer washing machine that my mother used, but what a joy it was when they became electrified, making the job of wringing clothes much easier. Later, when the even newer-fangled automatic machines came on the scene, it's hard to believe my husband had to actually talk me into getting one. I was really convinced that I enjoyed doing it in the wringer washer. Old habits die hard.

It hadn't seemed like too much work at the time, this primitive method of doing laundry, and it gave Mom (as well as me) a lot of pleasure to see her freshly-washed laundry flapping in the summer breeze, drying in the sunshine. Bringing that heavenly sweet "fresh-air-smell" into the house was so satisfying; most housewives considered it the most important reason for "hanging out." But the process was time-consuming.

According to the rules of laundry, it was absolutely necessary to wipe down the old wire clotheslines to make sure they were clean of dirt or rust before we could hang a garment. I was given a wet towel and sent out to do this job about every Monday. There were even special directions for the way the garments were hung: shirts by the tails, pants by the back of the waist, etc.

Then came the time we used a new device Mom had found—wire pant-stretchers—which were inserted into the wet legs of Dad's work pants so that when they dried the pants were automatically creased, reducing ironing time. They were awkward and hard to insert however, making it questionable as to whether or not the process had really been made easier.

Mom had another little cleaning remedy for an especially soiled, just-washed, garment or towel (it had to be a white piece though) and that was to lay the piece directly on the grass so the sun could shine fully on it. Amazingly, it worked, as the stains usually disappeared when they were sun-bleached. I was surprised, one night, as I was watching a TV documentary program set in Israel, to hear a reference to the "bleaching fields."

I'd never heard of these before; so, intrigued, I went to the Bible to see if I could find the specific reference. I could not find a reference to the exact term, "bleaching field", but I did find several references to the "Washerman's Field" in 2 Kings and in Isaiah. Going to another Bible I came across this reference in Isaiah 36:2 which said, "He camped near the outlet of the upper pool, along the road going past the field where cloth was bleached."

Voila! Checking another reference, here it was—in yet another Bible, Isaiah 7:3: "near the road that leads down to the bleaching field." Interesting—all this time I had thought this was Mom's idea. Oh well, nice to be reminded that women have been using their ingenuity for centuries. (However, I suspect it was done by men in those days).

Washdays held all sorts of unexpected surprises back then, like when the laundry froze on the clothesline. We kids were given to lots of crazy conjecture when the laundry stopped flapping in the breeze, and hung frozen, rigid, and drooping—strung together on the line. The clothes began looking to us like so many executed prisoners stiffened with rigor mortis. Our imaginations ran riot.

It turned even funnier when the suits of underwear that Dad (and we) wore froze into stiff pieces of white "cardboard." "Look at mom, she's going to break our underwear," someone would shout with a giggle as the rest of us raced to the window to catch sight of her struggling with a frozen stiff suit of underwear under her arm—its inflexible arms and legs jutting out in front and back, straight and unbending. It was even trickier trying to get the suits inside the house, as they were so awkward.

These "frozen billboards" didn't dare be bent or the frozen fabric would crack, tearing a hole in them, so iced-up laundry was taken indoors to thaw. Sometimes that sight got even funnier if it had been windy when the garments were hung, causing these wind-whipped items (especially things like overalls) to freeze into strange and grotesque shapes that caused them to look like objects of some demented torture.

Of course, these "freezings" usually only happened in early spring or very late fall; but not even the discomfort or inconvenience connected with this process was too daunting to discourage most of these laundresses from hanging their clothing outside to insure bringing that fresh odor into the house as long as possible.

During the winter months, in every house where we lived, Dad would rig up a system of clothesline ropes through the warmest rooms of the house, usually the kitchen, or the dining room with the pot-bellied stove, or both. We didn't have to be told that it was Monday when we came through the door after school; we could tell that by the odor of the still-damp or nearly dry clothing still hanging around the house.

The odor that permeated the house wasn't really that unpleasant, and it did have the additional medicinal advantage of keeping our sinuses open. Dodging the wet clothing was something like threading one's way through the rain forest. It didn't do too much for the decor, either, but we learned to tolerate it; and of course the ropes came down when the clothes were dry.

After Monday, came Tuesday—and the ironing. This meant that the clothes had to go through a lengthy process of being sprinkled from a bottle with a sprinkler head on top, until they were just wet enough to be rolled into tight little bundles and stacked into the clothes basket. There they remained until the pieces were thoroughly damp through—meaning they were just wet enough to be ironed dry again. The dampening process was especially necessary for the shirts, because they, as well as a few other pieces, had been so heavily starched they dried to a crisp.

I soon learned to do the sprinkling, which I quickly realized was a mistake, because from then on, Mother felt that the next logical step in my houswifely education was that I should inherit the ironing position. I learned to iron. This entire laundry procedure, which now seems very primitive, required not only a strong back and legs, but also plenty of time, and a colossal amount of stamina--both mental and physical. Who, back then, could have envisioned the joyous emancipation of women at the dawning of the era of "wash and wear?"

I suppose it was only inevitable, after learning to iron, that I would inherit this job on a pretty permanent basis. Mom's little bribery, to insure a more cooperative spirit from me, was to turn on the tube radio my dad had just gotten, to listen to my soap opera favorites such as: *Ma Perkins,* (with her faithful companion *Shuffle); One Man's Family; As The World Turns; Guiding Light; Stella Dallas; One Life to Live,* and others. It wasn't hard to iron my way through an entire basket of rolled-up clothing when the radio was on, distracting my mind from this otherwise monotonous job. I was even proud of the number of pieces hanging on the rack of hangers when the job was finished.

Mom had found the magical way of making me believe I actually enjoyed ironing; truth be told, I didn't actually mind it all that much. She also made sure to give me lots of praise. You don't even have be a child for that ploy to work. In fact, I'm certain of it, because after I'd grown into an adult I once overheard Mom saying to my grandfather, "Arlene can do anything." While we all know she was exaggerating (well, maybe slightly), those few words reinforced in me the confidence to believe that it was true.

Undoubtedly it gave me the spunk to tackle many of these "anythings" throughout my life that I might have otherwise thought were too difficult. Grandpa's retort to her was a pithy old-time farmer saying, "Yup, she's as independent as a hog on ice." I never quite knew what that meant, or if it even applied to what Mom had said, but it sounded to me like he was agreeing with her.

I learned a lot from my mother, without her even having to tell me. From observing her at work I learned a great psychological truth: that a clean and organized house was her loving gift to her husband. That became my motto when I married. If she was ever a bit late getting supper started at night, she would scurry around, setting the table so as to give the illusion at least, that dinner was in the works when Dad got home. Her housewifely lifestyle was the personification of the old adage: "an organized house is the reflection of an organized mind!"

These daytime soap operas came to us on a wonderful new invention, the radio. This large, tall, wooden piece of furniture that stood on the floor, bringing us these daytime favorites, also brought us many evening entertainments, as well. The entire family soon became addicted to the likes of *Amos and Andy, Fibber McGee and Molly, The Great Gildersleeve, George Burns and Gracie Allen, The Lone Ranger, Jack Benny, The Green Hornet, Lum and Abner* and a long list of thrilling and hilariously funny programs. For mystery fans there were *The Shadow, I Love a Mystery,* and *The Inner Sanctum*—the program that opened with the sound of a creaking door, causing one's nerves to tingle just by hearing it! This drawn-out squeak was setting the stage for the mysterious play following.

All of our radio programs were preceded by very appropriate music, much of it organ music, which set the mood for the programs they introduced. It was also the same format that was used to accompany the first silent movies—sad music for sad situations, excited music for cowboy chases, and tense music for spooky scenes. It seems rather obvious now, but back then, we were very aware of this music that heightened the mood of the scenes; this musical tone alone could send chills up one's spine. Come to think of it, isn't that exactly what's still happening as we sit, transfixed, watching our modern movies?

A favorite evening program of nearly everyone was *Little Theater Off Times Square,* starring Don Ameche. These were wonderful plays, and because they were so elegantly done, carried an aura of importance that set them apart from the others, making them even more special. We wouldn't have missed this program.

From the first words spoken, the announcer began setting in motion some magic of the mind, and we were literally hurled through time and space to this glamorous city out east. From that point on, it was easy to close our eyes and actually envision entering the theater in New York City, reveling in the pleasure of being ushered to our seats, "front row center."

Hearing the program, instead of actually seeing the play, had other subtle benefits, I believe, for it allowed us to *see* more, *hear* more and *imagine* more than if we had actually viewed it. This wonderful event was taking place in the creative world of our minds; a world custom-designed to look the way we wanted it to look, and be what we wanted it to be, instead of the way it might have actually taken place.

In this instance I'm afraid I would be hard pressed to agree with the old Chinese proverb: "A picture is worth a thousand words," because, like a good book which has the power to stretch, exercise and expand the mind, so did these radio programs have that same power, for they were taking us on fantastic "mini mind-trips."

It wasn't even necessary to dress up to "listen" to the show, and we could get as comfortable as we liked. It didn't make a difference if we sat, sprawled, or lay on the floor with our feet up, while we phased out the rest of the world. If a visitor had been watching us as we listened to *Little Theater* they would have given the same description of every facial expression in the room—"relaxed, contented, absorbed—with glazed-over eyes." We were lost in another world.

This image brings to mind my youngest son, Tom, who, as a boy, would flop on the floor wanting his back rubbed and scratched.

As I scratched, he became so relaxed that he literally drooled on the carpet. I wonder if there were any droolers in our home audience?

Public relations and advertising experts were not slow in recognizing this new medium as a potential gold mine, even in those years. It wasn't long before they began airing kids programs immediately after school hours. We were hooked. More often than not we left school on the run, bursting through the door at home fearful that we might not have made it in time for the start of *Jack Armstrong, the All-American Boy.*

This program even appealed to the girls, who like the boys, sat mesmerized in front of the radio hanging on every word. *Jack Armstrong,* was sponsored by the Wheaties Company; whose theme song was an easily memorized little jingle that was sung by every kid in America—often. *Little Orphan Annie,* and *The Lone Ranger* were more favorites not to be missed.

The radio sponsors didn't miss a trick when it came to holding our interest, because they offered things like secret decoder rings, and a 3-dimensional film in a viewing box. These could be ours free, the announcer told us, if we would send in only three box tops of their products, and our name and address. It would have been unthinkable for any kid in his right mind, not to beg his mom to buy the sponsor's cereal so he could save three box tops. We absolutely had to have the secret decoder ring to be able to decode the messages that were hidden in the story.

My all-time favorite special offer, though, was the viewing box, which gave a three-dimensional look at a dense, lush, green, jungle scene with the most beautiful trees and foliage I had ever seen. Looking through my viewing box, which was much on the order of the old stereoscopes, I could imagine myself in the heart of the jungle. As I viewed the scene, it was almost possible to see the exciting characters of our story moving through the jungle as well.

After eating as much cereal as possible, in order to collect the necessary three box tops, and dutifully sending them off to the proper address, the wait for our special offer became almost unbearable. The first question Mom was asked when we came dashing in the door after school was, "Did it come yet?" Of course it never came as soon as we thought it should, so we lived in a state of impatient, nervous anticipation for something like ten or twelve days.

In addition to the radio programs, we also loved the newspaper comics. That section was the first part of the newspaper we looked for every day, turning immediately to the comics the minute it came. The comics that made us laugh, then, were *Tillie The Toiler, Maggie and Jiggs, Popeye, Dick Tracy, The Katzenjammer Kids, Little Abner*, *Jane Arden, Flash Gordon, Smitty, and Mary Mixup.* And if one can believe it, *Blondie and Dagwood* was a favorite strip even as long ago as that; and Blondie has never needed to dye her hair, get a facelift, or go on a diet in all that time. Somehow funny papers seemed funnier then, but maybe that was because my sense of humor hadn't fully developed into the discriminating wit that it is now.

Our newspaper was the *Marshalltown Times Republican*, a paper that Maurice delivered in our town until he became tired of the route and no longer wanted to be the delivery boy. For weeks he kept begging me to deliver the papers for him, but I wasn't interested as it seemed like a pretty big commitment that I wasn't prepared to make.

Realizing that he had failed to foist the hated route off on me, he finally came up with a deal I couldn't refuse. Being certain there wasn't any other way to get me to take the route for him, he promised to give me his bicycle if I would do it. I didn't have a bicycle and had longed for one for ages. Figuring this would be a pretty sharp deal, I agreed.

It's just too bad I hadn't made him sign the agreement in blood because it wasn't too long after I had made a commitment to the newspaper office to become the carrier, that he reneged on our deal and I found myself delivering the papers—on foot. With every toss of the newspaper on every porch, his face became my target as I kept remembering my brother's treachery.

Why I didn't plead my case before Mom and Dad, I can't imagine. Perhaps I did and this was one of the times they let us work it out by ourselves. That would have been certain defeat for me as he usually found a way of outsmarting me, or perhaps it was out-tricking. I never did get the bicycle.

CHAPTER 15

Mom and Dad instilled a responsible sense of discipline in all of their children. We had great respect for most everyone, particularly adults. In school we respected and minded the teachers, and grades were important to me. So much so, that if I came home with a paper marked with anything less than 100%, I was devastated.

In that regard, I seemed to stay about even with Max Mabie (a boy on whom I had a crush through all of my younger school days—even though his response to that crush was, to my dismay, total indifference). Max and I, and also Clarice, received good grades throughout our school years. It wasn't in my nature to want to settle for being second place in the grade department, which meant that I kept careful track of everyone else's grades as well. Several new students moved to Whitten, during our senior high years, and they did as well which added to the competition.

Max (my unrequited heartthrob) and I were cast in the lead parts of our junior class play, "Don't Darken My Door." I was thrilled to be picked to play the part of Rosemary Kent to his Tom Garrick. Our yearbook, "Quivala," gave it the following review: "*It was a riotous comedy—a pinch of romance*, a *dash of laughter, resulting in a triumphant success.*" I remember the kissing scene, which I'm sure accounted for most of the laughter.

Even though it was a lot of work—building props, learning lines and constructing costumes—it was worth any amount of work just to be a part of the fun and excitement of being involved in the school play. The most obvious and spectacular prop for the play literally filled the stage. It was a tree, supposedly in full blossom. While the cast was busy making preparations, one day, a couple of the older boys came dragging a mammoth tree limb they had found into the auditorium and up on stage. After giving it the once-over we unanimously pronounced it "our tree."

Somehow the boys got it anchored so that it wouldn't fall over into the curtain, and we promptly set about turning it into a tree by tying pink crepe paper blossoms to even the smallest twigs and branches. It was a long and tedious job, but since we wanted the tree to look its best, we kept tying long after our fingers had cramped into knots. After each bit of pink paper was attached and fanned out to resemble blossoms; the tree took on enormous proportions. It was breathtaking! It looked like a mammoth pink cloud! In fact, it was the sight that first "socked you in the eye" as the curtain rose. The appreciative gasp from the audience told us the play was destined to be a hit.

Oh, that our performances had been as spectacular as the tree. The review in the *Quivala* was undoubtedly far more generous and charitable than we deserved, I suspect, written out of kindness for some very inexperienced thespians. Our performance that night seemed competent enough to us actors to humor our pride, and this review certainly stroked our egos. It is probably just as well that we weren't labeled "a raving success," for I would have unquestionably wound up in Hollywood; by now an aging, wrinkled, cigarette-smoking former-star, still clinging to that futile dream of "one more smash hit!" Think of the horrid role model I might have been instead of the mother of *excellence* my kids know me to be.

Our school was too small to have had a band or orchestra program, so few of us learned to play an instrument. Our big involvement was vocal. I was fortunate to be chosen to sing in the sextet and the chorus when I was in high school. The best times came when we got to travel to another town to compete. Usually it was only the smaller groups that got to make these trips. It was, however, on just such a trip that I was to suffer another of my youthful embarrassments. Mother had made a soft, mauve-pink, lightweight wool skirt for me to wear that day. From some obscure place I had found a pink, felt, picture hat that was a perfect match for the skirt. Obviously I had to have it to complete my ensemble.

The day of our trip found me wearing my beautiful mauve-pink skirt, a lovely white blouse, and—my outlandishly large, but matching, picture hat. Under more appropriate circumstances it's entirely possible the outfit would have been viewed as "quite charming". But as the others began getting into the car, it became obvious to me that this was not one of those charming moments. Only one girl present was wearing a hat, and that girl was me.

The moment had passed when I could have conveniently left the hat behind, and since I was assigned to the front middle seat of the car the hat most certainly obstructed the view of the person sitting behind me in the back seat—even, quite possibly, the entire back seat.

So it became necessary to continue to wear the hat, or toss it out the window, which would have been the ultimate insult to my frugal nature. Then too, throwing it out the window would have been a guilty admission to the rest of the group that I was totally stupid for wearing it in the first place; and I'd rather have had a root canal than admit that. So I rode along in the car hoping that at the very least, the "dumb, stupid hat" was hiding my flaming cheeks from the rest of them.

The seemingly endless trip became sheer torture for me as I imagined the disapproving eyes staring at my back—without any prospect of its getting better. I either had to wear the hat all day, or carry it, which to my mind seemed pretentious and equally as embarrassing. There was no way to extricate myself from the ordeal, so I compensated, first, by feeling mad at Mom because she had allowed me to embarrass myself this way (like she could have prevented it?) then by wearing myself out smiling all day in a self-deluded attempt at displaying what I hoped would pass for a nonchalant and self-confident air.

I wound up both wearing and carrying the hat all day; I couldn't have felt more conspicuous and uncomfortable if I'd been wearing only my underwear. Over the years this was probably not to be my only fashion faux pas, but for that moment, it satisfied any need I had for another.

In the wintertime, basketball was the magnet that drew the wild-eyed sports fans to the schoolhouse for both the boys' and girls' games. Nearly everyone in town supported the games, and the kids involved. Our greatest claim to fame was the year our boys made it to the State Basketball Tournament. What a coup for a bunch of greenhorn, small-town kids who could scarcely believe their good fortune at advancing this far, much less being assured of a trip to the finals. They were giddy to the point of craziness, and so was the entire town.

One of the boys on our team, Tom Long, a good-looking and rather mature-appearing boy, had grown a mustache that year. At some point, after they'd arrived in Iowa City, the original site of the State Championship Tournament games, Tom left the stadium. Returning shortly, he was refused re-admittance because the guards at the door believed he was too old to be a high school team member. Tom was resourceful, however, bought a program and showed them his picture. He was allowed back in.

Tom's younger brother, Dwight, was also a member of the team. It was he who created another memorable experience for the fans that night, which has amused the residents of Whitten for years. At one point in the game, young Dwight, a sub, was so flustered and excited at being allowed to join the team that he grabbed the ball, during one of the plays, and blindly dribbled down the floor to the opposing court, sinking a basket for the other team.

The fans, watching in astonished disbelief, began yelling, trying to get Dwight's attention; but he was so intent on making the basket that their warning screams fell on deaf ears. He had undoubtedly mistaken the calling of the crowd for cheering approval as he drove down the floor, making a flawless shot.

This totally unprecedented and hysterical maneuver earned him the title of, "Wrong Way Corrigan." Dwight has taken the teasing with amazingly good grace, and laughs along with the others over the incident. This is the same family from which later came the famous girl basketball player, Denise Long, well known throughout the state, who eventually went on to play professional women's basketball.

Like most of the girls in our class, I also played basketball. Tall and skinny throughout my basketball-playing years I was probably the most anorexic-appearing girl on our team, or on any of the other teams. As difficult as that image is for me to conjure up these days, "thinness" is now a deliberately unrecognized word in my dictionary—an impossible goal to dream about in these more "matronly" days. The agonizing reality of being the skinniest girl on the team made it painful for me to be seen in my short little suit on the basketball court. My love of playing forced me to make a choice—quit, or endure the embarrassment.

Given only those alternatives, there was no other option but to endure and bear up as stoically as possible. Oh, to have played in today's world, when being paper-thin and flat-as-a-pancake are prizes for which some girls now are literally willing to starve themselves to death.

Most of the girls had crushes on the coaches, which made us strive to do our best to impress them. Surprisingly, I was a starter on the team, and usually got to play most of the game; but our team never seemed to excel, and we girls never made it to State.

The experience was priceless, however, and we all felt like stars as we ran out onto the floor with the crowd going wild with enthusiasm. One's team doesn't even have to be great when the hometown fans appreciate you. In our own defense, we did win many of our games, but regardless of our record, our fans' ovation and support made us feel like tournament winners. My uniform number was thirty.

Maurice, on the other hand, was never interested in joining the boys' basketball team. Maybe his lack of interest resulted from his smaller stature. I always believed he would have done well in most any sport because of his scrappy nature. Perhaps if I had been more of an encouragement to him?

Maurice did play baseball, however, and we all played softball during those pick-up games in the cow pasture just west of town. These pick-up games were the most fun of all, particularly when you were lucky enough to be chosen right away for the team you mainly wanted to join. Somehow the word always seemed to get out to the rest of the kids when we were going to have a game, and enough of them showed up to make it happen. Then came the uneasy process of choosing up sides—holding one's breath until the team captain called your name.

The team captains were usually two self-appointed older boys who were the loudest and first to claim those positions by shouting, "I'll be the captain." Everyone was eventually chosen, however, and we all played, even those uncoordinated kids who stood around on one foot, looking pathetic until they were finally picked. I always felt a tad sorry for the little kids who were picked last; but once the game got underway, rejection was forgotten and the fun began.

We were an energetic bunch back then, pretty typical of most little rural community youths, I'd say. Our play times were usually physical—physical from necessity, for ours was not a world of computers, video games and television sets, but a world that became exciting only by what our imaginations could dream up for us to *do.* Perhaps all of the physical exertion was what made us "old-timers" the sturdy lot that we are.

CHAPTER 16

Maurice was the one assigned to do the milking when he grew up, and I was the one he coaxed to go along when he needed some help. The times he "needed my help" the most were the times he was late getting his chores done and the evenings were getting dark. Dad had rented a neighbor's barn, where he stabled the cow, and it was dark and creepy in that old barn at night. Maurice's last act on earth would have been to admit that he was afraid, so he had to find a logical reason for me to come along. Holding the lantern seemed to be his favorite one. I couldn't really blame him though because that gloomy old barn gave me a nervous feeling too.

My brother and I were closer in age than Maxine and I, and we were generally pretty good buddies; at least till something set one or the other of us off—then it was every man for himself. Like the time I threw a plate at him because he was mocking me.

That despicable act happened the night we were being forced to help Mom dry the dishes. Maurice decided to relieve his boredom by repeating every word that came out of my mouth. This hateful practice was a bona fide sore point with me (guaranteed to "get my dander up") and he had honed his performance to an art form. My patience, at least the miniscule amount I had that night, was stretched to the breaking point by his mocking me—and I threw the plate I'd been drying at him.

My hope was, at the very least, to teach him that I couldn't be messed with, or if I got lucky, to inflict a really serious wound. True to form, with his easy ability to turn my simple irritation into serious anger, he did it to me again—he caught the plate—and then stood there laughing at me. His mocking, taunting, laugh infuriated me so that I wanted to exterminate him. By that time the murderous intent of my heart was to remove him from the planet, or at least, hurt him enough to make him cry. He would have seen both outcomes as equally bad. I was hoping Mom would use a little brute force against him; but since that didn't happen, I had to be content with the scolding he (we) got. Brothers can be such a pain. Ask any sister.

After the dust settled from that skirmish we became friends once more. Some time later, on a typical hot July day, he even invited me to join him and his friends for an afternoon swim in the Iowa River west of town. The truce between us, at that point, seemed friendly enough that I was confident he hadn't asked me to come along to drown me.

Maurice drove us all in the car, because the river was located between Whitten and Union and the distance there was too far to walk. Could our parents, back then, have been more relaxed or more permissive than today's parents, by letting their kids go swimming in the river? I don't remember being told that we couldn't go; but neither do I remember being told we could. Or would that have been a time when we conveniently forgot to ask?

Recalling, now, that daring plunge into the swift current, it's certain that my own young'uns would never have received my permission to swim in this river. Piling out of the hot car, the lot of us streaked for the river. Making a mad dash to see who could be first to leap into the murky torrent, it was usually the more daring boys in the group who were faster, braver, and reckless enough (or maybe merely showing off) to throw themselves in first.

A revolting amount of arrogant bravado came from the wild bunch already splashing around in the water. With a smugly superior attitude they yelled up to the waiting, not-so-brave leapers who were standing high on the riverbank ledge trying to gather the courage to make that first jump. These exhibitionists would holler and goad the timid ones to "come on in." Their heckling taunt of "ninny," for anyone hesitating to make the jump into the rushing water, would eventually force the apprehensive to take their bait.

Once in, it was almost unnecessary to swim as the current immediately swept us out into the middle of the river. What a ride we had, until the rushing flow turned menacing and began sweeping us too far downstream. Then, "daring" quickly vanished as panic set in. Frenzied, we would streak for the riverbank like insane maniacs—thrashing wildly in the water, desperately reaching for overhanging branches, grasping at fallen logs and stumps, and frantically clutching at anything,—even the reedy weeds lining the water's edge—in a desperate attempt to stop the free fall.

How we survived those fool hardy, but tantalizingly hazardous days, is a wonder; but I don't recall ever "catching it" for these fetes of daring-do. If Mom reprimanded us, I'm betting that behind our backs Dad just gave her a conspiratorial smile of approval for what we'd done. Had he been our age, it's a sure bet he'd have been swimming with us.

Most of my children will remember their grandfather as a rather stern and gruff man in his later years, not the "cut-up" he was when he was younger. As a father, however, Dad was a strict disciplinarian who thought "children should always mind" and that meant, *instantly*. He would never tolerate "back-talk" or any disrespect to mom.

Dad suffered a stroke, later in life, which somewhat altered his personality. Noisy children seemed to bother him a great deal, which probably accounted for their seeing him as being so stern. It's also possible that any of his irritated frowns or quick scoldings might have been brought on by what he considered a parent's lack of the type of discipline he would have meted out when the grandchildren were getting too frisky.

Though we kids respected and loved our dad, we tried hard to stay out of trouble so as not to displease him. With his children, Roy was "all Dad;" but because of another wonderful quality he possessed—being part kid at heart—our growing up years were to be filled with memories of great fun when he was participating.

My grandfather, Robert E., or Rob, as his neighbors called him, loved to fish. He liked making plans for fishing expeditions with our dad, and any of his brood who wanted to come along. Many times Grandpa would get us up at dawn, having driven from the farm, near Laurel, to our home in Whitten, before sun up. Often he came and spent the night before with us. Then, it seems, he was there shaking us awake in the middle of the night so we could head for the river "while the fish were biting."

This was the same river that became our famous swimming hole when we grew older. Grandpa had a special formula for "doughball" that he mixed and brought from home, or concocted at our house. This was his sure-fire formula for catching fish. For me, the smell of dough ball, and grandpa Mann, are forever linked.

It was during one of Grandpa's famous fishing forays, that I was forced to deal with another of life's catastrophic, and near tragic, ordeals. This fateful pre-dawn fishing excursion found Grandpa tiptoeing into our bedrooms early that morning. After awakening three sleeping kids, he hurried us to dress. Reluctantly getting out of my bed, and only half-heartedly pulling on my clothes, he carried me to the car for the drowsy ride to the river.

Reaching the right fishing spot on the river, Dad plopped me down on a tall bank high above the water, handed me a fishing pole, baited my hook and got my line in the water. After I was settled he walked off down the shoreline a bit, thinking, I'm sure, that I was safe there and out of the way of the "real" fishermen.

How ironic, because the first hungry fish looking for his breakfast worm that morning, chose my hook. He was a pretty good-sized one, for he took the bait—and my hook—and tore off through the water, pulling vigorously on the line, with me hanging onto the pole for dear life.

The startling jolt instantly snapped me fully awake. This unfeeling creature, clinging so stubbornly to the other end of my line, prompted screams that grew loud enough to wake the dead. By screaming, however, I'd committed an unthinkable offense. One of the cardinal rules of the *fisherman's code* was that no one was allowed to talk above a whisper because loud talk would scare the fish away. Whooooa! And here I didn't even know fish had ears. Since Grandpa took it so seriously, however, we never talked above a whisper when we fished. He never wanted to run the risk of upsetting any other fishermen, or frightening off the fish.

That impossible rule began to put a real strain on me in this time of extreme peril (being rapidly drug toward the edge of the riverbank) and I ceased to care at all about any old rules. It no longer mattered to me who was upset by my yelling, because I was terrified—and I wanted someone to know it. By then that fear had grown into uncontrolled, frantic, earsplitting panic ......"Daaadeeee!!!!" The gathering speed at which I was sliding down the embankment was escalating into a major crisis of dire proportions. I was doomed—headed for certain immersion.

The water was frighteningly black and forbidding in that "dark-before-the-dawn" early morning. For some insane reason (probably from a previous lecture on never dropping your pole) I felt it would have been treasonable for me to let go of the pole; so my only option was to hang on, no matter what. It's even possible that through gripping the pole and hanging on this tightly I was given a small sense of security by having something solid to grasp. But by following orders, I was also sliding closer to the water's edge. I was now within a whisper of my unscheduled baptism.

Bracing myself for the overwhelming agony of being plunged into the cold, black, river water, my eyes were squeezed tightly shut, hoping to make it all disappear. Tensely holding my body as rigid as a board, I clung to the fishing pole, and the obviously futile notion that by gripping tight I might somehow prevent the fall.

Sensing that I was at the edge of the precipice, with all hope now gone, from out of nowhere two strong arms materialized grasping me firmly around the waist. Fright, it seems, had rendered me deaf as well as rigid in that awful moment, because I hadn't heard Dad—on a dead-run—coming to my rescue, snatching his terrified kid from the brink of disaster. Here was just one more reason for feeling safe and protected when "*my dad*" was around.

It proved to me, that morning, that Dad was close by and watching even when I couldn't see him. Somehow that incident is a vivid illustration of our Heavenly Father who is always close by and watching, but who sometimes waits until the need is critical to rescue us. I recently heard another great little quote that tickled me and seems to fit this fishing scenario: "Satan, like a fisherman, baits his hook according to the appetite of the fish." Fortunately I didn't become the catch of the day that morning.

That incident is reminiscent of another "Dad-to-the-rescue" story that Mother retold often. Living on a farm at the time of this happening, Mother decided that she and Maxine, around age one or two at the time, would drive the Model-T Ford out to the field where Dad was working and take him some lunch. Whether the road was muddy, or simply rutty, is unclear; but the deep ruts cut into those old, dirt country roads made driving treacherous at any time, coupled with the fact that the tall, top-heavy car, was very difficult to handle under these conditions.

As they were approaching the field, the wheels of the car dropped into a deep rut, causing Mom to lose control, and over they went. Maxine was thrown out of the car, and it tipped over onto her. Dad had been watching their approach from the field where he was working, and in Mom's words, "he came running over the field in about three giant steps."

Wild-eyed with fear and super-charged with adrenaline, Dad reached down, grabbed the car at the top, and lifted it back to its upright position, and off Maxine. With every nerve tingling the two of them examined her carefully, but determined she hadn't sustained any life-threatening injuries. Perhaps the roadside was muddy or marshy that day, accounting for a softer landing, which could have saved her life. Of course this happened before my birth, so my account is, of necessity, secondhand.

Maxine sustained a slight chest indentation that remained with her all of her life. I'm uncertain whether it was the result of Mom's smallpox when she was pregnant, or if it was diagnosed as a result of the crush of the car on her tiny body. At any rate, this was never confirmed—but seems likely.

At that point, Mom declared in no uncertain terms, that her driving career was finished, because of this terrible accident. She never touched the wheel again. No amount of coaxing could ever change her mind. Mother's retelling of the story always made me shiver; but I loved hearing over again how Dad had lifted the car off my sister. Who wouldn't be immensely proud to have a Dad who was strong enough to lift a car off the ground, single-handedly?

Not only was he strong, but Dad was also a quiet encourager. At one point he allowed me to bring my entire class, including our teacher, to our house to see the goats Dad had raised in a pen out in the orchard. Seems as though we had field trips then too. Dad raised goats primarily for the milk on which we children were raised for some time, or maybe when the cow went dry.

The goats had borne a few kids and I could hardly wait for my classmates to see them. I was elated when our teacher enthusiastically agreed to the visit. The trip was a rousing success, not only because they got to see something unusual, but because my schoolmates were always thrilled for the chance to get out of the classroom (and I suspect it was a welcome relief for the teacher as well). As an added bonus they got to see these adorable little goats wobbling around inside the pen alongside their mother. Before we left, everyone, of course, had the chance to pet the goats; and the cuddling, and fawning over these babies, the excited giggling, and the jumping and squealing, entertained us all.

From the sound of things, it might appear that we lived on a farm, but in our small town, zoning laws, as stated, were non-existent, or at least, hadn't been put into practice—if, indeed, these kinds of laws had even been heard of in rural Iowa. Many residents like us raised chickens, cows, goats, etc. This practice had more to do with sustaining life than winning Better-Homes awards.

Pets were a requirement in our home, it would seem, because we usually had at least one dog and cat in residence at all times. To our sorrow, our favorite dog, Spot, whom we'd had for years, was killed by a car. This sent us kids into a deep period of extended mourning. We were inconsolable, and cried for days.

Earlier, Maurice had built a box and mounted it on the front of his bicycle in which Spot could ride. This sight brought smiles to the faces of a lot of town folk as they watched him peddle down the street with his dog sitting snugly in his box seat. Overall clad men, in town from the country, along with anyone loafing on the town benches, would point and call out, "Hi Maurie, how's your dog like his ride?"

To these bystanders, the sight of Maurice, riding down the street with his dog perched regally in his box, head facing into the wind, surveying the scene with royal élan, gave them something new to look at, and talk about.

This scene seldom went unnoticed by our neighbors either, who smiled and shook their heads in passing, saying, "There goes Maurie and his dog." It was a phrase heard often, with amused and good-humored laughter on Main Street.

Because of our constant accumulation of cats, dogs, goats, and cows, it's understandable that the reason for my permanently altered attitude towards animals (I have no pets) now exists. Our collection, I believe, served to more than satisfy my need for a pet for all time.

As a kid in this family it was part of my responsibility to see to their care and feeding, and I now have neither the stamina, nor the desire, to repeat the experience, particularly when coupled with the genuine grief that accompanies their demise. As the Bible says, "Today has enough grief of it's own." (Paraphrased for scholars)

CHAPTER 17

Through the maturing process I came to a fuller realization and deeper appreciation of the ongoing and loving sacrifices my parents made for us through the years. Children, it seems, aren't always quick to sense the amount of sacrificial love made by their parents along the way; but I now recall many such incidents that prove the reliability of that statement.

One "proof-positive," of an ultimately supreme sacrifice made by my mother, was the time (actually the many times) Mom volunteered to be *the* sponsor of our church youth group at summer church camp. Camp was at the Methodist Campground at Clear Lake.

The role of sponsor required my mother to be "chief-cook-and-bottle-washer," as well as chaperone, counselor, probation officer, nurse and mother to the entire group. She was, indeed, the chief cook, as we were all attending camp on a shoestring and could ill afford the luxury of taking our meals in the dining hall. Instead, we ate our meals at our mess tent where mom cooked over open fires and a kerosene-burning stove, preparing three meals a day for up to ten or twelve ravenous kids for a week.

That act alone should give reverential pause for a "woman among women." At the very least, a medal for heroism should have been struck for her personal sacrifice above and beyond all expectations of duty, elevating her, in any other woman's eyes, to the role of superior sainthood.

It was a few of the men of our church, including Dad, who set up separate tents for the boys and girls. We slept on cots, which also had to be assembled. Mom supervised the operation and helped make up beds for everyone. The best part for me to remember is that she seemed to be having fun along with us kids. Was I really watching?

Our week at camp each year was pure bliss. We were treated to interesting classes, with missionaries sharing their wonderfully riveting stories of life in the jungles, and some seemingly impossible miracles God performed for them there in the field. And of course, everyone knows that missionaries, if they are "real" missionaries, are people serving in the jungles of some wildly remote country of headhunters.

The most vivid and unforgettable story I remember two of our missionaries telling us, was a time they were taking a foot trip through the jungle. Suddenly, without warning, they were caught in a blinding, torrential rainstorm, in the nature of a monsoon. This signaled real danger for them, and they began to pray for deliverance. At once they found themselves miraculously standing in a dry spot in the midst of the downpour. There they remained, safely shielded until the storm passed. It was then, even at my young age, that my faith in God became a real and personal possession through this powerful testimony.

That incredible happening was a deeply meaningful revelation to me. The missionaries' stories were spellbinding and memorable, making such an impact on me that early on, I seriously considered becoming a missionary myself. Circumstances and lack of opportunity directed my life elsewhere. It remains to this day an unanswered paradox—where would my life have led had I followed this different course? God obviously had other plans.

The usual crafts, games and socializing opportunities presented at most other camps, were offered at ours as well; we enthusiastically took full advantage of each one. Everyone took home handmade gifts for family, and mementos for themselves. My most eagerly looked-forward-to event, however, was not the crafts or the lessons, or even the eating, it was…the *lake*.

We were more than a little dejected, however, when we found out that we were not allowed to go swimming except at specifically designated times. Clearly, the consensus of our group was that a tyrant was in charge of the rules. With the lake just sitting there, beckoning to us to come on in, this odious decree seemed somehow comparable to spitefully dangling a huge steak in front of a starving man.

We were positively giddy with excitement that first moment we were allowed to pull on our scratchy woolen swimsuits and head for the lake. We were off and running. The first swim of the day was scheduled early, before classes started in the morning. This meant a nearly heart-stopping plunge into what seemed like ice water. But who would let such an insignificant thing as a little discomfort keep us out of the lake?

It took some time before our young, pre-teen body-thermostats adjusted to the near-hypothermic level of the frigid water; but even before they'd adapted, we were jumping off the dock and leaping into the freezing water as though our nerve endings had been anesthetized and destitute of feeling.

In reality, these sub-zero plunges of ecstasy became challenges of endurance for us. Our icy plunges were possible only because of our youthful stamina, and lustful desire for being in the lake. But we were determined to stay "up" for these daring flings—we weren't about to surrender. Nothing could have convinced us that this wasn't really fun!

Streaking back to our tents after our swims, we ran barefoot across a campground that was still covered with cold, early-morning dew. Dripping hair sprayed icy drops over our already frigid bodies—still wrapped in wet swimsuits that clung to us like the peel on an onion—with the wind cooling us even more as we ran. We were quivering and shaking, but we remained undaunted and exhilarated.

Shivering lips stretched over chattering teeth, remained blue, hands stayed cold and wrinkled, and goose bumps continued to rack our pubescent frames long after we'd struggled into some warm, dry clothing. But we were in heaven. This was what life was meant to be. Of course, this exercise was repeated two or three more times every day, never missing! The water temperature did manage to rise a bit as the sun shone on the lake.

Fortunately there weren't many distressing camping experiences at Clear Lake that I can recall; but there was one, and it was a doozie! This shocker took place on an evening that we had been looking forward to for the entire week we'd been at camp. We were going to be treated to a Christian movie. A movie (wow) of any type was a rare event for us. We were lucky to find a good seat in the Conference Center, and we busied ourselves chatting with friends while waiting for the main attraction to begin.

After the call for quiet, the movie began. Right from the start, alarm bells began to sound in my head as they began showing scenes of inhumane treatment of the Christians.

Already feeling uneasy about the initial violence being shown on the screen, my body went rigid with terror at that moment when a captive Christian was taken by the arms by two "evil" Roman soldiers and placed, on his bare back, atop a metal plate that had been heated to red hot. It's possible my screams might have drowned out the captive's screams right then.

Propelled out of my seat by an overpowering force, I turned and bolted out of the Conference Center with the speed of the quarry at a foxhunt. There, sitting on a low bench, sobbing and shaking, Mom found me completely dissolved into a pathetic, quivering heap. Needless to say, the two of us sat outside the building for the rest of the movie.

I thought that traumatic incident would probably scar me for life, but the memories finally faded and the years have mercifully softened the horror of the scene. Now I only feel a bit of righteous indignation for the inappropriateness of the leadership's choice of movie for such a young audience. Compared to the media offering being fed to young people today, however, it's apparent just how naive and unsophisticated we kids were in my day—or at least me!

Recalling the incident now, I don't remember seeing many other kids leaving the movie that night. Wouldn't that say something about my much more sensitive nature than the rest? At least that explanation works for me, and excuses any cowardice on my part, reassuring me that my reaction must have been more righteous than the others.

A conclusion might be drawn that this shattering incident would end my fun at camp, but it didn't. Instead, it left only a long-standing aversion for the Conference Center. I only had to look at the building to feel a chill run through my body, which no amount of parental counseling could eliminate. Though the incident didn't manage to completely wreck my camp experience, it did put an end to the evening events (of the movie type) at the Conference Center. About then, Mom was probably wishing I were someone else's kid, but she willingly became a sacrificial lamb who stoically sat them out with me.

No accounting of our wonderful life at camp would be complete without admitting the rest of the sordid story. Our trips to summer camp were the culmination of a year of impatient waiting for those lucky enough to get to go, that most perfect time which we'd been dreaming of all year. That is, it would have been perfect except for yet another unbreakable rule that was posted and enforced, seemingly, to mar this most perfect time.

The town of Clear Lake was located almost directly across the lake and a little to the right, as we viewed it from our campsite. From the time we were old enough to be campers, we were painfully aware of the existence of the amusement park that stood at the edge of the city proper, partially visible from our camp. Although we knew of it, and longed to go there to see, and be part of all of the excitement, we had no hopes or expectations of ever being allowed to visit the park because of…the *rule*.

How could we not be aware of the glittering lights of the amusement park, which cast their seductive, sparkling reflections our direction across the water? How could we not be attracted by the "siren song" of the carnival music, wafting over the lake, beckoning us to come?

It seemed only natural that curiosity and desire would eventually begin to stir in us some of the similar desires that Adam and Eve must have experienced in the Garden of Eden. Like those two, who were overcome with the desire to taste the forbidden fruit, we, too, eventually began to experience the same first rush of Satan's evil influence. Yet, the rules of the camp were clearly posted for all to see—and strictly enforced. Leaving the grounds was "Verboten."

Maturing as we were with each passing year, growing in confidence and becoming more adventurous, this rule was becoming more oppressively restrictive. It wasn't long before the restraint began acting like a catalyst, fueling an already-smoldering desire in us that was yearning to be set free.

During the spare time we occasionally had after classes, our small group of restless friends began hatching a plan whereby we would throw caution to the wind and discover these hidden and forbidden delights for ourselves—regardless of the consequences. We'd been intolerably tested, and found wanting.

So it came about during a rare free time in camp one balmy summer evening, that this deceitful band of pleasure-seeking protesters, having grown weary of waiting, decided to put our hastily-thought-out plan into practice. We would find a way across the lake to the amusement park this very night.

So anxious were we to go that the possibility of being expelled from camp held no fear for us (although we'd spent little time thinking about possible repercussions). The thrill of personally experiencing the illicit pleasures of the amusement park was reason enough to take the risk. In fact, the bravado the group managed to pull together, through our mutual conspiracy, made us feel invincible that night. The possibility of our nefarious scheme being discovered seemed too remote to even warrant discussion.

Fortunately, depending on how you look at it, one of the more resourceful boys in our group was able to confiscate a boat (not one among us was sufficiently interested in questioning the source) into which we all piled, and set off rowing. Since there were about seven or eight of us we were obviously overloaded and it remains a mystery, or perhaps a miracle, why some night fisherman didn't have the unfortunate duty of reporting a mass drowning in the middle of the lake.

In spite of our youthful exuberance it wasn't long before the trip across the lake turned into an exhaustive chore requiring more effort than we'd expected when we'd pushed off from shore. Two by two we took turns rowing our small but unwieldy craft across the lake in the fading light. The boat tipped dangerously as we stepped and stumbled over one another trying to change seats to take our turn at the oars.

Not surprisingly, we had seriously underestimated the distance from our camp to the amusement park. It had looked so close as we viewed it from camp! But it was a long, hard, pull, trying to cross the lake. Having only reached the mid-way point, a few began to have doubts, but the rest felt too seriously committed to turn back for any reason, even exhaustion (which everyone felt but no one would admit).

Even though our energy was severely drained, the sound of the boat scraping on wet sand brought us a huge sense of relief and revitalized our spirits as our boat slid to a sudden halt, telling us that we had made it safely to the forbidden shore. Recovering quickly, we were instantly reenergized by the sights and sounds of the park. We jumped from the boat onto the sandy beach for our long-anticipated visit to the Amusement Park at Clear Lake. This was it! We were actually here! We were ready for the fun to begin.

Perhaps it was due to our slim-to-non-existent funds, or quite possibly the flagging confidence we were beginning to feel as we now thought of the fate that might be waiting for us back at camp, or it could have even been the grim prospect of having to make that long trip back across the lake, whose horizon had now become one with the black night sky, that caused us to cut our trip short.

We must have appeared like pathetic, homeless, orphans wandering around the park with no money to spend on rides that looked so agonizingly attractive. After all, wasn't that the point of our coming to the amusement park? But with little money we were obliged to stroll among the rides and concessions pretending to be having a good time, while dripping disappointment from every pore.

Our high hopes had turned into a disaster, which really shouldn't have surprised us, for if we'd been a little less eager to transgress, and a little more realistic about our finances, we might have saved ourselves a colossal amount of heartache as well as some throbbing backs and arms.

It wasn't long (still green-eyed with envy as we circled these "unavailable-to-us" rides) until this alluring temptress, who, for years, had beckoned us to come over to the other side, began loosing much of her appeal. One glance back over the ghostly darkness of the lake, and the park's swiftly fading glamour turned positively alarming Reality had replaced lust, thoroughly robbing us of the anticipated joy we had expected would be ours at the amusement park. Crestfallen, and sobered by our experience, we took our disappointment (and a certain uneasiness) with us back across the lake.

Our trip back, guided only by the lights from our camp, was again exhausting, but accomplished without disaster. Once safely back at camp, however, we began building up the adventure in our minds, fibbing to each other about how much fun it had been, and telling ourselves that we wouldn't have missed it. Truth be told, most all of us were relieved and overjoyed to be back where we belonged, but no one wanted to say it out loud. We were too busy congratulating ourselves on the fact that we'd even done this daring deed, and for the fact that we hadn't gotten caught, and, oh yes, for not drowning.

We all pitched in to help the boys get the boat back into its original position at the dock. Then, as quietly as it's possible for a group of bone-weary kids to tiptoe over a darkened campground covered with dry, crackling, pinecones and needles while furtively whispering "shushings" at each other, we stealthily headed for our tents. Once there, we fumbled around in the dark searching for our pajamas, struggling to get them on. Falling onto our cots, exhausted, and harboring the smug notion that we'd pulled off this little caper completely undetected, we slept like the dead.

We had completely deluded ourselves, of course, because Mom had learned of our unauthorized trip. She said nothing until we guilty truants had had our breakfast the next morning. Then she called us all together for a major talk in which she confronted us with our little deceit. We got a lecture on responsibility and honesty that day, and while we were embarrassed and remorseful, we were also relieved that she didn't exact too great a punishment from us, like placing the lake off limits, which would have been too cruel.

My admiration for Mom grew by leaps and bounds, that day, having been totally impressed by her controlled self-restraint. Without as many fireworks as we deserved, she made her point, and luckily, she didn't report us to the "rule-makers" who would most surely have expelled us. We never did it again; but then again, who among us really wanted to?

The focal point of the last night of our camping week was traditionally the most dramatic, designed to give us campers a memorable sendoff. Of all of these last nights, one outshone the rest. It happened at sunset. All of the campers, chaperones and counselors were assembled on the wide lawn leading down to the beach. As we stood watching to see what was about to happen, the camp director called for silence, then directed our attention to a point up along the water's edge in the direction of the setting sun. We were straining to see what might be coming.

It wasn't long before we could make out the outline of two canoes. Inside each boat sat an Indian (in reality, camp personnel in costume) paddling his boat along the shoreline, silhouetted against the last of a sun that was just beginning its evening dip into the water.

Moving silently through a long reflection made by the shimmering rays of the setting sun on the water, the "Indians" continued advancing down this brilliantly lit path of red and yellow, now gradually softening into a serene and beautiful shade of mauve. There was scarcely a sound to be heard while we watched and waited.

The majestic bearing, and imperial entrance of the Indians, was a sight to behold. As the Indians reached the shoreline, they stepped out of their canoes onto the shore. From their positions on the sandy beach they raised their hands in salutation, calling out an Indian greeting and blessing. After a small ceremony, they ending their official visit with an Indian prayer.

Their presence, in full regalia, was tremendously impressive to this group of wide-eyed kids in that solemn moment. Then, as quietly as they had appeared, the visitors stepped back into their canoes and departed in the direction from which they'd come, again following the now fading, silver-lit path along the shoreline, until they disappeared.

The sun, which by this time was nearly out of sight as it sank into the water, pointed to the darkening sky and the early stars that were beginning to blink in the gathering dusk. Those who had been watching the entire spectacle that night remained still, seemingly reluctant to move—still marveling over the Indians' appearance.

Next, we were instructed to light the candles we had been given earlier. The candles were wedged into small white cardboard "boats," and were lit by passing the flame from person to person. When all of the candles had been lit, the entire group moved down to the shoreline, walking slowly amidst the glow of the flickering candlelight,. Each stooped to place their burning candles on the water, setting them adrift on the lake.

What an amazing sight those hundreds of burning candles made, bobbing, rocking, and swaying over the calm water as they drifted leisurely out onto the lake, carried along by the gentle swells and natural motion of the water. It made a stunning picture that caused us to gasp in awe, as the candles headed out onto the dark lake. Of course there were a few mishaps as some of the "boats" capsized and were extinguished. But the total experience was awesome! The atypical (for a camp full of kids) silence was broken only by the normal lake sounds: water lapping onto the beach, the call of a lonesome loon, and the customary noises common to wildlife in the lake area.

The occurrences we'd just witnessed made most of us feel as though we'd burst with a holy emotion we could only feel—not explain. After the Indians' visit, the candle lighting ceremony, the songs and prayers, the evening ended. Merely being part of the throng, that night, was too impressive for description. Even the smallest kids in the crowd could hardly have missed sensing God's hand in this beautiful display of His world.

We left the lakeshore knowing that we had been a part of something very unique and special, something I would later come to recognize as a "mountain-top experience." It was obvious that everyone present had been touched in a very personal and meaningful way. The lakeshore had become an almost hallowed place in those minutes as we stood in the presence of our Maker. It must certainly be times such as this that are responsible for bringing people into a closer relationship with God; becoming the building blocks which form the foundational basis for our moral judgments, and the framers of our code of ethics for a lifetime. Somehow I felt this never-to-be-forgotten event that night, would somehow change my life forever.

CHAPTER 18

Our path to school each day went past Doc Blaha's house, past Ada Essig's house, then on to the town pump that stood on the corner, on Main Street, and diagonally across the intersection, to the town park. Following the diagonal path through the park made the walk shorter. Several blocks later we passed what was to become our new house. From that house it was only a short trip up to the end of the block where it stopped at the fenced-in schoolyard. Because we were almost never driven to school, we actually walked those proverbial "five miles through the snow to school." In reality, it was, at most, eight or ten blocks from any point in town. Weather was never considered a necessary excuse for a ride, so we walked the path in every kind of condition—hot, rainy, cold, or snowy.

Ada Essig, was a friend and neighbor, and from my perspective, seemed always to have been an old lady. Her continual fascination, for me, was her ears. Mrs. Essig's ears must have been pierced at birth, because the holes accommodating those ever-present heavy, old-fashioned, ornate drop earrings were, by then, long slits. And no matter how hard I tried not to look at her ears, my eyes were irresistibly drawn to them. Because of the length of her lobes, her earrings nearly reached her shoulders.

Ada was usually up and stirring around by the time we were on our way to school and she would give us a cheery smile and a wave as we walked by. I looked forward to seeing her, not just to look at her ears, but because she was sweet and friendly and it was nice to talk to people on the way to school. Many times we'd find her outside sweeping off her front porch, or the sidewalk in front of her house. But always we'd receive her cheerful "Good Morning, now have a nice day in school," spoken in her soft grandmotherly voice.

On the last block, just before the fenced-in schoolyard, stood the last house on the street in which lived a man named Vanny Snyder. He was a small good-natured man who liked the school children. We kids liked him too, and loved to drop by his shed, which stood only a short distance from his house, on rendering day. Once in a while, if he saw us on our way to school, he would call out for us to stop by on our way home. On the days when we weren't invited, he didn't shoo us away if we simply dropped in anyway.

It was in this little shed that Vanny rendered lard. We always knew we were in for a special treat if we had walked by Vanny's house in the morning and had seen that this was the day he was rendering. Lard was rendered by cooking pork fat until most of it became liquid. The liquefied lard was then poured into smaller containers and set aside to harden. The residue, or what was left of the pork fat after the rendering process, was called "cracklings," or "cracklins," depending on the person with whom you were talking.

We left school a bit faster on the days Vanny rendered, making our way straight for his house. That was because Vanny made cakes out of the cracklings. These caramel-colored cakes were approximately twelve to fourteen inches across, and six or eight inches deep, and were bite-sized chips that had been compressed into larger cakes. Vanny was prepared for us when school let out. With his wry little smile, he allowed us to "cool our heels" a bit while he waited for our not-so-subtle hints for a handout. He doled out little handfuls of these crisp cracklings to every one of us who stopped by.

I'm sure this delicacy sounds gross and unappetizing to many, considering its source. Au Contraire! To us kids it was delectable.

Although cracklings were pork fat that was rendered to a hotter degree by far than crisp bacon, the taste was similar to the fat part of crispy-fried bacon. Happily, we worried not a whit about cholesterol or fat calories—and why should we when we'd never even heard of such things as calories or cholesterol. Life was good—happily munching on one of life's unusual treats. How is it possible that I ever made it to so great an age?

When I was ten, our family moved from our beloved little house (leaving memories tucked away in every nook and corner) to this larger house on the other side of town, very close to school—which incidentally made us neighbors to Vanny Snyder. I rather missed my old familiar trek each day, waving at Ada and giving the old pump handle a couple of pumps as we passed by. I missed taking that walk with my friend Clarice.

The only advantage I could see to the shorter walk was that I'd be less likely to freeze to death in the winter—unlike some of the times I "knew" it would happen when we lived further away. Even then Mom believed in dressing us for the weather, and it wasn't unusual for us to arrive at school with an ice-caked scarf tied tightly around our noses and mouths. The moisture from our breath froze on the scarf, causing one of the nastiest cold feelings in the world, unless, of course, you were also suffering from a runny nose.

Boots and mittens were occasionally pulled off by an obliging teacher who took pity on little kids who were too bundled up and stiff with cold to manage the job themselves. Both school entrances became mini-ponds, as scattered, ice-encrusted boots and clothing were left there to melt.

Any misery of those winter treks was long forgotten, however, when it came time for the ultimate and absolutely most exciting event of our entire school year. This biggest-of-all-extravaganza was the last day of school—a celebration guaranteed to bring out the entire town!

Unfortunately, in sharp contrast to the miserable winters we'd been forced to endure (and as wonderful as this school event was) this annual event was not without its own peculiar discomfort. For it seemed decreed somewhere that the temperature for this grand send-off needed to be another of the hottest days of the year—and it seldom missed!

Be that as it may, this was still the day all of our parents came to see, and be part of the end of that year's school activities—the big picnic, the big ballgame, the big "run-ourselves-ragged" day, and the biggest "no-more-school-tomorrow" day (the day we lived for, and the reason why lots of the kids endured school the rest of the year).

The main feature of the morning's entertainment, given by the students, was first on the program. For weeks, students practiced in the gymnasium, working on the main attraction—the Maypole Dance. Of course it was a special honor to be chosen as a dancer. Representatives from each class were selected for this prized position. But in order for this dance to be performed around the Maypole it was first necessary for someone to climb the designated Maypole to attach the ribbons.

Our Maypole was always the flagpole standing out in front of the school, and the job of climbing the pole usually fell to the school janitor. A large part of our excitement came from the fact that our teacher usually allowed us to watch the janitor from the classroom windows as he climbed the pole. We would watch as he attached sixteen or eighteen colored crepe-paper streamers, to the very top of the pole. Each streamer then fell to the ground in a four or five foot long puddle of additional streamer. After the streamers had all been securely anchored, the janitor, would then duck down beneath the ribbons of paper, wrap his legs around the pole, and slide down to the ground amidst a lot of wild cheers of approval from the row of "peewees" lining the windows.

The dancer's job was to take up the end of one of the perfectly color-coordinated streamers—usually pale green, yellow, pink and white—with half of the dancers facing one way, and the alternating half facing the opposite direction. When the music began, the dancers would start weaving over and under the heads and arms of the dancer approaching them so that a woven pattern began to emerge down the flagpole. This continued until the flagpole was completely encased in braided, multi-colored, crepe paper ribbons, giving the pole the appearance of a basket-woven obelisk.

The music came to an end only after the pole was completely covered. When the streamers reached the bottom of the pole, the dancers ended the drill with a flourish, to enthusiastic applause. Our teachers made sure we were carefully choreographed, so this part of the program usually went off without a hitch. Our beautifully decorated Maypole then became the royal scepter reigning over the day's activities, for a very appreciative group of loyal subjects.

Last-day-of-school events always seemed to follow the same pattern each year, but the predictability and anticipation of these events only added to the excitement for us. The day's schedule of entertainment started first thing in the morning and lasted until late afternoon. It would have taken a mini-catastrophe for anyone from the community to have missed this event. After the dance around the flagpole, came such energetic games as sack races, tug-of-war, relay races, softball games and any physical activity designed to keep the kids entertained.

Tucked in between the Maypole dance and the very important afternoon baseball game, was the most anticipated event of all, the impressive noontime potluck dinner. This was an eating extravaganza to boggle the mind and send everyone sprawling under a shade tree afterward. Tables were stretched out beneath the trees on the schoolhouse lawn, then draped with each lady's favorite tablecloth, and laden with her most special dishes. Families attending this event weren't stingy with the amount of food they brought.

Moms didn't usually call on their kids to help on this special day, so after the program (which had required us to look neat) we ceased to care about our appearance, and took up the chase, wildly running in hot pursuit of one another. As the heat-index of the day continued to climb, it was generally sweltering by lunchtime, when most all of us kids were totally disheveled and dirty, our hair wet with sweat and plastered to our heads. The noisy, feverish activity of these rowdy, over-stimulated, bunch of boisterous celebrants, continued until someone mercifully announced that dinner was served.

As memorable as all of those days were, one particular last-day-of-school-dinner stands out above the rest. The food was plentiful and inviting, and our entire family was there. It was heady stuff, to be part of the festivities, and everyone was enjoying the picnic, until that earth-shattering moment when Maurice came running up to Mother, thrusting his plate of food at her with a stricken look on his face. With his face screwed into a ridiculous shape, he loudly announced that he HAD FOUND A HAIR IN HIS FOOD! Maurice had done some preliminary investigation into whose food the culprit hair had been found, and he "knew for a fact" that "she was a poor housekeeper"—and "the hair had to be dirty."

That was it for him! Every year, from that point on, Maurice tried to beg off going to the picnics. Anticipating the tug-of-war between Mom and Maurice was the first thing that popped into my mind on picnic mornings, and I was up early to witness the skirmish to come. Secretly relishing any incident that got him into trouble, I wasn't about to miss the commotion Maurice's stubborn refusal would make again this year. I was never disappointed; what a fuss he made with his exaggerated gagging, coughing and all of the melodramatic gyrations that he went through in an attempt to impress Mom with just how sick he would be if he had to go to the picnic and eat the food.

Of course we always had a good laugh at his expense because he tried every ploy he could think of to avoid the potluck every year; but our gentle Mother was still a force to be reckoned with (backed up by Dad) and she wasn't being taken in at all. Every picnic found him there. Such was his stubborn nature, however, that every year found him being marched off to the picnic with all of the zeal, and the crazed expression of a martyr being led off to a firing squad. His retaliation for this indignity was to eat only the food that mother had brought.

It was hard for me, his little sister, not to enjoy the secret pleasure of seeing him sitting under a tree, off by himself, skimping along with his meager little plate of food when there were heaping tables of wonderful food spread out before him. After a bit of coaxing by the family, we resignedly learned to ignore him, shaking our heads in disbelief because he was missing all of the bountiful goodies available to him—and all on account of his own stubbornness.

It was colossal fun for me to exaggerate, for his benefit, just how wonderful everything tasted as he sat eating his one lone chicken leg and a bit of the other things Mother had brought. He was determined, though, to remain unimpressed through all of my taunting, and never again ate anything at the school picnics but what Mother brought.

Maurice remained a finicky eater to his last days. Now, the imponderable question—is it possible that such a life-altering destiny could occur because of one lonely, misplaced hair?

CHAPTER 19

The new house quickly became home, due to Mom's efficient homemaking instinct. This house had a large eat-in kitchen, a dining room, living room and music room on the first floor and four bedrooms upstairs. In this, as in all of our homes, part of its charm, aside from her ability to make each house cozy, came from the fact that Mom insisted on absolute cleanliness. She didn't achieve this look on her own, however, because she made sure we kids were present and involved in every bout of cleaning frenzy. She managed the platoon when it came time to man the brooms, mops and polishing rags.

One might have noticed, in my description of our house, the absence of a bathroom. Typical of this era, our "bathroom" could be found some thirty feet outside the house and was called by the charming name, "Outhouse." Of course, the outhouse was equipped with the mandatory, multi-purpose, Sears and Roebuck catalogue—used for reading, or for any other "necessary." Flowering bushes, of the large variety, surrounded the main house. They looked nice, but may have been planted for more than one purpose since they hid the outhouse from view.

It may not have been typical, but it did seem a necessity for us to have a music room in our home; necessary, because Maxine needed the room to practice, and also because Mother gave piano lessons at home. Mom, an accomplished musician, was the pianist for many occasions in and around our community.

Who could forget the march she played (probably a bazillion times) as a member, and official musician of the Royal Neighbors Club. The ladies wore matching white uniforms and white caps, and at the first chord of Mother's music they would all jump to their feet and march round the large hall in perfect time until the music ended in a rousing crescendo. The melody she played, entitled *"Rustic Dance,"* by C.R. Howell, will live in my head, possibly even into eternity. This lively piece was always the first order of business on the agenda.

Aside from the spirited music Mom played for the group, and the riveting sight of the ladies marching around the room in perfect cadence, my trips with Mom to any of their meetings was completely underwhelming. Again, there was nothing for me to do but sit and be quiet as the ladies conducted one of the dullest and most uninteresting business meetings in the annals of recorded history.

Perhaps it was the treats at the end of the meeting that helped me to endure the anguish of my mega-boredom. Why Mother insisted on taking me along eludes me. Perhaps her only other alternative was to leave me home alone.

Mother taught Maxine to play the piano. In our home there were piano lessons, piano practice, or some form of musical distraction, incessantly. We ate, worked, and slept to piano music. Mom gave me piano lessons too, and I felt my lessons were going along rather well until the day she dropped the bomb that she would no longer be my teacher, and my sister would be taking over that duty.

I loved my sister, but the idea of taking lessons from her was like getting booted off a moving train. I did not want to lose Mother as my teacher. What have I done to deserve this, I remember thinking, and here I was doing so well. She must have either become discouraged with my progress, or had just grown weary with struggling with me, I reasoned. Or, she may have felt that Maxine was now accomplished enough to take over this chore.

My zeal for learning the piano seemed to flag from the day Mother dismissed me as her student. Maxine and I never seemed to click as teacher and student, and the lessons gradually dwindled off until they stopped completely. As a result, I have been left with a great void in my life resulting from my truncated education in piano training, the lack of which still distresses me greatly, particularly while sitting at the piano.

While Maxine's talent soared, her musical ability was given a higher priority in our home, greatly overshadowing my own thwarted effort at the keyboard. One reward of being dropped as a piano student, I suppose, meant that I no longer had to practice, for which I probably thanked my sister, at the time. We were all proud of Maxine. Her talent was recognized throughout our town, and she was chosen to play for many of our school and community activities. Maxine spent a great deal of time practicing, that being my most enduring memory of my sister during our growing-up years.

Since she was six years older than I, and very mature for her age, Maxine and Mother were far more companionable than my sister and I in our younger years. That early bond forged between Maxine and Mother, remained constant throughout their lives. However, as we sisters grew older, married, and had children, we too became even closer friends.

The things Maxine and I did together, as children, are not as clear to me as the relationship that existed between Maurice and me. This can probably be explained by the fact that both Maurice and I were more play-oriented, while Maxine was studious and serious.

Because of that six-year age difference between us, she probably saw me as a nuisance more often than not. Occasionally, mom would urge Maxine to take me with her as she was leaving the house, and just as often she would ask Mom, "Does she always have to tag along?" Even so, I loved being with her and was always excited by those times when she gave in and allowed me to come along, particularly when she was meeting her friend, Hoveta Lyons. Their conversation was always far more grown-up and interesting, and sometimes I even got to hear them talking about boys.

As Maxine progressed on the piano, Mother felt it was necessary to find her a more advanced teacher. Her new teacher was impressive. Her name was Mrs. Crosswaite, a talented and beautiful lady of color, whose husband was an executive at the Dunham Corporation in Marshalltown. She reminded us of a young Lena Horne.

Surprisingly, Maxine occasionally allowed me—I assume at Mother's forceful urging—to come along when she went to Marshalltown for her piano lesson. While the trip to Marshalltown was always exciting, sitting in Mrs. Crosswaite's pristine living room with nothing to do but wait while Maxine received her lesson, on the impressive grand piano that sat so imposingly in their home, became the ultimate challenge to my ability to remain absolutely quiet. Looking back, it seems there were many of these moments in my young life. Once again, the urge to fidget became like an itch screaming to be scratched.

Looking around, trying to distract myself from the dreadful tedium of simply waiting and listening, I once picked up a magazine from the rack next to the chair I was given to sit in, and started turning the pages so quietly that I was sure no one could possibly hear me. By simply turning those pages I had unknowingly disobeyed Mrs. Crosswaite's ironclad rule that there be absolute silence in the room when she was giving a piano lesson.

The result of committing this unspeakable deed was the stern look I received from Mrs. C, which was as caustic as any spoken reprimand could be. Wishing, at that point, to be anywhere else but here, it would be a pretty good guess Mrs. Crosswaite shared my feelings. I now wonder how she really felt when Maxine arrived for a lesson, to find me standing on the doorstep too? Mrs. Crosswaite's demeanor was always most cordial, but she tolerated no interference, noise, or distraction during the course of a piano lesson.

Her striking appearance quickly attracted one's attention, not only because of the beauty and poise she possessed, but also for the easy grace of her movements. We often compared her elegance to the most glamorous movie stars of that day, but her style was more subtle, serene and quiet. It seemed heady stuff to be in her presence. She had taken a particular interest in Maxine, because of her talent, and over time, saw to it that Maxine competed in competitions as far away as the University in Iowa City. Because of this close connection with Maxine, our family formed a fast friendship with both Mr. and Mrs. Crosswaite. They were charming and friendly people.

Whether it was Maxine or Mom's idea, it was decided to invite the Crosswaites for dinner one night as part of a celebration for some honor Maxine had won on the piano. While I was totally excited at the prospect, a surprising question seemed to form somewhere in the recesses of my youthful mind as to how these people might be received in our small WASP community if folks knew they were coming. The Crosswaites were black and everyone else in town was white.

I wasn't aware of it at the time, but this could have been viewed as a racist thought, although innocently inspired. It held no significance for me, I assume, since I had put it out of my mind almost as soon as I thought of it, replacing it with the more important plans for the party. It was totally forgotten in the dusting, scrubbing, and shining routine of making those plans happen. In truth, I was colossally proud of the fact that these prominent black people had accepted an invitation to come for dinner, particularly since they would have to drive all the way from their home in Marshalltown—at night.

The fact that I could entertain even the slightest question about the Crosswaite's visit should have been a good indicator that racism, in all of its ugliness, did exist. On some level, those of my generation must have had an awareness of it; but for me, it seemed remote, a foreign concept. The ramifications of the inhumane acts that were taking place in the country at large, while heart breaking, were apparently not brought into our home in any substantive way by my parents. This might very well have been a protective measure for their children, or an oversight viewed from the perspective of the times.

It should be remembered that worldwide news came to us in limited doses, either over our few radio news broadcasts, or from our provincial newspaper, the *Marshalltown Times Republican*. The feeding frenzy of media coverage, as we know it today, did not exist in the form to which we have become accustomed. From our rural position in the world of ideas and issues, racism and other global conflicts seemed light years away from our calm and stable, though isolated, existence.

We can shake our heads at these seeming naive and isolationist attitudes that may have existed in our area, in our generation, but for lack of a better definition or explanation, the truism "Out of sight, out of mind," seems to me a more applicable condemnation. Few, if any, black men, women, or children had ever set foot in our town. It's doubtful, also, that any of our townsfolk knew a black person personally, or even had the opportunity of meeting one. Not, as I choose to think, because it would have been an unwelcome concept, but because our tiny town offered precious little by way of economic opportunity, an important commodity necessary for attracting newcomers. Since our little berg was miles off the beaten path, it was highly unlikely that strangers would seek us out deliberately. Stumble upon us, perhaps.

When the Crosswaites accepted the invitation I was elated because I loved having company and was totally awestruck by Mrs. Crosswaite, in spite of my discomfort while at her home during piano lessons. Mom outdid herself that night preparing dinner. I must have checked my wardrobe at least a dozen times before choosing just the right thing to wear for this much-anticipated occasion.

The night of their visit finally came, and the Crosswaites arrived on time. Our entire family turned out to greet them on the front porch. Their warmth and charm captivated us all. From there we moved into the house for some lively pre-dinner conversation. Seated at dinner, the spirited talk continued in the same relaxed mood as it had from the moment of their arrival.

After dinner, Mrs. C. suggested that Maxine play the piano for us. After several numbers, Mr. Crosswaite urged his wife to play also; so she joined Maxine at the piano and the two of them began playing duets. Everyone got into the spirit as the two of them sat together on the piano bench, playing with complete enjoyment and a total lack of inhibitions. One duet led to another, then another—on and on into the evening. Watching the two of them at the keyboard, it wasn't hard to see they were having fun; which made it just as great fun for the rest of us.

Occasionally they would burst out laughing as one or the other would stumble over a note. No one wanted the music to stop, least of all Mr. Crosswaite. His face was set in a continual smile as he watched his wife; it was obvious that he was very much in love, and very proud of her. The girls, finally tired after the long concert, threw up their hands, signaling the end. Mr. Crosswaite commented about how happy it had made him just to sit and listen to his wife's playing. This was evidently a rare happening in their household—not unusual in a piano teacher's home. The time for them to leave came all too soon, and we reluctantly stood on the porch waving them off as they departed.

Another top-ranking occasion on my wonderful events list, was the unusual evening lawn party Verna Hauser, her husband, Howard, and their daughter Winifred, hosted on July 6, 1933, from 8:00 to 10:00 PM. (I still have the invitation.) What a thrill it was to be invited to this most glamorous event, the likes of which was not to be duplicated again in our town.

Our first indication of the lovely evening awaiting us, as we approached the Hauser home, was the location of the party. It had been set up on the lawn at the side of their house. The thing that first caught our attention was the lighting. The entire lawn had been festooned with Japanese lanterns that were hanging everywhere, a startling innovation at the time.

Most of the guests came on foot because they were town folks, but a number arrived by car from the country. As we walked to the Hauser house, the gentle darkness of late evening was beginning to fall. Mother had to constantly remind me to remember my ladylike manners and my party demeanor, for I wanted to run on ahead in my haste to get to the party. The softly glowing, colorful, lanterns, transformed the summer evening setting into a magical vision as they swayed in the gentle breeze, lending extra importance to this already thrilling occasion. I was thrilled to be going to such a special party.

Ladies, dressed in their finest summer voile, organdy, and silk gowns, children in their Sunday best, and men, properly attired, although undoubtedly uncomfortable in suits and neckties, mingled to socialize and partake of the delicacies set out on tables.

The gathering darkness carried sounds of soft voices and laughter over the stillness of a night seemingly made-to-order for this gala event. Milling around in dress clothing these normally hard-working men and women—usually overall-clad farmers and working people—rarely had occasion to attend a fancy party. But here they were. These same folks, who had shed the identifying trappings of their work-a-day worlds and donned their Sunday best, were indulging in an uncustomary, frivolous good time. They were at a party and it was pleasurable—they were among friends. Tomorrow would bring its ordinary work—later.

"Later" didn't find this young girl remembering anything ordinary the next day. Her thoughts were on every detail of the exciting party she'd been part of the night before.

CHAPTER 20

My father, as well as my mother, must have been responsible, in large part, for my own children's interest in music. When I was still a very young girl, Dad and a few other local musicians formed a band to play for community dances. They were held weekly in one of the vacant business buildings on Main Street. The dances were remarkably well attended, and jolly good fun, from Dad's reports.

Dad played the guitar and practicing for him often took the form of playing for us at home. After tightening the keys, listening carefully as he tuned the strings, he would begin playing such songs as, *She'll Be Cummin' Round The Mountain, If I Had The Wings of an Angel, When The Moon Comes Over The Mountain,* and others.

Dad had a soft way of caressing the strings of his guitar, which made his music very pleasurable to listen to. Those nights when he got out the guitar and began tightening the strings we knew that it was sing-along-time at home. With the first note, all of us would immediately take up the beat and sing along with enthusiasm, sometimes at the top of our lungs. We knew his full repertoire and could sing every word of each song by heart.

Ours was one of the fortunate homes that had a Victrola—perhaps that was because music was such a large part of our lives. Another evening's entertainment for us, after the dishes were done and we'd settled down for a quiet time, was putting a record on the machine. After carefully placing the record on the turntable, one of us would have to give the Victrola a good cranking so the turntable could start turning. Even that was part of our fun and we argued over who would get to do it.

There were those extremely rare evenings when Mom and Dad would drive to Eldora, some twelve or fifteen miles away (the site of my beloved Pine Lake) to run an errand or see a movie. We kids didn't feel altogether deprived when we weren't allowed to come along, because, after everyone had gone, Maurice and I would open up the lid of the Victrola, put on a record, crank it up, set the needle in place and listen to some great golden oldies. More often than not we chose to listen to the mellow voice of Kate Smith singing, *"When The Moon Comes Over The Mountain."* When silly moods overcame us we danced around, gesturing and pantomiming the words. These great songs were sometimes catchy and funny (like the ridiculous record, *"Quit your kiddin' Jack*) or dreamlike and romantic, but always soul satisfying. The best part of all, one could understand *all* of the words.

As a child I spent a good deal of time in the music room of our new house. Filling the room with big bowls of flowers, setting the stage for my glamorous, make-believe piano concerts, became a regular event for me on the days when the piano wasn't otherwise in use. It seems I was continually harboring some mistaken illusion of my keyboard prowess since I spent so many grand times playing the piano there.

Of course, these grandiose concerts were always given for an audience of one, unless you counted all of my dolls, and maybe Mom (if she hadn't escaped outside the house). But somehow, even this fantasy fun fulfilled a need of mine to be on stage, in a theatrical setting with an adoring audience (if even imaginary) who greatly appreciated my talent. I came to realize early on that this was never to become a reality, so I settled for dreaming and making believe. At least Mom always knew where I was.

The move into our new house made us neighbors to Bertha and Robie Prim, and their children Howard and Ruby, who lived across the street. This was the lady who told exciting stories to us kids on her front porch many evenings—the one who unintentionally, I'm sure, instilled in me this great fear of being buried alive. Even so, it seemed to be an evening ritual to congregate on their porch after dinner for more stories, and great games.

We always knew when Mrs. Prim's husband would be coming home from work at night (and sometimes we even watched for him). The sound of his honk as he reached the corner by our house, would send Mrs. Prim flying out their back door, running down the path to the barn where he kept his car. She always arrived in time to have the barn door standing open for Robie to drive right in.

Not only did Mr. Prim have his wife trained for his arrival, but us as well, it seems, for it never failed to attract our attention when we heard his horn blast signaling his wife. This announcement would send us scurrying to the window to watch the evening ritual, prompting many joshing comments like "Hey, Mrs. Prim made it in time!" We often conjectured about whether this was an act of love, or duty demanded.

Their son, Howard, was my age and we palled around in the summertime after we moved into that part of town. We liked to go exploring, which found us walking down the railroad tracks to the trestle, and climbing the big tree that stood in front of our house. It's a wonder there was any bark left on that tree from the many times we shinnied up its heights, stretching lazily out on its limbs, viewing the village scene from above. From up in the tree we could watch the clouds as they collided, meshed, and melded together, forming shifting images in the sky, while still being able to keep an eye on the comings and goings of any unsuspecting traffic below. Hanging from the tree limbs gave us the necessary dreaming time to hatch up more fantastic plans for future expeditions.

My farm cousins were great pals who made visits to their farm energetic and fun. My cousin Max Appel and I were born two days apart. The circumstances, surrounding that particular incident, have long been a happier part of the family tradition.

The day Max was born, January 25th, my Aunt Louise, his mother, sent Mom and Dad a letter announcing the news that she had just had a little boy. The day my folks got the letter, January 27th, I was born, a fact that is giggled about regularly by Max and I.

One of our favorite places to visit on Sunday, when we were kids, was my Aunt Louise and Uncle Cordie Appel's farm. From the minute Dad turned the car into their driveway, the car doors were flying open spilling out kids. After some quick hugs for the grownups, we cousins were off and running—any place out of sight of the adults.

Carrol, Max and Raymond, my cousins, had ingeniously scraped a roadway among the trees in the huge grove behind their house, probably with their dad's help. This eighth wonder of the world was a thing of pure sheer joy as we drove our wagons, scooters and trikes in, out, around, and among the trees. After we'd "burned up the road" for a while, it was necessary to drive our conveyances to a spot where weary travelers could park and have a treat—although the treat was usually imaginary since we didn't want to risk going to the house for something to eat, and be tagged for some chore.

Uncle Cordie, had conveniently cut a few of the trees to chair height (and some of these chairs even had built-in backs) so we drivers could find a comfortable place to sit when we got out of our vehicles to stretch our legs, or to park before heading to the house for a meal. There seemed to be no end to their ingenuity, and we played there until we dropped or were forced to leave for home, whichever came first. Again, it was an unsightly set of disheveled, grimy kids our parents took home with them after these arduous visits.

I was often invited to spend a week on the farm; but due to my chronic homesickness I couldn't agree to stay without my sister or brother. To appease me, since Cousin Carrol always wanted me to stay, Aunt Louise would also invite either Maxine or Maurice, or sometimes both of them.

A daily event on the farm was chore time, happening both morning and night. It was Carrol's job to feed the chickens and geese; the look and smell of the feed she mixed up couldn't go unnoticed. Into huge buckets of sour milk Carrol ladled big scoops of dry meal that she mixed with her bare hands submerged to the elbows. While messy, the results produced an almost edible-looking mixture called mash, which was fed to the chickens. I even liked the smell of the stuff. When the buckets were fully mixed she took one bucket in each hand and staggered off to the feeding troughs. That was an amazing feat, because, try as I would, it was impossible for me to pick up even one pail with both hands. I was more than impressed by her strength.

Carrol was often assigned the job of "shepherd," which meant she tended their cows along the country roads as they grazed in the ditches in search of greener grass. Of course she insisted that I come along with her on these grazing forays, which I always wanted to do because the two of us were bosom buddies and these expeditions were unusual and fun. Then too, I knew it would be more fun lazily meandering along the roadside with Carrol than it would be if I'd stayed behind and ran the risk being assigned some inside household chores.

As the days grew hotter, she stopped us at certain designated places along the road. Going to a secret hiding place, Carrol would find a little tool she'd hidden there and begin digging. Deeper and deeper she dug until she uncovered her treasure. The treasure was a buried box containing a fruit jar full of very cold water; the principle being that the deeper she buried her little "refrigerator" in the ground the colder it remained. It worked! I was in total awe of this clever *invention* and came to the conclusion that country kids had more fun, at least they were stronger and smarter.

Carrol and I were given the job of driving the hay wagon one summer while the farmers cut hay at the farm. Carrol was used to driving a team of horses, but riding on a hay wagon was new to me. We stood up front—just inside the large hay wagon directly behind the horses—while she drove the team and wagon slowly along so the men could begin filling it with freshly cut hay. As we moved slowly down the field, making pass after pass, the men, using pitchforks, gathered up the loose hay and tossed it onto the wagon.

By the time the wagon started filling up we were already sweltering under the blistering summer sun. Appearing to be as loaded as I thought the wagon could possibly get, I falsely assumed we would be heading back to the barn about then. But the men kept tossing more hay onto the wagon until it reached a point more than twice as high as our heads. Then they tossed in some more. The stack got so high we had to lean forward, out over the horses as far as we could stretch, to keep our heads free enough from the hay to be able to breathe.

The odor of the hay, by then, had become so overpowering I was convinced that if the heat didn't get me I would certainly choke to death from the seemingly lethal fumes of the toxic-smelling hay. Wrestling with that unnerving thought brought on a near a panic attack, telling me that I either needed to bail out, or stay with it, in which case I wouldn't last long enough to get back to the barn.

It's been said that the odor of fresh-cut hay is comparable to the smell of Phosgene Gas; an agent designed and used for chemical warfare. I found the smell of the hay to be so smothering, so intense and objectionable that I wanted to bolt the wagon and run back to the house. But I wasn't about to admit that I couldn't take as much as Carrol, so I stuck to the bitter end.

About the time I was absolutely certain we were in real danger of being asphyxiated, Carrol thankfully turned the horses around and we headed for the barn. Once there, thoroughly bushed and gasping for fresh air, I promptly bailed out. I tried to make my exit off the wagon appear as casual as possible in an effort to keep my honor and reputation in tact. I had no intention of being teased about that forever.

Never have I experienced nights so still and quiet as the nights at Aunt Louise's farm. I refer to it as Aunt Louise's farm as I scarcely remember Uncle Cordie, who died at the young age of forty. Aunt Louise, with my oldest cousin Raymond, continued to work the farm, with the help of the other two.

It was so quiet there in the country at night that I found it a tremendous relief to hear an occasional hoot owl hooting, or a dog barking somewhere in the distance. It was hard to admit to everyone that the oppressive stillness upset me, so I gamely suffered in silence through the long, dark nights, waiting and praying for the sun to come up. For that reason alone, I was always glad when it came time to head home where things sounded normal at night. But while I was happy to leave the intimidating quietness of the farm, it was hard to leave my cousins and the unusual super fun we had.

CHAPTER 21

My occasional overnights at Grandma and Grandpa Mann's farm, at Laurel, gave me the chance to play with my cousin Bob Ward. He lived in Laurel with his parents, and when we came to visit, his parents usually brought him out to spend time with us.

The two of us were approximately the same age. Typical of our routine while on the farm, one lazy summer day found us stretched out on the sprawling green lawn under the shade of a giant oak tree. We were reveling in the sheer delight of being alive, luxuriating in the satisfying fact of having nothing to do but enjoy each other's company for the entire day. But kids can remain inert and passive for only so long before they become restless and begin mentally sorting through their options of really keen and "neat-o" things to do.

It was Bob who came up with this daring and risky, but totally fantastic, idea. He assured me that he'd pulled it off before without getting caught, so it didn't take much convincing to get me to agree to the scheme. With plan in mind, we two eagerly motivated conspirators jumped up from the ground and immediately began putting our plan of attack into action.

After collecting the necessary equipment, we walked down the road a bit until we came to a culvert—a large round cement tube that formed a tunnel under the road to drain off excess rain water from the fields and ditches. Bob had borrowed one of Grandma's old purses to which he attached a long cord to the handle. Laying the purse in the middle of the road, the two of us then worked feverishly covering the cord with gravel The cord, now out of sight, reached from the purse, lying in the middle of the road, to the culvert, where we had gone into hiding.

The purpose of the game was to stop an unsuspecting driver, who had thought he'd seen a purse lying in the road, only to find, after he had gotten out of his car, that there was no purse (because we had jerked it back into the culvert). It was expected that his reaction would be to merely scratch his head, get back into the car and go on his way.

Since there were so few automobiles in existence those days, we had quite a wait for our intended victim to come along. Although the mid-day sun was relentlessly beating down on the gravel road, the two of us sat rather comfortably, loafing away the time in the cool of the shady culvert, chattering and wishing our prey would hurry and come along.

Suddenly we were alerted to the sound of an approaching car far off in the distance, tearing down the road heading our way. We immediately jumped up, peering down the road from our hidden vantage point, nervously anticipating the thrill of finally getting some action—and at last capturing our target in our nefarious trap.

As the car sped past the purse we groaned with disappointment at not having caught our quarry after all the hard work of our preparation. Within seconds, however, the driver jammed on his brakes, coming to a screeching halt that sent gravel flying in a colossal cloud of dust.

Before the driver was even out of the car, of course, the two of us had begun frantically yanking and pulling the cord until we'd drug the purse back into the culvert, a move that left our surprised-looking target wondering if he had seen an apparition. Bob had earlier taken extraordinary pains to convince me that that would be the end of it; but on this day it appeared that our intended target's attitude did not support Bob's optimistically reassuring theory.

Crouching nervously in the culvert, trying as hard as possible to appear invisible, we suddenly felt the man's presence, having seen his shadow falling over the ditch beside us. Sheepishly looking up from our embarrassed, squatting positions, we beheld a very agitated and burly, but well dressed and official-looking man towering over us, his white-knuckled hands firmly gripping his hips.

Contrary to what we had thought was a foolproof scheme, he'd been keen enough to follow the cord-drawn path of the purse to the culvert. Having no place to hide, we were caught dead to rights. From his towering position over us, the red-faced man loomed ferociously large and frightening, breathing nasty threats, promising to contact our parents, the police, the truant officers, and probably the Army, Navy and the Marines. We squirmed with fright.

Further threats of jail, shouted angrily at us, were lost in the wind as we raced through the weed-choked ditch with pounding hearts, back to the safety of Grandma's arms. Expecting to see the car come turning into the driveway at any moment, with its occupant breathing fire, we stayed inside, nervously watching the road. He didn't come to the house. As far as we knew there were no repercussions from our misbegotten little escapade; in retrospect, it would seem the man only intended to scare the daylights out of us, and he succeeded! He undoubtedly went chuckling down the road, anxious to spin this yarn to his friends. This wild adventure, however, successfully ended my life of crime in that realm.

Bob's mother, my Aunt Mayme, was an artist and I loved going to her home because it was filled with her own interesting paintings, and her collection of delicately hand-painted china. She was a gentle, sweet woman, the epitome of graciousness.

Aunt Mayme and Cousin Bob Ward
my co-conspirator on the "road job."

Aunt Mayme usually had some little snack waiting for us when Bob and I came into town after our afternoons at the farm.

One could almost imagine stepping back in time, to the days of genteel southern ladies, when one entered the warmth of her home. She spoke in a soft voice, and her loving tone assured me that she was delighted to have me there. There were many interesting things to see in her house. I believe her artistic ability somehow found its way into my genes, and any skills I now possess as an artist, I credit in large part to her, second to God.

My aunt Ida Williams, Dad's younger sister, was a great storyteller. It was through her that I learned what happened to my Dad's career as a veterinarian. Through tears of laughter she gave me a detailed explanation about how Dad, and their cousin, Homer Bill, had decided to pursue careers as veterinarians. Both of the boys enrolled at a college in Missouri. Dad and Homer Bill were enjoying their time in college immensely, did well in their studies, and things were looking very promising for their new careers.

Their time in school was flourishing until the night they decided things needed a little livening up. This didn't surprise me, knowing of my Dad's restless nature and the ever-present need for action that stirred in both of these farm lads. Ida didn't have a clue about whose idea it had been, but she knew they were in it together.

Dad and Homer Bill had gone to the animal barns where they found a Billy goat. What followed wasn't a question of being tempted into doing this act—it was intentional. They led the goat into the dormitory and managed to smuggle him into their room. This outrageous accomplishment made an immediate hit with their fellow students. They were enormously rewarded for their reckless, daring deed by the wild cheers and applause of all their dorm mates. From that point, bedlam broke loose. Unfortunately, the prank did nothing favorable for the dispositions of the "powers that be" of the college when they found out about it.

The boys were promptly expelled from school. How unfortunate for them, because this "knee-jerk" reaction would scarcely have drawn a comment today. In fact, one day as I was watching a news broadcast on TV, announcing the death of Steve Allen, it was reported that he was responsible for placing a goat on top of the roof of one of the buildings of the Drake University campus in Des Moines, when he attended there. He denied it, of course, but the incident evidently happened. I immediately thought of my poor, luckless Dad. In his day this practical joke was viewed as a felonious high crime.

Getting expelled from school was bad enough, but it was made all the more alarming because neither of them had money enough to pay for transportation home. From Aunt Ida's boisterously rousing details, it's probably safe to assume that regardless of their alarming state of "pennilessness" they didn't contact either set of parents for traveling money. Given their pauper status it was impossible for them to return home immediately, which may have been a good thing. It's possible they were even grateful for the few extra days this gave them to keep their shameful exploits hidden from disapproving parents, at least temporarily.

There was nothing left to do but start walking and hitchhiking, which was exactly what they did for the better part of the trip home. Aunt Ida nearly collapsed with laughter remembering the story, which I'm sure was funny to almost no one else concerned at the time. To me this sounded suspiciously like the reaction of a kid sister thoroughly enjoying the disastrous predicament and embarrassment of an older brother.

How their parents received the truants was left out of the account. We had never heard about the incident from anyone else in the family, least of all, Dad. Later it was impossible to get more information from him since the story was relayed to me only after his death, and the deaths of everyone else directly involved.

Many of Aunt Ida's riotous stories were told about herself; like the time grandpa R.E.L. had sent her into Laurel for some lumber he needed for the project he was working on. By today's standards, Aunt Ida would have been considered a "women's libber," for she insisted on learning to drive her dad's new Model-T Ford as soon as he drove it home—at a time when almost no other "ladylike" women drove.

Grandpa owned the first automobile in Marshall County, and at that time, few women would have been brave enough to defy convention by daring such a thing as driving a car. With her high spirits, though, she didn't give a fig what others thought about her taking the wheel.

Therefore, having only recently mastered the rudimentary elements of driving, she happily took off in the new car and headed for Laurel to pick up the lumber. The men at the lumberyard, having been equally blessed with little or no experience loading lumber onto a car, decided to place the boards through the open back door windows so that the boards projected out both sides of the car.

Once the car was loaded, Ida began driving down the gravel country road toward home. Driving was pure ecstasy for Ida because it gave her this great new sense of freedom, a fact that totally appealed to her fiercely independent nature. Knowing my aunt for the free spirit she was, it would not be inconceivable to imagine she'd been pushing the foot-pedal to the floorboard, or (in the vernacular of our day "putting the pedal to the metal") moving along as fast as the car could possibly go.

Somewhere between Laurel and the farm, Ida came to a bridge. Flying along, feeling supremely invincible, oblivious to any impending disaster, she headed into the bridge with characteristic coolness and self-confidence. Her description of what happened next, through her many recitations to an ever-appreciative audience, never ceased to double the listener over into fits of laughter.

Of course it's easy to guess that the lumber caught on each side of the bridge and stopped the car dead in its tracks. Her recall of the horrendous jolt, and the neck-snapping whiplash that ensued were second only to the wild thoughts that flashed through her head (damage to the car, her dad's reaction, etc.). Her skillfully phrased description of this preposterous event was hilarious. It still amuses me to mentally visualize the ludicrous scene this catastrophe must have created that day, as well as recalling her delight in telling it. Fortunately she suffered no injuries, and neither did the car. Anyone hearing her tell the story for the first time would laugh until the tears flowed, including Ida.

As I think about my dad's sisters and brother, it would have to be assumed that the same daring blood coursing through Aunt Ida's veins also ran through my dad's. Aunt Mayme and Uncle Claude, on the other hand, were calm, quiet, and gentle, the reverse of their younger siblings in nature. Neither had probably caused Grandma and Grandpa a moment's worry, as opposed to Dad and Ida who probably made up for the other two.

L to R: Uncle Claude Mann, quiet and dignified; Aunt Ida, strong-willed and "fun"...the gal who loved to drive the car; Aunt Mayme Ward, quiet, gentle, artistic; LeRoy Thomas Mann, the cut-up, my Dad

Aunt Ida's next major thrilling encounter with the subtleties of driving involved a little excursion she took to visit her sister Mayme, who was by then married and living a good many miles from the family farm. The weather had not looked promising that day, and Grandma Hannah had warned Ida against making the trip. However, this iron-willed, highly motivated, and, at times, overly-confident young woman, took no heed of the warning. She wanted to go—and go she went.

Even though the weather had turned threatening during her visit, Ida lingered, staying as long as it pleased her for most of the day. She simply took no notice of the snow beginning to fall—undoubtedly because of her inexperience with driving in snow. Eventually, she was faced with the reality of having to drive home, alone, and it was getting darker. But she was fearless and had no doubt that she would be able to make the trip easily.

After many "goodbyes," and much vigorous cranking of the car (that's the way we started our cars back then—we cranked them) to get it started, she jumped in, ready to leave. With the side curtains snapped tightly shut, to keep out the freezing wind, she started off.

That trip home, down roads that were fast becoming snow-clogged, had suddenly became a force with which she now had to reckon.

Suddenly, now painfully aware of the looming dangers that lay ahead, the chilling realization brought skin-prickly, panicky warning sensations that began to warm her most uncomfortably beneath her heavy coat. The car was slipping, sliding, and lunging through drifts of snow that were growing alarmingly deeper, and she realized just how treacherous the road she was traveling had become. Finally that sturdy car, which had been so valiantly trying to keep moving against the odds of a road that was too deep with snow, gave up the battle and stopped. She was stuck! No doubt about it!

Sensibly realizing the pointlessness of panic, since she was too far from help in either direction, she was soon forced to accept the fact that her only salvation for rescue rested in her own ingenuity and perseverance. Grandpa had fortuitously placed a shovel in the back seat of the car and so she began the seemingly impossible job of shoveling two paths, one in front of each tire.

Following this pattern, she shoveled for a distance, re-started the car, got back in and drove forward until it could go no further. This process was repeated over and over until, hours later, by some unbelievably marvelous feat of strength, and sheer, persistent willpower, she got herself and the car home. Fear, in this case, was obviously far more than an exceptional motivator—it had become her life preserver.

I learned a new respect for my aunt as I sat listening to this new story. Realistically, how many men would have been equal to that task? (I'm guessing a man would have just given up and tried to walk home.) But her determination to conquer the gargantuan roadblock that stood between her and the safety of home, for a girl of her inclination, stemmed not only from her fear of freezing to death, but also from her anxious need to avoid any lecture about the foolishness of her trip, or, worst of all, being grounded from future driving.

It's difficult to imagine that many women in the world today would even try, or could manage such a Herculean effort. Three cheers for Aunt Ida! In defense of females everywhere, however, it's pretty certain that most women wouldn't have insisted on making the foolhardy trip in the first place, having been warned by "Mom" not to go.

Be that as it may, a word of praise, here, must now be included proclaiming the excellence, endurance, vigor, strength and reliability of the Model-T Ford. The many glorified stories told about the stalwart exploits of this dependable and reliable old "workhorse" of the automotive industry, give proof that it has unquestionably earned its impeccable automotive reputation.

Aunt Ida loved to snitch on my dad, especially on those occasions when he had been guilty of teasing his younger sister. It seems he once carried her to the roof of a shed where he left her stranded, bloomers caught on a nail, wailing and screaming for help. He must have been the proverbial "terrible tease," and gotten into trouble with my grandparents more than a little. It's a good thing his kids didn't learn of his antics until they were grown. By then it was only the cause of laughter, and not an enticement to go and do likewise. How I appreciate her wonderful stories of my dad as he was when a kid.

As he grew older, Dad met my Aunt Pauline, Mother's twin sister, and he asked to date her. Then he met Mom! She evidently must have made his heart beat a bit faster, bringing more of a twinkle to his eyes. I don't know how he managed to gracefully make the transition from Pauline to Alvina, but it happened. I have often wondered how Aunt Pauline felt by my dad's change of heart. Although they looked quite a bit alike he must have sensed some uniquely different qualities between the two girls—one of the hazards of being a twin I would guess. Obviously Aunt Pauline survived the disappointment, for she and Mom remained devoted sisters.

The twins lived on a farm near Melbourne-Baxter, which meant a trip of at least twenty miles by horse and buggy for Dad to "come-a-courtin'." Dad obviously didn't consider it a great inconvenience to make the long trip. I can picture him now, dressed in a suit and tie, with high stiff collar, in a shiny buggy with a high-stepping horse prancing down the road, calling on his "gal." Mom never mentioned the nature of their dates, but once talked about the Chautauquas she'd attended. Whatever their form of entertainment, it would seem that they found a way to enjoy each other's company doing the things young couples found to do in that era, for love flourished.

CHAPTER 22

We're often reminded that nothing stays the same, a truism of which I am all too aware after recently hearing my granddaughter, Kristen, talking about her Family Consumer Science Class. In my school days, this class was called Home Economics, or Home Ec.

As we discussed her assignments, I became more acutely aware of the proliferation of technical cooking skills separating her world from mine. Cooking, however, regardless of the terminology and the technology, will probably always require a certain amount of hands-on, labor-intensive preparation in order to produce something edible. That fact will undoubtedly remain unchanged unless in some far distant, future galaxy they invent a way to circumvent this step.

In my first Home Economics cooking class at school we were given the assignment of making salmon croquettes. For all I knew at the time, a croquette could have been something you played on the lawn. I learned in a hurry about croquettes and what it meant to create something with a class.

Under the teacher's intimidating and close supervision, we thoroughly studied the recipe. The instructions told us to roll soda crackers into crumbs, assemble and mix the rest of the ingredients: salmon, eggs, flour, etc., which we were then to hand-form into small shapes resembling cones. That was probably the most fun part of the exercise for me.

After a good deal of smirking about the shapes our croquettes had taken, they were then dipped into the beaten eggs, rolled in the cracker crumbs, and after all of that, deep-fried in hot oil. Our first effort reminds me of the old proverb, "A camel is a horse made by a committee." I remember thinking, at the time, that if cooking in general, and salmon croquettes in particular, took this much time and planning to execute, I was never going to make my living as a chef.

What a slow and mind-numbing, orderly procedure was required for cooking, I thought. Who could possibly want to put up with this tiresome routine was my final judgment of the culinary arts process. Each step had to be performed precisely, according to the teacher's instruction, and every student was required to take part in the assembling of this dubious project. Needless to say, our cooking experiment consumed the entire class period. Surprisingly, the croquettes turned out pretty well, and even tasted good. Now, after years of honing my culinary skills—as a "pinch of this" and a "little of that," type cook—my sympathies still lie with the students. Incidentally, I have never made salmon croquettes, at least not in that form, again.

Because we got to use the sewing machines, the prospect of sewing class promised to be a bit more rewarding. However, the class size and the shortage of machines made it necessary for us to wait to use a machine until a classmate had finished her daily project. (Notice the single gender reference, there were no boys in this class.) This meant, for the rest of the time we were to busy ourselves with pinning, cutting and construction.

Again, cutting out the pattern had to be done in precise order, which for me again proved tedious and monotonous, being the hyper-energetic girl who always wanted to go faster than the teacher. Pinning and basting became twin nightmares of frustration that spoiled my classroom expectations, turning what could have been a gratifying time into a semester-long sentence.

My first project was a pinafore, which proved to be another drawn out task that took the entire semester. It can probably be quite accurately assumed that every bad sewing habit I now possess, beginning with wanting to take every shortcut possible, can be traced back to the unrelenting regimen forced upon us by our teacher. *Note: By my very nature, which today would undoubtedly be described as a Type-A personality, coupled with a possible impulsive persona, I am now an official, card-carrying member of the "sew-first, then rip-out-seams," or "cut in haste, regret in leisure," or, "measure once, cut twice " school of seamstressing.

Mother had taught me to sew at an early age, and it wasn't long before I insisted on doing everything myself, *(see previous note). Golly, I must have been an impossible child. (I'm much more wonderful now!) Mother, who was a beautiful seamstress, was much in demand to sew for the ladies with lesser skill in our town.

Mrs. Hauser was one of her regular clients, as well as several of the teachers in our school. How vividly one particularly length of silver lame', brought to Mom by one of our young schoolteachers, stands out in my mind. The teacher had wanted her to make it into an evening blouse to be worn over a long black velvet skirt--very chic in those days—and, it should be noted, very much in vogue again. It was exquisite.

Another wonderful piece of navy blue semi-sheer fabric, printed with tulips, was a particular favorite of mine. Mrs. Hauser had brought that piece to Mom to make into a summer dress. I had never seen a more exquisite piece of fabric, including the silver lame'. I'm not able to account for the reason why this particular piece of material appealed to me so much, but it did. Any print resembling that dress today takes me back to my mother's sewing room, and I find myself wishing I could find this exact piece of fabric again in some store.

It was actually some of mother's beautiful leftover scraps that got my sewing career underway. Making dresses for my dolls, with the barest minimum of input from Mom, became my rather deep-seated passion. I designed, cut, fit and sewed these creations at warp speed. It was only when my frustration level over a problem had risen to industrial strength anger, that I would stomp into the room where Mother was working and ask for her help. According to me, I didn't need anybody else's advice! Had I gone to her for more of that advice, it's entirely possible that my skill as a seamstress would have improved a lot faster, saving myself many exasperating and costly failures.

Mom's sewing was beautifully precise and efficient, and always professional-looking. She didn't mind working for days on a dress, basting, pressing and carefully measuring (the things I abhor). I, on the other hand, had to complete most of the garment the same day it was started, a requirement I still find necessary on the rare occasions that I actually sew a garment.

Working too long on any piece usually insured my losing interest in it and took the fun out of making it. But then, I guess I didn't really think of sewing as being exactly fun, because, for me, it was merely a means to an end—a necessary task to be tolerated in order to turn out something "really great" for me, or my dolls to wear.

Lest one begins, here, to get a picture of the author as some sort of impossible, crazy, impatient, impulsive, ole' ding-bat, let me hasten to add that with age has come far greater wisdom than I possessed in those long gone days of my youth. Back then I was most always in too much of a hurry, and far too self-sufficient to ask for, or accept anyone else's help. But without apology, I still lay claim to the right to be impossible, impulsive and impatient—but never crazy, and certainly not a ding-bat.

One of my first *spectacular* doll dress creations was an ice-skating costume made of stiff navy blue satin trimmed with white cotton to resemble white mink. I sewed the rows of "mink" to the bottom of the short skirt, around the wrists and neck of the costume, and even made a hat for her head. How proud I was of my grand design; I thought it was brilliant. I made many other pieces of doll clothing, but the skating costume is the most memorable.

My inspiration for the skating outfit undoubtedly came from the costumes of ice-skating movie star, Sonja Henie. We were awestruck by her movies that featured her Olympic-winning skating style, the likes of which we'd never before witnessed. If we hadn't seen it with our own eyes it would have been hard to believe that this young lady could spin and twirl and make the astonishing moves on the ice that she did.

Her skating was spectacular, and her expertise on the ice undoubtedly blazed the trail for all of the unbelievable performances we are seeing in today's skating stars. She had the power to completely mesmerize all of us who were sitting in the majestic and darkened Grand Theater in Eldora, watching this doll-like creature skate like an angel.

Aside from her skating, the dazzling costumes she wore were the things that interested me the most. With each new movie my full attention was given to mentally filing away every detail of every costume. I never wanted these movies to end. It follows, then, that my next ambition would be to become the same kind of divine ice skater as Sonja.

Like the brilliant piano career I had so mistakenly envisioned for myself, ice skating fame would also elude my grasp. I'd like to think that quite possibly a small part of that failure could be attributed to the clamp-on skates we had to wear, as opposed to the custom-fitted, spectacular white shoe skates on Miss Henie's tiny feet. With the completion of each of my doll's costumes, however, I could immediately imagine my brilliant, skating-star idol (or even myself) wearing my creation. Sonja became the mental mannequin for most of the costumes I designed from then on.

Movies, as I've indicated, were a rare commodity when we were young. We didn't have movies in Whitten; but several times, while visiting my Aunt Anna and Uncle Gus Osterhagen in Melbourne, Iowa, on a summer's day, an enterprising young movie operator happened to be in town. He had rigged up a movie screen from a large sheet that he'd hung among the trees in the park. Backless benches were set up in rows for the audience. After dark, when the townspeople had gathered, purchased their tickets and were seated, the projectionist started the movie. Once the movie began, we lost all conscious recognition of the fact that we were sitting outside in the dark, on hard park benches, watching a sheet. Rather, we'd become as absorbed in the movie as if we were viewing it in a beautifully comfortable theater. However, this audience undoubtedly went home with more than an evening's entertainment—most likely some colossal mosquito bites as well.

The movies that we watched in the park were usually of the spooky kind; often featuring Zazu Pitts, a damsel who seemed forever, to be in distress. One of the scariest and most memorable scenes for me was a time Miss Pitts went up into a dark, haunted attic where she stepped into a bucket of tar. Now how logical is that—first, that she'd be in a haunted attic by herself, and that she'd just happen to step into a bucket of soft tar? It could only happen in the movies!

However, unbeknownst to her, also stuck in the bucket of tar was the foot of a skeleton. Every time Zazu took a step, the skeleton just naturally followed close behind. The eerie dark setting of the park, the spooky attic, and the shadowy movements of the actors on screen, including the backward glances of the "google-eyed" heroine when she finally realized that a skeleton was following her, brought screams not only from Zazu, but also from most of those of us in the audience as well.

In addition to that movie we also got to see our heroine tied to the proverbial train tracks—terrorized, waiting for the hero to come and rescue her. There were the predictable boos and hisses directed at the villains by nearly everyone in the audience. We really "got into" the movies back then; the experience was new and exciting, and they were thrilling. You knew you'd had an experience when the movie was over. Now I'll bet my young readers are jealous of the unusual fun we had. How many movies has any one of them ever seen in a park? At the time, it was a great way—if not our only way—of seeing them. Later on, as movies became a bit more sophisticated, we too were happy for the luxury of sitting on cushy seats in our movie theaters, although we saw precious few of them.

The year I turned fourteen, our family was involved in a third move. Dad decided to open a grocery store in an empty building on Main Street, between the creamery, owned by Enos Fouts, and the barbershop where Roy Eggleston gave the traditional shave and a haircut. The only other store carrying groceries in town was Charley Long's Drug Store, which stocked a limited inventory, if you didn't count Fred and Martha Long's tiny café and gas station that handled a few snack items.

On the second floor of our projected store was an empty apartment, and Dad thought it made economic sense for us to move in. It was a hard job, but we made the move into the apartment even while moving into and stocking the store. It was probably the only "high rise" apartment in town. While it was comfortable enough and not too unattractive inside, I was never quite sure whether I was embarrassed or happy about it. After all, no one else lived in such a strange place as a second floor apartment.

Dad equipped and stocked the store very well. His ongoing pride was the fact that we sold Hadley Ice Cream, which came from Ackley, Iowa (almost a sister city to Faulkner, that wide place in the road--my birthplace). We bought a great deal of Hadley Ice Cream because we sold a lot of it, probably due to the fact that we hand-packed the containers ourselves, and gave people more than their money's worth. We, on the other hand, undoubtedly lost money on every sale because of the generous servings.

Since the few other businesses in town had been established for many years when Dad opened the store, and given the size of the town, it was tough going for us to compete for quite some time. Dad often chaffed over the fact that a large number of customers shopped with us when they were out of money and could charge their purchases at our store. Collecting these accounts was not easy during these depression years, and Dad sometimes lost money owed to him.

To enhance sales, Dad and Maurice developed the novel idea of starting a grocery route to serve the folks living in the country. Being the imaginative and innovative guys they were, they managed to come up with a panel truck and outfitted it with staples: bread, sugar, flour, canned goods, etc.

Maurice, the designated route-driver, started combing the back roads and country lanes, canvassing all of the farm homes with his stock of groceries. This was quite an enterprising and visionary idea at the time. It's likely that the idea was too unique for it's day; because the venture proved convenient for the farm ladies when they were out of something, but it wasn't how they chose to do the bulk of their shopping. The grocery route was not a huge inflationary addition to our income.

It was about that time that Dad bought the vacant gas station, which was also located on Main Street, across the street and a half-block north of our store. Everyone in the family took turns servicing cars, trucks, and tractors with gasoline at the station, as well as manning the grocery store. It was important to Dad that he was able to purchase Skelly gasoline, as he thought it to be the best gasoline available. Dad was fiercely loyal to any product of which he approved, and seldom compromised when he thought he was right.

These years were most certainly an era of "firsts." One day a salesman came into the store, asking Mom and Dad if he could set up a customer-sampling display of a brand new product. How grand and impressive this stainless steel, electrified warming pot looked as he set up his wares.

We waited expectantly to see what he was going to put into it. He had already told us it was a brand new product that had never before been on the market. When he told us the name, "Campbell's Cream of Mushroom Soup," my enthusiasm took a nosedive since the prospect of this strange sounding soup didn't appeal to me. But once it was heated and ready to serve, I was willing to try a tiny taste along with everybody else. Surprisingly, everyone loved it, including me. Still do.

In fact, there wasn't much in the store (that I liked) that I didn't sample. My parents liked to tease me by saying that when I helped in the grocery store, I ate all of the profits. Perhaps it was true because my favorite treat was a grape or orange float. Neither Mom nor Dad ever put a limit on how much of it I could have, so I indulged myself whenever I wanted.

Unfortunately, from my point of view at the time, these indulgent treats didn't add an ounce to my tall, lanky frame. That came much later. The fates are cruel, for what I had hoped for then, now requires only a glance at picture of a piece of pecan pie to add a pound.

Our pop (referred to now by the "hip" name, *soda*) came in glass bottles in those days; and after prying off the cap it became a challenge to see just how much pop I could pour into a tall glass already packed with as much ice cream as I could squeeze in, without running the glass over. In my opinion, the store had many great qualities.

CHAPTER 23

A backward glance at the last three-quarters of the previous century must certainly prove to anyone the unprecedented number of astonishing and life-changing innovations that did indeed take place during that period of time. It soon becomes clear that this phase of our world's history—a time in which it was my good fortune to have been born—produced more significant contributions to family enrichment, economic, scientific, medical, industrial, technical and social progress than any other period in history to date.

This meteoric advancement, however, continues to rise, involving every aspect of our lives today. Soaring progress is proving to be a phenomenal achievement that keeps reinventing itself almost daily. Take, for example, the computer. Almost as soon as one is purchased it becomes obsolete; being replaced by a smaller, faster, more detailed, more sophisticated and technical model—an improvement, undoubtedly, but one which comes with a price, to the dismay of many consumers. Think also of the telephone—now everyone carries one in their pocket, and can not only talk, but see the one they've called—and it sometimes has computer qualities—taking, storing and sending messages to their computers—hardly the telephone of my day.

During my lifetime it's been my privilege to witness the introduction of many of the world's "firsts." The telephone first became available for general use, as well as the electric light bulb, radio, typewriters, automobiles (later, even, with balloon tires), heaters, fans and air conditioners, airplanes, indoor plumbing, automatic washers and dryers, microwaves, gas and electric stoves—in fact, electrical "anything." Speaking of the computer world, I'm sure that by accessing one of the websites, I would be able to come up with dozens more of the world's " firsts." Who knew?

In more recent years, man has walked on the moon, and circled the earth from outer space. Medicine and science have made gigantic strides; legal, business, and communication technology have undergone such dramatic changes that we are now hurtling down the information highway at a dizzying rate, leaving many folks my age gasping for breath.

From our vantage point, scores of us believe the world to be careening down that road at too frantic and crazy a pace. However, when we receive that first picture coming to us via the computer, with its capability of instantly showing us the sweet little squished-up eyes and red face of a newborn grandchild the moment it arrives, we're willing to admit that this might just be a good thing. Given this kind of evidence, we'll even concede that this marvel has somewhat mollified our doubts, conditioning us old geezers into at least tolerating this intimidating new-fangled gizmo—some (more every day) even becoming adventurous enough to use one.

Not only was it a thrilling luxury to own our first telephone, but it represented only one of these many "firsts" mentioned here. We got our first telephone when Dad opened the grocery store. It would be hard for anyone of this generation to understand the awe, and sense of wonder we felt at being joined to so strange a concept as this sort of communication. My, how important we felt—having *a telephone*! Then imagine how nervous we were about making that first call. But whom did one call? That dilemma presented an even greater predicament because not everyone had a telephone.

The phone was a tall, black tube-like piece that fit onto a heavy base, which sat on the desk. The speaker cup was at the top of the tube. The receiver we listened through was placed on a hook and connected to the telephone by an electrical cord.

Since there weren't any private lines in our area at that time, it was necessary for us to make sure no one else was talking on their telephone before we tried to ring someone. If they chose, those customers sharing the same line could hear everyone else's conversation, so we had to be careful about what we said as it could very likely be passed on.

We heard the telephone ring every time anyone on our line got a call so we had to listen carefully for our own ring, such as two shorts and a long (or two short cranks and a long crank) when someone was calling you. Because it was necessary to count the number of rings each time the phone rang, it wasn't long before we had memorized each person's code, and always knew who was receiving a call.

Our calls were made through the use of a small crank attached to the phone, so you had to know your party's private ring to know how many cranks to give. Because of some unsteady hands and a few unusual cranking interpretations, one couldn't always be sure who was receiving a call. Then too, you never had any privacy. If some curious neighbor heard the phone ring and wanted to listen in they could—and often did. It was open season on one's conversations, and it was risky not to care what people heard us say. But for us, having a phone at the store, regardless of who listened in, meant we were able to receive grocery orders over our phone.

It was, in fact, a phone order at the store that set off a series of events leading to another of my many brushes with the grim reaper (it's beginning to look like there have been an unusual number of them for my age.) . It was summertime and someone had called in an order for a box of strawberries (by phone, oh joy). Mother gave me the strawberries and asked me to make the delivery to the lady who lived about four blocks away. This was like a reprieve from jail for me, getting this chance to be outside on a nice day and away from work.

Reaching for a small package of hard butterscotch balls on my way out of the store, I quickly slipped a ball from its cellophane sleeve (containing about five or six balls) and popped it into my mouth. I needed no urging to make the delivery. This momentary official pardon from my store duties was a welcome diversion.

The delivery took me past the town pump, diagonally across the intersection, and then past the park. At about the halfway point of the park, the hard candy ball I'd been sucking slipped down my throat, closing my windpipe. I was immediately immobilized with fear, and terror stricken at the morbid prospect of choking to death right here on the sidewalk, with a candy ball stuck in my throat. I flushed with anxiety. Struggling for breath, while nearing hysteria, I swiftly set the box of strawberries on the sidewalk and took off at the speed of light, running back to the store, wheezing and straining for air, confident that if I could reach Mom, she would save me.

The candy ball miraculously popped out of my mouth just as I reached the town pump (undoubtedly the result of being jolted by the running). I was limp with relief over this good turn of events. Still shaken and badly frightened by the near catastrophe, however, I continued running back to the store, gasping and panting. In a trembling voice, I raced through the line of customers and spilled out my shocking story to Mom.

How I could have run so far with my windpipe blocked is still a mystery; but once again, fear was the great motivator, and I was more than a little motivated to get home to Mom because I "knew" she would fix it. After a bit of tender sympathy, however, I was sent back to retrieve the berries and complete my delivery. Some consolation.

It was after we had moved into the upstairs apartment over the store that Maxine went off to what was then Iowa State Teacher's College, now the University of Northern Iowa (UNI) in Cedar Falls, where our granddaughter Abby is currently enrolled. Maxine had been home for a visit one weekend, and Dad was ready to drive her back to college in his shiny, black 1938 Hudson Terreplane, our wonderful new car that made us a mobile family once more. Dad had invited me (or more likely, allowed me) to make the trip with them.

It was joyous experience, taking a car trip with Dad in those days, because it so seldom happened. It took us some time to get to

Cedar Falls, and when we arrived on campus we delivered Maxine to her dorm. It's hard to say what prompted the next move because it was so unexpected, not at all characteristic of something I imagined Dad would do. He decided that the two of us would go to a movie. This was the first and only time Dad and I ever went to a movie together, by ourselves.

The sheer elation I felt at this unexpected bolt from the blue was almost too good to be true and I could hardly believe it was happening. Perhaps his grand gesture was prompted by the simple fact that there was a movie theatre in Cedar Falls—and we were there! A slightly guilty feeling began to nag at my conscience, however, because the rest of the family wouldn't get to see the picture.

Quickly consoling myself, figuring that Dad knew what he was doing since his conscience didn't seem to be causing him any remorse, I was more than happy to mind my dad without hesitation that day. My guilty feeling lasted about as long as it took us to take our seats and get ready for the movie.

The typically wonderful and unique smell of the theater, the plush seats, and the lowered lights all worked their magic as the curtains parted and the screen lit up. We settled down in our seats for the awesome experience. The movie was, *The Good Earth*, starring Miss Louise Reiner.

Set in China at the turn of the 20th century, the film was the story of a family of Chinese peasants and their struggle for existence during a drought-stricken time of famine. It was beautifully acted, and a stunningly unforgettable story. Miss Reiner won an academy award for her performance in that role.

Because of the intenseness of the movie we had just seen, it was like entering a different world, moving out of the theater into late afternoon sunlight. It took a few moments to adjust to the daylight and to reality. It was hard to think of anything else on the drive home but this soul-stirring film. The distance didn't seem nearly so long as we clicked off the miles, talking and recalling every scene of the amazing story.

That was a day to be cherished, probably for several reasons: because it was a once-only treat, and because of the powerful message of the story. One seldom hears this movie mentioned, these days—like almost never—but if in any serendipitous moment one does hear the title again, I'm once again that little girl seeing a movie with her daddy.

We were also living in the upstairs apartment when Maurice developed an interest in raising and selling domestic white rabbits. During his youthful venture into this entrepreneurial project, not only did he sell his rabbits, but he cured and saved a number of pelts as well. Typical of his interest in learning how to do everything, Maurice learned the art of tanning rabbit hides, and they became quite lovely white fur pieces—the poor man's "ermine."

Maxine, now through "Teacher's College" and on to her first teaching job at Yale, Iowa, developed a real flair for style, and a keen shopping sense. When at last she became solvent, due to her now-regular paychecks, she bought herself a stylishly fitted, black crushed velvet coat. On a visit home Maxine brought her purchase to Mom and together they designed, and Mom fashioned, a white fur collar and cuffs for the coat.

Maxine shopped until she found a pair of white, high-heeled snow boots that came up over the ankles—boots, at that time, were really rubber overshoes designed to slip over one's shoes and featured many different height of heels. These boots were also trimmed with white fur at the top around the ankles. They matched the coat exactly.

The first time Maxine put on the newly-designed coat we were all "wowed" by her glamorous appearance. To us, she looked like a movie star! She couldn't have been more proud of the coat, or we of her. Mom, too, gained a momentary celebrity for having created such a dramatic garment. As styles go, however, things change, and this "costume" would probably be considered corny and out-of-date now; but for then, she was a knockout.

Just after I'd finished my junior year at Whitten High School, I was faced with another startling tragedy. Dad sold the store and the gas station and took a job at the John Deere Company in Waterloo. For a brief time, the prospect of having to move to another town was absolutely heart wrenching for a young girl with expectations of graduating with the classmates she'd known her entire school life.

I sat stunned after hearing the news that we were to move to Waterloo. How could Dad do this to me, was the first thing that popped into my head. For a time I didn't think I'd be able cope with the disappointment—trying, with every argument I could come up with, to convince him that I needed to live in Whitten at least one more year. My friends, too, were shocked when I told them my news. There was concern and bewilderment as we talked over this "unbelievable" turn of events. Before long, the news was all over town.

Dad had been offered a better opportunity in Waterloo, which was too good for him to pass up, and there was no changing his mind. So, in an effort to win my cooperation, Dad began telling me stories about Waterloo and the excitement of living in the city, the house he had gotten for us, and my new school. It must have worked because before long the prospect of living in this decidedly more exciting place gave me something new to think about. Gradually I began to warm to the idea.

Having been born with a fairly optimistic nature, it wasn't in my makeup to spend too much time looking back, or fussing over regrets. With Dad's advance publicity eliciting the many benefits of the move—the exciting possibilities available in a larger city, going to a larger school, and meeting new friends—suddenly made the prospect of the move seem brighter than remaining in Whitten. I was now ready to go.

We moved into a house quite near the place where Dad worked, at John Deere, and it wasn't long before I had made friends in the neighborhood. About three or four of the girls in the area actively sought me out and took me under their wings, and seemed happy to include me in their group of friends. On my first day of school they walked with me to West High School, showed me around, and acquainted me with the building, the rules, and other kids. We became fast friends. Although we see each other infrequently, we remain friends.

Our house was located thirteen blocks from school. During the winter months, we walked to school. Just as irrational as some traditions can be, but as rigorously upheld by schoolgirls of every age, it would have meant social death to appear at school in snow pants (a popular outside play garment at the time) even if the temperature dropped to a dangerous 30 degrees below zero. Making matters worse, neither did the girls of our day ever wear jeans or long pants to school, which meant exposing our bare legs to any and all extremes of the elements.

Our compromise to the weather was to wear knee socks, and walk as fast as we could. Fortunately there was an apartment building about half way to school, and as soon as it came into sight we girls would start racing to get inside the heated lobby to thaw our frozen knees. Why we aren't all crippled with arthritis is unfathomable, or more likely a miracle. Surely there must have been some cases of frostbite, or very nearly so. "Coolness," among the young of any age, has the ability to override sensibility, one might say. It must be noticed here, that again, we *always* walked to school. It was a rare thing to be chauffeured to school. Kids were expected to be up every morning in time to walk to school. Never would we have harbored the thought of begging for a ride because it would have been a pointless request anyway.

The change of schools for me was not, in every instance, as successful as I had thought it was going to be. Scholastically my grades dropped and I was no longer one of the "brighter" kids in the class. I soon realized how much more advanced the classes and the students were in this larger school. I felt a wide disparity in the instruction given here, than that which I'd received in our small rural town school, and I began to doubt the abilities of the old teachers I had left behind.

In retrospect, it was possible that the size of the new classes and the lesser amount of attention given each student, could have accounted for part of the inconsistency in my grades. The difference in the size of the two schools, which at the time appeared as intimidating to me as one might experience in changing from high school to college, could have also been responsible for my slipping grades. *It certainly couldn't have been me*!

As the year wore on, however, I began to catch on to the system and was relieved when my grades began to improve considerably. Things seemed to begin leveling out for me from then on. The change of schools proved to be difficult in many other ways as well.

Coming into this new situation during my senior year made it nearly impossible for me to feel like a real part of the class, especially since the classes were so large and most of the students remained strangers to me. However, I adjusted well enough, and dealt with it.

This wasn't the happy conclusion I had envisioned for my last year of school; but with the new friends I had made, and having learned a new way to study, I was not unhappy. I finished the academic part of my senior year at least satisfactorily, if not great.

CHAPTER 24

Unlike the less personal, more distant relationships with my teachers in Waterloo, we students in Whitten had been well acquainted and at ease with our teachers. They became our friends and we felt connected to them. So much so, in fact, that after Maxine graduated from high school, she began dating the boys' basketball coach, George Pederson. He was, in the vernacular of today, a "cool guy," "a hunk," or "hot," and every girl in school had a huge crush on him. I was no exception.

He came to our house one day (to call on my sister) and found me ironing Dad's shirts. He was so impressed with my work that he "hinted" he wished he had someone who could iron his shirts as well. Any thinly-veiled request from this "Greek god" would have been reason enough for me to have knocked down, trampled, or stomped roughshod (with cleated shoes) over anyone standing in the way of my haste to volunteer for the job.

No amount of work, no sacrifice, no inconvenience, would have been too great for the privilege of becoming this gorgeous guy's slave. Being asked to iron his shirts was compliment enough to make me want to faint, certain that my hard work would assure his notice of me and win his approval.

But, alas, ironing coach Pederson's shirts, and knowing I had done them to perfection, was to be my only payment. Through all of my hours of hard work (taking extra care to do the job perfectly) he remained interested only in his stupid shirts, and in my sister. I found it necessary to satisfy myself with his many enthusiastic "thanks" and the fact that, at least, he did come to our house—if only to see my sister—and to drop off more shirts.

But the reward I'd been looking forward to the most, was expecting many of my classmates to drop dead with envy; this would serve as the ultimate consolation prize. I took elaborate care, going out of my way to "drop" little tidbits about being given the "honor" of ironing our teacher's shirts.

My superior status, as chief-ironer for the coach, was obviously a complete figment of my naiveté—completely wasted on my peers—because it went totally unrecognized by those I most wanted to impress. On the contrary, my friends undoubtedly considered me a bit "touched in the head" to want to work that hard, and for what—a benevolent pat on the ego?

So, it seems, my ironing expertise gained me very little by way of attracting Mr. Pederson's attention. Now I smile at this absurd notion—that I could have even entertained the impossible notion of attracting a teacher's (or any man's) attention at such an immature age. It's even funnier to think about what I was expecting would happen if he had noticed me. I'm sure if I had found myself in that situation, I'd have become the silly, giggling, nervous, teenager that I was, completely at a loss to know how to cope. So much for teen crushes.

My sister dated Coach Pederson between high school and the time she started to college at UNI; and the interest continued when she went away to college and for a while when she came home on weekends. I don't remember much about the breakup. It seemed more like it just fizzled out—possibly because of the distance between them, or her increasing involvement with school. I don't recall that she was devastated about it.

I do, however, know several classes of teenage girls, at the time, who would have gladly walked over hot coals for the privilege of having a date with him. The entire experience of a first crush was not a total waste, however, for it taught me to be a bit more sympathetic with my own children when they were going through those first major school infatuations.

The only teacher I recall by name at my new school, Waterloo West High, will be forever remembered, not for her teaching skills, her charisma, or her personality, but for one systematic, precise, and predictable quirk in her behavior. Miss Clara Hansmeier taught History with all of the enthusiasm and appeal of reading aloud the National Registry. This, one could expect from a teacher, but it was not her most memorable feature.

The unforgettable thing about Miss Hansmeier was her actions in the classroom. It was her daily practice, when entering the classroom, to turn on the overhead lights by using a key that she inserted in the connection located by the door. She would then move over to the windows and lower the blinds closing out any possibility of sunlight. After five or ten minutes into her lecture (in her monotonous voice, devoid of inflection—never rising or falling over a half centimeter) she would return to the windows and raise the shades. This, then, made it necessary for her to go back to the door, take out her key and turn off the lights.

After sitting in Miss Hansmeier's class for more than a day, it soon became apparent that a rhythm, a pattern, was emerging in her movements as she repeated the key/shade exercise at least four or five times each class period. Watching her strange behavior, and predicting her eccentric movements, became far more mentally stimulating and challenging for most of us than her rote-delivered lecture.

The only other teacher who stands out in my mind at the new school was the science teacher. He was a rather timid and shy man whose greatest impact on the class came the day he collapsed in class—and died. On that day he had everyone's undivided attention. He was a pleasant man and a gentle soul, if less than a stimulating teacher.

Aside from these two riveting classes, the academic side of my senior year of high school seemed less than motivating, for my attention had turned to the acquisition of as many friends as possible.

One of my greatest disappointments at West High came because they had no organized basketball team, and no one trained to coach it. Our gym classes became an exercise in frustration for me as the girls in the class acted silly and girlish when throwing the ball, pretending only to play a game which I had played in competition. Gym class held no fascination for me.

I graduated high school at the age of seventeen. Because our graduating class in Waterloo was so large, the ceremony was held in the high school stadium. Since we were relatively new to Waterloo, my family didn't make any grand celebration plans after the event. This was due in part because the ceremony was held at night and most of our relatives would have had to come from too far a distance; night driving seemed to be considered a risky venture at that time. Obviously so, because we never went anywhere but what my dad would eventually say, "We need to leave now so we can get home before dark." We heard that phrase from all of our visitors as well. Might as well not have put headlights on those old cars.

Dad picked out a lovely small gold locket on a chain, from both Mom and Dad, for my graduation, which I treasured. Mom did her best to make it a time of celebration for me by decorating the table and making a special cake and a few other treats for our family after we got home from the ceremony. As small a celebration as it was, my parents still made it an event by inviting a few of my friends as well. Somehow, though, I couldn't stop thinking about the celebration that must have been going on in Whitten, which found me missing all of the friends who were graduating without me.

To my sorrow, the locket was lost, on an antique-hunting junket to Walnut, Iowa, the spring of 1998. Bob and I were in and out of the car at various times on the way to Walnut and it was during one of those times we realized the locket was missing. Frantically retracing our steps, our search proved fruitless. The loss of this little gold locket was like losing a part of my past; a treasure valued like few other items in my possession. However, the unusually sweet and fond remembrance of my father and mother having given me this gift will always be cherished in my heart.

The summer before starting college, found me working at the Maid-Rite Cafe in Waterloo. It was there that I first met my future husband. Interestingly enough, Robert Harry Kelly had stopped in to see his girlfriend, Dorothy, who was also working there. At that point ours was a casual acquaintance, and we didn't meet again until years later. From the first, however, I had been totally aware of this cocky, self-assured kid when he came into the restaurant. Right away my assessment of him was that he was really cute, and I wished he hadn't been there to see Dorothy.

Working at the Maid-Rite was a new, but not unpleasant experience. My responsibilities involved working until the 2:00 a.m. closing—the time when we all pitched in with the cleaning before we could leave. I never left the restaurant until around 2:30 or 3:00 in the morning. It seems inconceivable to me now that I was allowed to walk home alone at this very early-morning hour—a walk of at least ten or twelve blocks. Almost no one my age had a car or even access to a car, so walking was my only option. Young people (and parents) of today would find this unacceptable, and rightfully so, but it was a reasonable and expected thing to do, then.

Because I wasn't afraid of walking alone in the dark, these homeward treks became mini mind excursions whereby it was possible to imagine myself totally alone in a solitary world (not too hard to do when everyone else in the universe appeared to be in bed). Somehow the quiet intensified in these late night hours, with only the sound of my own footsteps disturbing the silence.

Objects appeared to take on larger dimensions—the stars sparkled a bit brighter, and the moon appeared much bigger in those dark, still, night skies. The silence itself was a bizarre anomaly since we lived on a busy street that was usually bustling with traffic. Only occasionally would a car pass me by, on these solitary hikes, their drivers usually paying scant attention—completely unmindful of my presence. So contrary to feeling threatened by it, I rather welcomed the company.

Foot traffic also was non-existent at that hour, because I never saw another walker. But then, the world was still a less threatening, significantly less populated, and a vastly friendlier place than it is now. It was correctly assumed, by my parents, that I would make my way home safely, confident of my arriving there in one piece. Instead of dreading this long walk home, I usually found myself looking forward to these late night, or early morning, hikes. No doubt this news will come as a shocking revelation to current readers, so it makes one wonder if things really have changed for the better!

CHAPTER 25

They say it isn't unusual to remember where you were, and what you were doing at the time you heard an enormously shocking piece of news. On December 7, 1941, our family was visiting Aunt Louise and Uncle John Frericks, and my cousins. (Aunt Louise had, by then, remarried and they were all living in Grundy Center). We had just finished Sunday dinner and everyone was lounging around, recovering from the oversized meal we'd just consumed.

Comfortably relaxed, everyone visiting, we were all within earshot of the tall floor-model console radio that was sending out soothing music from deep within its innards, creating the right background for our conversations.

The setting is as clear and vivid to me as the day it happened. Sitting on a hassock I was nearest the radio when suddenly a solemn-voiced announcer interrupted the music to deliver an almost heart-stopping news announcement. In the next moment we heard the strong, but obviously shaken voice of the President of the United States, Franklin Delano Roosevelt, coming on air. In his unmistakably familiar voice we were stunned to hear him make the pronouncement that on that Sunday morning, December 7th, the Japanese had bombed our naval base at Pearl Harbor. With the words: "This is a date which will live in infamy," we learned that America was at war.

We sat, for a time, in silent disbelief after hearing the news—looking around at each other, trying to imagine what this ominous revelation could mean for all of us and for our familiar, predictable world. Somehow the seriousness of the announcement seemed to suggest that our visit was at an end and we needed to return home at once to try and sort out this ominous news.

What had started out as a carefree and happy Sunday visit had turned into a somber ride home with very little conversation on the way. Somehow this horrendous news appeared strangely worse at that moment than hearing about a death in the family. At least it seemed larger. What was to become of us? While it was impossible to take in all of the consequences of what we'd heard that day, it was certain that this news meant different things to each of us, and would affect every one of us differently.

Pure, fearful, emotion ran unbridled in the hearts of both young and old following the announcement. For the young, who were unwillingly losing control of their lives due to the insatiable appetite of some unknown power-mad aggressor, it meant being catapulted into uncharted waters. For the older, more experienced receivers of this chilling news, visions of dark and heartbreaking days loomed large on the horizon. Life as we had known it was never to be the same again—a disquieting phrase we're prophetically hearing again after the terrorist attack on the World Trade Center on September 11, 2001.

Like most people, when faced with untenable obstacles, we soon learned to accept the inevitability of the situation even though we were, as yet, innocently unaware of the shortages, deprivations, and heartaches to come.

The disruption in everyone's lives, the uncertainties, the fears, worry, and the shedding of too many tears while saying too many "good-byes," too many times, were, as yet, unmet strangers at our doors. Very soon they would become all too familiar intruders.

In our own family, time, from then on, would forever be measured by long days of hopeful anticipation as we looked forward to a few days furlough for my brother Maurice, and Edgar Smith, my sister Maxine's husband. These too rare visits brought with them the tumultuous joy of reunion, as well as the sadness and despair of the unknown that went with their departure.

On one of these furloughs, Maxine and Edgar were married, in Waterloo, in the same church where Bob and I were married. She spent several years moving with him to a number of military bases in the States before he was sent overseas.

After graduating from high school and spending the summer at the Maid-Rite, I enrolled at the University of Northern Iowa. By then our world had taken on a somber mood with our entry into World War II, and everyone was quickly thrust into disturbing and unfamiliar new roles. We eager young students had graduated, not only from school, but also from our position as happy, fun-loving, carefree kids. This theft of our age of innocence, brought on by the war, came with a thud, hurtling us into an adulthood for which many of us were unprepared.

No longer were we in charge of our own destinies; our lives now seemed redirected by circumstances beyond our control. Many of our male friends were promptly inducted into active military service. This meant they were to be shipped to distant destinations in the United States, and eventually overseas. Not only was this a heartache for their families, but for the remaining young female contingent left at home.

The war years, while frightening, exciting, or traumatic for the young men who were called to serve, were difficult and depressing for those left behind, especially the young single girls. Graduation from high school was supposed to have meant we could eagerly look forward to the exciting prospect of college and all of the anticipated joy connected with it (meaning dates and parties). To say that this was a low point in our lives was an understatement, particularly since we realized how helpless we were to change or correct the situation. The only sensible thing to do was to yield gracefully and adapt to our present, if thoroughly unfair circumstances.

With the encroachment of the war into our lives, and the military machine indiscriminately ensnaring all of the eligible young men, the dating scene grew more dismal each day. At the risk of sounding totally self-absorbed and selfish, life for young ladies suddenly took on a bleakness that seemed cruelly unjust. This heartless situation was made even worse when our suspicions led us to believe that the young men in our lives were secretly thrilled and excited at the prospect of this man-thing called "defending one's country and marching off to war."

We had only reached our time of graduation from high school. The youth of our day (or any day for that matter) could be likened to seeds that had been carefully planted in the garden—tenderly nurtured and watered, and were just now reaching the budding stage. This was to have been our time to flower, having so recently attained our long-awaited adult status. We both, girls and boys, were allowed to enjoy that "budding-into-flower" stage for too brief a time. Too many would soon be required to assume an adult role in ways they could not have envisioned.

To have had this monstrously barbaric tragedy thrust upon us, through no less effort than every major world power, caused anguish for many young people, largely because of their powerlessness to prevent it. The frustration of it all stirred powerful emotions, which led us to directing all of our energies into hoping for an early end of the war.

Not only did our social lives suffer, but we soon became acquainted with such things as shortages and ration stamps. Since many items we had taken for granted were now being rerouted to supply the war machine, we soon learned about doing without.

Gasoline was probably the first necessity to be rationed. We, on the home front, were issued gasoline ration cards. One's driving needs determined the type of sticker that would be issued to them. An A-stamp allowed the driver of a private car to purchase three gallons of gasoline a week. A B-stamp was issued to those whose businesses and livelihoods depended on their driving needs, allowing them a greater amount. An R-stamp was the best stamp one could have, but was generally attainable only for those who needed unlimited use of their car, such as doctors or emergency vehicles.

Soon, and quite possibly the most nerve-wracking item of all to be rationed (threatening near-panic among the addicted) was cigarettes. Dad was a dedicated smoker. This shortage brought him intense pain. By devious cunning, plotting, and planning, I soon found myself conscripted into Dad's army, as a pseudo-smoker.

He assigned me to cigarette-sentry-duty, meaning that I was drafted to stand in line to obtain cigarettes for him so he would be assured of a few extra packs a week. Individuals were allowed to purchase only two packs of cigarettes at a time, thus my involvement.

This bitter state of affairs for Dad (the unnatural deprivation and forced self-denial) did nothing to persuade him to quit smoking. It only managed to compel him to adopt a more frugal lifestyle. Many times I watched him carefully tap the burning end off any cigarette (longer than an inch or maybe even less) and put it back in the pack. He did this when he was required to stop smoking for any reason, such as being called to dinner. After all, there were still a few puffs left in the butt, and for the addicted, even one puff was preferable to no puffs, regardless of how stale it might be. I don't believe Dad's cigarette butts were ever left around long enough to get too stale.

Although I was coerced into becoming a co-conspirator, I wasn't an altogether unwilling accomplice for supplying Dad's habit. In fact, it made me feel quite grown-up to be waiting in line along with the other adults to buy something as wicked as cigarettes. Since we weren't questioned about our age at the counter, obtaining cigarettes was easy.

Neither was it totally disagreeable having to put up with the inconvenience of my task; for what usually happens among people with a common (though miserable) goal—like being forced to wait in long lines—passing the time together usually took on a surprisingly convivial tone, unless one was dying for a smoke, and waiting was becoming unbearable.

It wasn't unusual to strike up some companionable, good-natured, conversation among the nail-biters. Perhaps adversity really does act as a catalyst for drawing people together, or using the same analogy, it could mean that misery surely does love company.

Silk hose was another luxury to be snatched from us women during these wartime years. This "comfort" was taken from our list of necessary items in order to provide material for making parachutes. Women, however, being the resourceful creatures they are, came up with their own version of faux-stockings in the form of leg makeup.

Applying the makeup was a rather messy procedure but when one got the hang of it the results weren't too bad. While this imperfect ordeal was time-consuming and far from tidy, it surely beat going without stockings completely or, heaven forbid, having to wear cotton stockings. We learned to refine the method of applying leg makeup so we could appear in public without looking as though we'd contracted a flesh-eating disease. The trick was to pour out a small handful of the makeup, and apply it quickly with long, sweeping, even strokes. You couldn't do it in dibs and dabs or you'd appear blotched.

While it was still wet, we smoothed it around over any spots that had been missed until the entire leg was evenly covered to just over the knee. Then we had to allow it to dry. At this point, washing the gooey stuff off one's hands meant a mess in the sink as well as on the towel. It took about as much time to clean up the bathroom as it took to apply the makeup to our legs.

We had to lightly towel our legs after they dried so the makeup wouldn't rub off on our clothing; even this cosmetic treatment had its downside. Getting dressed, to appear in public, wasn't simply a matter of throwing on some clothes and running out the door in those days, it took lots of intense concentration and plenty of vanity to accomplish the job!

This lengthy process completed our grooming ritual, and we were ready for the day. While it was an ordeal going through this messy technique, we endured it because it was the only help we had for improving our looks. It was the final much-needed touch that boosted our morale, enabling us to face the world even in our bogus socks. Sometimes it isn't easy being a woman!

The best present a furloughed serviceman could bring home was a pair of hose for each lady. They were able to buy them at their PX (post exchange).

Coffee, sugar, and other food staples soon became rationed items as well, making life on the home front a good deal less satisfying than we'd been used to.

Although we sometimes moaned about the things we'd run out of, we seldom complained. We were proud of our soldiers, and there wasn't one mom who wouldn't gladly have made any sacrifice necessary for her boy away from home.

CHAPTER 26

It was during this unfamiliar and troubling period of war years that I attended college in Cedar Falls. Aside from the gloom of the times, my first college experience got off to a less than appealing start when I moved into the dorm on campus.

My roommate was a stranger to me who seemed rather aloof; and, while she was not unfriendly, didn't appear to be terribly interested in getting to know me either. The outlook seemed rather bleak for a great future here—for a warm and lasting friendship—because each day we went to separate classes, and the rest of the time found us going our own way, spending little time together in our room.

My new roommate was, in general, not the type of gregarious person I would naturally have been drawn to either, if given a choice. It appeared from the outset that the feeling would probably remain rather permanently mutual. We were roommates who politely tolerated each other and shared the same small space—strangers whose personalities were too dissimilar to find that warm bonding shared by friends. Hardly the happy college beginning I'd expected. But having had no choice in the selection of roommates, we were forced to endure the luck of the draw.

After starting classes, it was suggested by my parents that perhaps I should look into getting a job at the Hillside Cafe, the same restaurant where my sister worked when she was in college there. The cafe was just off campus and was mostly frequented by college students.

Starting from a position of hating the idea, I did get a job there, but went to work every day with little eagerness. Compounding the problem, I left work every night with eyes that were swollen and red from the unbelievably thick clouds of cigarette smoke that continually smothered the entire restaurant.

It wasn't long before I quit the job in self-defense, which was probably just as well. In addition to the miserable smoky situation in the cafe, my old nemesis (homesickness) returned with a vengeance, adding one more reason why I found it necessary to return to living at home. I've since wondered if things might have turned out differently if I'd had a friend for a roommate. Come to think of it, few of my friends attended the college, which left me feeling quite alone and friendless.

Leaving campus life, I eagerly returned to home base, although I continued to commute to school with acquaintances. No longer was the college experience a thing of which I had dreamed for years. It had now settled down into a dreary routine from which there was little reprieve. Campus life had become businesslike and uninteresting as a result of the war. Factored into that equation, for me, was the inconvenience and dismal nature of those dark, gloomy, early-morning winter trips to Cedar Falls that had begun to make the entire experience thoroughly disagreeable. Eventually I transferred from UNI to Gates Business College, in Waterloo, where I was able to walk to school.

The strange and uncertain events of that period took a great toll; exacerbating a restlessness whereby decisions were made which might not have been considered under normal circumstances. Nothing was really right with our world. It was as if we were suspended in limbo for an unforeseeable amount of time. All of the carefully laid plans we had made for our futures were subverted by this unseen, but glaringly obvious monster, called war.

To many of us, the prospect of prolonging our educations became tantamount to a desertion of the war effort. Feelings were that the time spent in college could be put to better and more immediate use.

I wanted to get my education over with and get on with the business of at least becoming a wage-earning contributor to society as soon as possible.

I was not unhappy, making the transfer of schools, for I made many friends at Gates College. This smaller student body had managed to submit to the change in their fortunes, and actually found ways to have a good deal of fun. My best friend at college, Margaret Willey, went on to become a teacher at Gates College, and we remained friends until her death, in 1993.

Margaret and I were both members of Alpha Theta Chi Sorority; and even though it seemed incongruous in light of the times, we had occasion to attend many formal dinners and parties where everyone dressed in evening attire.

Perhaps these formal occasions were designed to offset the desultory and austere effects of the days in which we were living. They were, in fact, really quite grand occasions that gave us continued high hopes for the future, and despite the lack of escorts, we "dressed to the nines."

At any of our balls, parties, or other special events, as could be expected, the ladies consistently outnumbered the men by a large majority. Though modest in number, these few men determinedly presented their gentlemanly best as they valiantly squired as many of the ladies as possible onto the dance floor, assuring most of us at least one dance (with a man) during the evening.

Somehow, that bit of gracious, elegant living seemed to have mostly disappeared somewhere around that period, and I miss it. For there is nothing that makes a woman feel more elegant and feminine than when she is wearing a lovely evening gown.

During the course of our routine days, the abnormal was steadily becoming the norm. With our social lives dwindling, out of necessity we girls learned to adjust our expectations of fun, accepting the fact that it was to be mostly of the girl-variety.

The few remaining young men of eligible age were usually classified as 4-F, which meant they were physically unable to serve in the armed forces. The rest were either too young or too old to be of interest. To those of us who were left behind, these were extremely depressing, but vital statistics.

World War II, finally came to an end on V-J Day, August 14, 1945, the day Japan surrendered. Just months before that, our President, Franklin D. Roosevelt, had died, on April 12, 1945, in Warm Springs, Georgia, sending shock waves and sadness throughout the country, and indeed, the entire world. Of course that also left us all wondering what course the war would now take. He was succeeded by then, Vice President Harry S. Truman.

After assuming the presidency, it was President Truman who was largely responsible for the war's end by issuing the order to drop the atom bomb on Hiroshima on August 6, 1945, and then on Nagasaki on August 9, 1945. The hand-picked crew for the grim assignment of the bombing of Hiroshima, flew aboard the bomber "Enola Gay." It was the catastrophic demolition of those cities that became the vital component for breaking the aggressive back of the Imperial Japanese Government.

The surrender of Japan was formally signed on September 2, 1945 on board the battleship Missouri. As devastating as these bombings were for the Japanese people, and shocking to even most Americans, the majority of Americans and their Allies still believed the bombings were necessary in order to shorten the war and spare the many lives which might have been lost if the hostilities hadn't ended soon.

When that long-awaited moment came, announcing the joyous news of the war's end, euphoric mania swept the nation. Everyone seemed to feel a compelling need to share their joy with anyone they could find. The announcement brought people pouring out of their homes and into the streets. Americans felt caught up in the contagious elation and wanted to be a part of the jubilant celebration.

The victory earlier in Europe (V-E Day, on May 8, 1945) and subsequent official Japanese surrender (V-J Day) completed hostilities. This official and final surrender of the Japanese brought the return of America's remaining sons, and our friends and brothers, back from the four corners of the earth, along with our eternal gratitude. Their welcome home was doubly gratifying knowing they were here to stay.

The economy remained sluggish on the home front for some time, but eventually began a slow upturn. The war's end also brought with it the gradual phasing out of rationing and the shortages that had become second nature to us. But what should have brought us total ecstasy—the end of this monstrous conflagration—instead had a twofold deleterious effect—it reminded us of the many sons, fathers and husbands who would not be coming home, and left countless others feeling they had also been deprived and cheated of life. This void could be likened to someone who'd recovered from a very long illness—happy and relieved that it's over—but desolately aware that a large chunk of one's normal life has been lost forever, never to be recovered.

Although they both saw service in Europe, my brother Maurice, and my brother-in-law, Ed, (who received a battlefield commission) both came home unscathed. For that we sent many heavenly thanks to God our Father. As the war came to a close, however, we were to learn of the loss of many friends and acquaintances.

Next began the long process of restoration and readjustment for soldiers and civilians alike. It was time for jobs to be found, families to become reacquainted, and "soldier-indoctrination training" to be redirected to peacetime objectives.

Although jubilant at being home once more, many of our veterans brought with them harrowing experiences that left them troubled and in need of finding ways to cope.

Now began the uphill struggle of relearning the meaning of a normal existence. Searching for emotional stability—in their lives, jobs, and relationships—wasn't always readily found for all of our returning soldiers; and for some their search for this uneasy truce would never be realized.

Over time, however, most were able to overcome the memory of the obscene spectacles they had left on the battlefield. But for others, new disappointments were to be found at their homecoming. Time and distance had tested the mettle of some marriages and, unfortunately, found them sadly unable to cope. For the great majority of our returning soldiers, it meant deliberately putting their war experiences behind them and gradually easing back into what outwardly appeared to be a typical existence.

Eager, once again, to take up life where it had been so brutally interrupted, Wednesday and Saturday nights found many young returning soldiers and girls again at the dances at the Electric Park Ballroom, our favorite places for dates.

In the ballroom, with its well-polished dance floor, hung the typical overhead large, mirrored rotating ball, reflecting hundreds of lights that danced around the room and sparkled on the ceiling. The dance floor stopped in front of a wrought-iron railing, beyond which was a step up into a large carpeted lounge complete with tables and chairs.

This was the place for friends to gather and chat, or just listen to the band. Other than the movies, these dances were the main sources of entertainment for nearly every young person in and around Waterloo. We were there for every dance, either with a date or in a group. Because my parents had forbidden it, I was not allowed to attend the dances on Sunday nights.

We didn't realize just how fortunate we were to have had the top names of our time performing at the ballroom. It was commonplace to be able to dance to such bands as Woody Herman, Les Brown, Tommy or Jimmy Dorsey, Cab Calloway, Harry James, Vaughn Monroe, and others who were regular performers there, as well as many local favorites.

My husband, Bob, mentioned that he remembers the time he was standing directly in front of the bandstand, being merely one of dozens who were crowded around, when Vaughn Monroe sang his theme song, *Racing with the Moon.* Fact was, having the opportunity to stand directly in front of the bandstand when any group was performing, even the great ones, was not unusual. All this was available to us for the price of a reasonable general admission. Every Wednesday night was 20-cent night, and admission for a name band rarely exceeded two and a half to three dollars.

Everyone went, whether or not we had dates. Missing a dance at Electric Park Ballroom on dance night meant that you'd died an hour before. Making friends at the ballroom was easy and our circle of friends continually widened into an ever-enlarging group of congenial young adults who eventually danced with each person in our group at some time during the night.

One bona fide "character" who consistently frequented the dances, was a young man everyone called "Steamer." He was tagged with that nickname because of his energetic style of dancing, and the fact that he perspired excessively as he danced. We were dancing the jitterbug in those days and Steamer loved to show off his vigorous expertise with any girl who was equally as skilled and up for a marathon dance experience.

Since he was rather short and stout, Steamer's choice of dance partners was usually the shorter girls. It would have to be noted, however, that although Steamer's dancing ability fascinated nearly everyone, most of the girls present were reluctant to be thrown around the floor by this human dynamo, dripping from every pore.

I, like everyone else, was captivated by Steamer's dancing and found myself watching him in the ambivalent hope that he would validate my dancing skill by asking me to dance, while at the same time, apprehensive that he might.

I danced with Steamer only one time, but his asking me was enough to lend me dancing credibility in the eyes of my friends. I had been chosen. It was exhausting! Up until then, I believe I had convinced myself that the reason he had never asked me to dance was probably because I was a head taller then he. Then, who knows?

I met and dated a number of young men over the course of those turbulent years, which was the custom of the time. I also became engaged for a period to a young man whom I met through my sister, Maxine.

She was teaching in the small town of Rolfe, Iowa, at the time, and introduced us on one of my visits. Unfortunately, I met him during the war years and it wasn't long before he joined the Marines, which meant he was gone for much of what was to have been our courtship. The engagement was broken soon after he came home from the service. The object of his next engagement, the girl he subsequently married, was the girl he'd known all his life, and who's family farm adjoined theirs.

While the breaking off seemed enormously devastating to me at the time, I survived, eventually coming to the realization that, like a duck out of water, I was hardly prepared to become a farmer's wife.

Time, of course, has a wonderful way of healing the raw wounds of lost loves and infatuations, and successfully blurring their memory. Time, in its mercy, also deals mercilessly with the past, when *THE ONE* comes along! Of course that *ONE* was Robert Kelly, whom I had met while I was working at the Maid-Rite Cafe. Bob was dating Dorothy Newkirk, a dark-haired, dark-eyed, slim, pretty girl who also worked at the café, and who, incidentally, was one of the smartest girls in school.

After leaving my job at the Maid Rite and heading for college, I lost contact with both Dorothy and Bob. During those intervening years, Bob had volunteered for military service, where, after basic training at Amarillo, Texas, he entered the Air Cadet Training Program to become a pilot and an officer. It was to become the bitterest disappointment of his war years when they eliminated ("washed out," as they called it) the entire cadet-training program because the need for pilots had drastically diminished, dashing his hopes of his becoming a military pilot.

Instead, he was sent to Sioux Falls, S.D., for Radio School training. After radio training he was sent to Las Vegas, to B-17 Gunnery School; Rapid City, S.D., for Combat Crew Training; then on to the Lincoln, Nebraska, Staging Area; and finally to Harlingen, Texas, for B-29 Training. From there he went to Clark Field in the Philippines, where he served for fourteen months as a tail gunner as well as a scanner gunner, two of the most vulnerable positions on a B29 during combat.

CHAPTER 27

After returning to the United States, Bob and I met again—where else but at the Electric Park Ballroom. His relationship with Dorothy had ended and he asked me for a date. Still seeing him as this really cute, fascinating, and funny guy, I was intrigued and attracted; I eagerly accepted.

Our plan for that first date was to attend a major basketball game at the University of Northern Iowa. Bob's dad, Harry, one of the world's most, if not the most, avid (meaning really rabid) sports fans, wanted to see the game as well, and somehow managed to be invited along. I suspected, at the time, that it was at his own instigation that he was permitted to tag along on the date, and Bob later confirmed it. This was not a great beginning.

We arrived at the gymnasium only to find the place already packed. Spotting two seats in the middle section of the bleachers, Harry decided one of them was his, and Bob graciously suggested I sit with his dad.

If it had been possible for me to walk home I would have left at that moment, but I was stuck. So I reluctantly climbed over countless knees to take my seat with my new "date." Having lost all interest in the game by now, I spent the rest of the time looking around trying to find Bob in the crowd, where he was forced to stand. I found myself wondering how I had gotten myself into this situation, and whatever had I seen in him to make me put up with this ridiculous circumstance.

We only occasionally made eye contact during the game, which was probably just as well, given my present mood. Forcing a few brave smiles, in a desperate attempt to recoup the rest of the evening, required a lot of effort since my every inclination was to bolt and run. The drive back to Waterloo, to deliver his dad home, was uncomfortable and rather cool. More or less understandable when you consider the fact that I was forced to endure a running commentary by his father about the plays and eventual outcome of the game for the entire trip.

It is difficult to believe that there could have been a second date. But ever the optimist, I must have sensed some redeeming quality in this young man for I accepted a second date. This date, as well, turned out to be no more promising than the first. In fact, the date was so forgettable it's impossible to remember what we did. I just remember that during the entire evening, Bob was quiet, not at all as I remembered him at the Maid Rite where he was happy-go-lucky and self-assured, the very qualities that had attracted me to him in the first place. Perhaps he was reliving the embarrassment of bringing his father along on our first date. Whatever the cause, I was having difficulty understanding how he could have changed so much as this thoroughly uneventful evening came to a joyless end.

While I had other opportunities to date, for some inexplicable reason I continued to see Bob, even though it took some time for him to become relaxed in my company. It's hard to imagine having such a persevering nature that I would have given him so many chances.

Things gradually began to improve as we saw more of each other. As we dated, and mixed with friends, Bob began lightening up and we found ourselves laughing and having fun again. Bob had (and still has) a unique and totally delightful sense of humor that appealed to me right from the start. His ability to diffuse the heat of any tense or irritating situation, with his masterfully artful, and disarmingly spontaneous remarks, has saved the day on more than one occasion. Our dating took the form of movies, dinner, dances, and quiet talks while sitting on my parents' front porch in our "courting swing." Romance began to blossom, and it was on one of these romantic evenings that Bob proposed, and I accepted.

We had been dating about a year when he asked me to marry him, surprising me with a diamond ring. I knew then that this was a case of true love on Bob's part, as the diamond ring he gave me was bought by selling his prized, hand-made, Olds Trumpet. Bob cherished that trumpet, and for him it was the ultimate sacrifice. He was the one!

Our wedding took place in the evening at First Methodist Church in Waterloo, Iowa, June 25, 1948. The Rev. Gilbert S. Cox performed the wedding ceremony. Once again the sports world played a prominent, but unwelcome, role in our story by intruding even on so special and momentous an occasion as this.

As it happened, out in the East, during this time, Joe Louis and Jersey Joe Walcott were scheduled to fight for the eagerly awaited Heavyweight Championship of the World. This fight was no small event for sports fans, and was of particular interest to almost everyone those days, given the few entertainment opportunities available. The fight had been scheduled to take place in Yankee Stadium around the middle of June. Unfortunately, the rains came and came and came, canceling the fight, night after night, until when?... of course... the 25th of June.

The day broke to a fresh, cloudless, deep-blue sky; but by late afternoon the temperature had managed to climb to an uncomfortable level. The church was a big and beautiful old building, but without air conditioning, and few fans in the sanctuary. Eventually all was ready for the evening wedding, in spite of the heat which was taking a toll on the wedding party and guests alike.

It was difficult getting ready in the airless dressings rooms, coupled by the nerve-racking fact that once I had my full wedding gown on, the bridesmaids decided you could see through the filmy material. Quickly finding the slip she'd come in with, my sister Maxine helped me put it on under the long slip beneath my gown, and the day was saved. By the time we were all properly attired, the wedding party created a lovely scene. My father had injured his arm earlier in the week, and escorted me down the aisle sporting an arm sling over his new suit. He managed to perform his formal "father of the bride" best in spite of the handicap.

Despite the heat the guests seemed to endure the ceremony with good grace, and the wedding proceeded without a hitch, that is, if you didn't count the fact that I had to whisper to my groom to "kiss me" when it was over, to the guest's great amusement. He seemed to be in catatonic shock.

It was almost immediately after the ceremony that the seeming disaster set in. The party began disintegrating alarmingly when, immediately after passing through the reception line, most of the male guests rushed through the doors of the church, heading for their car radios to "catch the fight." For a period it seemed as though the wedding reception would consist of mostly female guests.

This new development was totally emotionally upsetting for a new bride whose elaborate plans for her perfect wedding had taken this disgraceful turn. Looking around for my groom, I happened to wander into the kitchen to find his bottom half dangling from a small kitchen window. His top half was draped through that window and he was listening to the fight being broadcast from the radio of a car parked half a story below.

Of course, "The Brown Bomber" won the fight that night, "in the eleventh round, before a crowd of 42,667 cheering fans who paid the outrageous sum of $841,739 to watch him land the blow that knocked Jersey Joe Walcott unconscious." Although he retained his crown, the mighty Joe Louis announced his retirement shortly after that fight.

It's fortunate for my descendants that I didn't take the word "fight" literally that night. For a fleeting moment it crossed my mind to hoist Bob's remaining bottom half out the window as well. Love must have restrained me. Seems like my mom wasn't the only one whose wedding started on a rocky note. This was another "like-mother-like-daughter" episode in our life and times. Eventually, the fight, which was ***the*** sports event of the year, ended and the men sheepishly rejoined their wives for the festivities.

Another tense, almost catastrophic, moment occurred during the wedding reception, however. My cousin Raymond Appel's son, Gary, a small boy at the time, began to choke on some nuts from the reception table. A frantic search was made for my dad, who always seemed to know just how to handle most any emergency.

Dad came running, saw the problem, and there, amidst a bunch of screaming, excited, women, calmly cleared Gary's windpipe. He began breathing and the reception returned to normal, or as normal as all of the preceding strange "going's-on" allowed it to be.

A little aside, here: Dad possessed another talent, or gift, if you will, which was the ability to stop the flow of blood for anyone who was bleeding profusely. This gift seemed always surrounded by an aura of secretiveness, for he was able to do it without touching the victim.

This gift garnered for him a great deal of awe and respect from anyone privy to witnessing the miracles. He could not be coaxed or persuaded to part with the secret, however. He would only say that "someday he would pass it on." On whom he intended to bestow this *gift* was never made known to the family. To my knowledge, it never was passed on, and the "secret" obviously died with him.

Bob and I bought a used, red, 1939 Ford convertible, with a rumble seat, for our wedding trip to the Black Hills. To ensure its safety from pranksters, we had hidden the car in the garage of my boss, Dr. Seymour Krantz, who, along with his wife, Belle, also attended the wedding. I was proud of him that night since he was one of the few men whom I described as classy enough not to desert the reception for the boxing match. I feel confident in making that statement, as most of the men who were at the wedding are no longer living, so they will not be stung by my accusation; and if they are, they might as well try the shoe on for fit.

My going-away outfit (we had such things in those days) was a dark green pique two-piece fitted suit with a swing skirt, complete with green lizard shoes and bag, and a large-brimmed brown hat. I retrieved the corsage of gardenias that had been positioned into my wedding bouquet, pinned it on my dress, and we were set to leave.

Having picked up our car from the Krantz's garage, we were off. We weren't long on the road when the rain came in a deluge. We made it only as far as Iowa Falls. Having heard somewhere that rain on your wedding day was a lucky sign, made the downpour somehow easier to bear.

Our room for the first night of our marriage was in the only hotel in Iowa Falls, and was typical of many hotel rooms of that age. There was a transom with a window over the door of our room. Overcome with shyness, I insisted that Bob climb up on a chair and cover the window with a blanket to shut out the light that was streaming like a beacon into our room from the hallway outside.

Our trip to the Black Hills was memorable and fun, but we didn't find a vast improvement in the hotel scene heading out West. Our hotel, while we were there, was also a typical old western hotel (the only one in town) that was neither glamorous nor especially comfortable. Its best feature was that it was clean.

Tourism in those days was not the multi-billion dollar business it has become today, and we were obliged to take what was available. To reach our room it was necessary for us to pass through another bedroom, a rather disturbing state of affairs for a new bride and groom. Had there been a fire in the hotel, our fate may have been questionable due to the room placement.

The bathroom was located down the hall and around the corner from our Siamese rooms. This meant that when we wanted to use the facilities it was necessary to traipse through the adjoining room to reach the hallway.

The final indignity in this scenario was our bed. While comfortable enough, its springs squeaked unmercifully. It was impossible to blink one's eyes without making the bed squeak. This is not a desirable feature newlyweds look for in accommodations. Lest I forget, the other room was unoccupied.

Three great kids were born of this union. First, was Timothy Robert, a sturdy little brick right from the beginning. Next came his sister, Sydney Kay, and according to her Aunt Mary, "the most beautiful baby she had ever seen." Last, but hardly least, came their brother, Thomas Patrick. Tom was our Cesarean baby, in such a hurry to be born that he came six weeks early. Typically, ten or fifteen minutes after boarding the car for any kind of a trip, it was always Tommy who wanted to know, "Are we there yet?"

Our Growing Family

Tom on the floor
Sydney with the cat
Tim behind Dad
Mom on the left

Any mother who claims that her children gave her no problems through their growing up years simply doesn't recognize the truth. Problems presented themselves for our clan as well. Fortunately, the Kelly household managed, somehow, to remain on an even (if sometimes wobbly) keel and continue to stay afloat, weathering the stormy tempests that afflict even the greatest of households.

Now, after the growing up years, it is even possible to laugh and tease and embarrass each other over our youthful (or parental) indiscretions. We, too, had our share of heartbreak, sadness, disappointment, anger, rebelliousness, temper tantrums, discipline, and forgiveness, as well as the good-natured roughhousing and hilariously funny and loving times that bring joy to heart and home, reinforcing family ties. All this sponsored by the grace of our loving Heavenly Father.

Now, I speak not only for myself, but for my husband Bob as well, as I acknowledge the way we rejoice over the lives of our three remarkable children. Each has brought a new, original and interesting dimension into our lives that would have been enormously missed without them. What a loss not to have known them.

To their extraordinary credit, it must be noted that each one has made the world a better place; for they are all loving and kind; interested in fairness and justice; and, to the best of my knowledge, are law-abiding and honest.

Because of their upright, spiritual characters, every one of them will leave a legacy for the world as a positive and loving contributor to the human condition.

This amazing trio has, individually, embraced the Christian faith, and strives to live according to the tenants of that faith—a comfort to hopeful parents—and my desire for everyone who reads this account. God has given us three immeasurably precious gifts that we continue to love and treasure through the years.

As of this writing, this account brings us to a grand total of fourteen spectacular grandchildren; all as smart as their moms and dads, and as beautiful as their grandparents.

Our "grown up" Kids
Timothy, Sydney and Thomas

CHAPTER 28

This chronicle must include one last episode relating to World War II, for I would have stopped short without recounting this closing incident. In 1994, Bob and I took a vacation trip to Hawaii. While there, we drove out to Pearl Harbor to view the original site of the horrifying bombing of the United States. How vividly that stressful message coming over my Aunt Louise's radio some fifty years before, flashed back into my mind.

Our tour through the buildings at the site was thought-provoking. The gift shop contained not only the usual souvenirs but also a display of ship models, photos and memorabilia of the war. Connected to that building was a theater. At the appropriate moment we were directed to enter the theater and take a seat before boarding the launches waiting in the harbor to take us out to the war memorial standing in the water.

Once inside the theater, we became aware of the large number of Japanese people who were in the audience. It seemed natural to speculate as to what their interest in this presentation might be. Was it, perhaps, to pay homage out of feelings of sorrow and guilt for the insidious attack perpetrated upon the U.S. by their country, or could it have been to smugly gloat over their superior air attack? We felt their attention was respectful and sincere, at least outwardly.

Undoubtedly, most of the Japanese in the audience were too young to have witnessed, or been part of the war, so it's very possible their interest was more historical than vindictive. At least that is what we chose to believe.

The theater was full, and as the lights went down, a hush descended upon the audience. Battle scenes and sounds, complete with intense narration, filled the screen for almost an hour, during which time not a sound could be heard from the audience.

The presentation riveted us to our seats with drama, horror, and electrifying historical commentary. When the film ended and the lights returned it was as though everyone in the audience had been hypnotized. We remained seated and still—stunned—until at last someone stirred. It was only then that we began moving outside the building, in a silence broken only by the muffled tempo of the group's movement.

Had I been pressed for a description of the emotional atmosphere charging the room at that moment, I would have had to say that it could best be described as reverential.

The audience slowly filed out, going directly from the theater to a number of launches standing by. Climbing aboard we were ferried out to the Memorial standing in the middle of Pearl Harbor. This gleaming white structure was built on either side of, and spanning the sunken hull of the famed battleship, Arizona, with its connecting bridge leading to exhibit rooms, one on either side of this gallant, old warrior..

As we walked over the bridge, looking down into the murky water, we could see not only the rusty outline of the ship, but parts of the ship itself sticking out of the water. This supernatural view of the ill-fated ship brought a chilling reminder of its history.

At some point near the ship, could be seen a very small circle of oil. We were told that this spot of oil came from a leak somewhere deep within the remains of the ship, and that it had been leaking continuous from the day the doomed vessel went down.

Governmental groups had conferred about whether or not to try to stop the spill, but it was their unanimous decision to let the seeping oil continue as a living memorial to these gallant heroes, reminiscent of the eternal flame that burns at the gravesite of John F. Kennedy at Arlington National Cemetery in Washington, DC.

We were also told that these same officials, who decided not to stop the oil spill or resurrect the ship, made these decisions so as not to disturb the bodies of the sailors who had died there. It was their opinion that disturbing the ship in any way would be a desecration of the dead.

The guide's sober explanation of this important resolution came with the additional grim news that most of the casualties' bodies were either burned, mangled, or blown apart so extensively that they were beyond recognition, making identification impossible. To this day, the remaining bodies of these heroic victims are still entombed there in their fitting and appropriate burial site.

Several visitors had thrown leis, as floral tributes, onto the water at the memorial site; the garlands floated near a protruding stack pipe, presenting an incongruous picture. The contrasting beauty of the flowers somehow heightened the somber eeriness of the scene: a rusty, tortured, helpless, ship, resting in a watery grave of dark stagnant water that would forever roll and swirl, back and forth, over and around it's lifeless, yet gallant, remains.

It was impossible not to notice the subdued, introspective mood of all of the other visitors to the Memorial that day. They, too, seemed lost in thought, obviously having carried with them the stunning presentation we had all witnessed in the theatre. Like us, they too were contemplating their own version of the events that had transpired there so many years ago.

Lingering on the connecting bridge, staring down into the shadowy water that cradled this once proud, but now tragically rusting hulk resting on the harbor floor, we were trying to memorize every detail of the remains. Reluctantly we moved over the bridge to the second side of the impressive building. Entering this room we were instantly awed by the sight of the chief exhibit prominently displayed on a large pristine wall. On this wall was written the names of all those whose lives were lost on the Arizona. We found the name of our sister-in-law, Mary Manske Kelly's brother, Robert Francis Manske Y2c, written there. Although we didn't know him personally, it was a touching moment for us.

The memorial trip came full circle with our visit to the Punch Bowl. The Punch Bowl is the well-groomed cemetery, sitting high on a hill overlooking Pearl Harbor, in which many servicemen, as well as local Hawaiians, are buried.

Walking among the gravesites, we were seeing the evidence of another facet of the war experience. The overwhelming nature of this memorial site, the beauty of its setting, and the remembrance of the heroes present in these graves, reminded us that not all of our men were lost at sea.

We moved quietly through this revered site, because our presence here demanded no less than our full respect as we paid homage to the memory of our fallen countrymen. Reading names, conjecturing, remembering, and pausing to sense the fundamental nature of this historic shrine, dictated our leisurely pace.

Another surprising view from this impressive place, as one travels up the road to, or down from the cemetery, is the sight of that steep hill completely covered with Christmas Cactus growing in a tangle of mass profusion. This unusual sight reminded us once more that we were in Hawaii. What we work so hard to grow at home needs no attention there.

While the pilgrimage to Pearl Harbor brought home to us the reality of what had only been, until that time, an imaginary place—light years away from our small and isolated Iowa town—it now, strangely, brought an unexpected sense of reality, and closed the book.

CHAPTER 29

The Gospel of John, Chapter 21, verse 25, makes an interesting observation; one which mirrors my thoughts as I attempt to bring this labor of love to a close. It states: "If all the other events in Jesus' life were written, the whole world could hardly contain the books."

Now it would be a presumptuous and sinful arrogance for me to claim anything close to equality with this divine record. But in recalling the events and people, who, like the many brilliantly colored stones that are so carefully, conspicuously, and masterfully set into the mosaic of my life, it becomes evident that there were legions who have influenced, enriched and given meaning and substance to my existence. To record them all, I realize, would have taken a book of vastly larger proportion.

But what a bumpy, exhilarating, trip this has been, traveling down the memory lane of my personal momentous past—penning yet another version of the "hard years." Those years demanded a resourcefulness from people they might otherwise not have known they possessed, but for these hard years. Struggle and austerity proved to be the catalyst for strengthening their will to survive and flourish. Certainly, the strife and misfortunes of that day required a colossal amount of strength, an extraordinary amount of courage, unbelievable stamina, and bushel baskets full of faith, hope, and trust.

I will consider the time and effort required to put this narrative on paper to be well spent if you've learned a bit, laughed a little, and enjoyed discovering my part of the past as much as I enjoyed living it.

Now, as I bid a fond and loving farewell, we part company through the conclusion of this book. It will be my great joy if my readers have gained a deeper insight into the way things were in the early to middle-part of the 1900's.

It will be my even greater joy if you have also glimpsed, even briefly through the pages of this book, that shining pathway of unlimited potential that stretches before you—the future generation—as you search for success. The sweat, tears, and tenacity of your courageous forefathers, who struggled to insure a brighter future for those of your generation, have bequeathed this inheritance of opportunity to you. Out of the darkness of unbelievable struggle has come the dawning of a bright new day, lighting your way as you walk with God.

About the Author

Having lived most of the experiences written about here, that which started as lively entertainment for family progressed into a full-fledged book by the author. The idea caught fire through the encouragement of her family who thought her stories needed to be told to a wider audience. Having written, and rewritten the book at least eight times, this comes as a warning to anyone who becomes bitten by the writing bug. One memory after another keeps the juices flowing, and the helpful criticism of scholarly friends brings many re-writes. Once inspired, it is impossible to put down this obsessive task, forcing one to stay the course to the end.

Because she lived in part through the Great Depression, flourished in spite of it, she now sees much value in such humble beginnings. Writing about living through these years reminded her that despite its negative spot in history, for her life was a joy—contrary to what one might expect. In fact, her observation is that the kids of that period learned a lot more about making-do, inventiveness, creativity, self-sufficiency and a sense of community—because of this very lack of many of the things that are considered "necessary" for our children today. Their lowered expectation for material things didn't result in a lack of drive or a striving to succeed, but merely became a catalyst for reinforcing them.

Having studied at the University of Northern Iowa, and graduating from Gates Business College as well, Arlene held many diverse jobs, eventually becoming the Assistant Manager of Plymouth Place, a retirement home for the well-elderly in Des Moines, Iowa, for over twenty years!

In addition to writing, Arlene is an accomplished watercolor artist, decorator, and is involved in many things creative. She and her husband, Bob, love to travel, usually spending the winter months in Florida soaking up the sun, and, hopefully, more inspiration for the challenge of any new interests.

With the coming of the computer age, writing had become her main focus; and for over three years she has sent a daily Bible verse, and commentary, to a group of interested people across the country.